The Alienated "Loyal" Opposition

The Alienated "Loyal" Opposition

MEXICO'S
PARTIDO ACCION NACIONAL

Franz A. von Sauer

UNIVERSITY OF NEW MEXICO PRESS
Albuquerque

Photographs from *La Nación* by courtesy of Juan Manuel Gómez Morín

Manufactured in the United States of America
Library of Congress Catalog Card No. 74–80743
International Standard Book Number 0–8263–0341–2
First Edition

To my mother, Angélica Morales de von Sauer

Contents

TABLES

ILLUSTRATIONS

Following p. 140

9. Sr. Alfonso Ituarte Servín, national president of PAN, 1955–57. He has twice been a federal deputy.
10. Lic. Adolfo Christlieb Ibarrola, national president of PAN, 1961–65, and federal deputy, 1963–67.
11. Arquitecto Ignacio Limón Maurer, national president of PAN, 1968.
12. Lic. Manuel González Hinojosa, national president of PAN, 1969–71, and federal deputy, 1967–70.
13. Efraín González Morfín, presidential candidate in 1970 and federal deputy from 1967 to 1970.
14. Lic. José Angel Conchello, presently serving as PAN president and federal deputy.
15. Rally in Ciudad Delicias, Chih. during 1958 presidential campaign of Luis H. Alvarez.
16. Rally in Monterrey, N. L. during 1952 presidential campaign of Lic. González Luna.

Preface

This study attempts to provide a balance sheet of over thirty years of intense effort and activity by Mexico's most important minority party, the Partido Acción Nacional (PAN), and to dispel some serious misconceptions about PAN and contemporary Mexican politics. When I first undertook this study in the spring of 1968, I was convinced that the real nature of the Mexican political system could not be investigated solely from the perspective of "official" sources and pronouncements. Perhaps the prestige involved in securing interviews with high officials of the "revolutionary family" has tempted many students of Mexican government to discard the potential relevance of associations commonly referred to as out-groups. Certainly, the prospect of an appointment at the Secretaría de Gobernación is more attractive than that of a visit to the comparatively primitive headquarters of PAN or the Partido Popular Socialista (PPS).

Actually, however, contemporary Mexican politics seem to take on added meaning when viewed from an out-group perspective; that is, comprehensive analyses of the activities of minority parties indicate that the Westernization of the Mexican political system will ultimately depend on the effective legitimization of non-official pressures and demands. It is herein assumed, therefore, that Westernization must involve the recognition of pluralist interests, the emergence of a genuinely competitive political dialogue, and the gradual disappearance of tutelary-authoritarian practices common in so-called guided democracies.

This is not to say that scholars who have relied on sources provided by members of the ruling coalition are not to be commended for their important contributions to the understanding of the dynamics of Mexican political life. As all who have engaged in field research know, it is not easy to secure appointments in Mexico, either with individuals who hold, or have held, important government posts or with members of minority parties and associations. *Antesalas,* or antechambers, are common everywhere in Mexico, and I had to sit through many days before I finally was admitted to the office of PAN's founder, the late Manuel Gómez Morín. I recall that first of many meetings vividly. I was very cordially received, yet I knew that Gómez Morín would be reserved toward an outsider and that I must convince him that my interest in his party was purely academic. Fortunately, Gómez Morín had always felt that a comprehensive study of PAN would be beneficial to the party, even if the results of such a study should not be complimentary. So, after the initial "ice" had melted, the academic goals of my research posed no real problems for me, since Gómez Morín's personal endorsement was much like a passport in Panista country. I came to regard PAN sympathetically only as a result of five years of research; my sympathy, therefore, should not be interpreted as an indication of party affiliation.

In addition to my face-to-face encounters with several prominent members of PAN, I relied heavily on PAN's weekly publication, *La Nación,* and other Mexican newspapers, notably *Excélsior, Novedades,* and *El Universal.* There are few other publications that relate directly to PAN. In Mexico such works are usually printed at the author's expense. PAN's leading publicist, Luis Calderón Vega, for example, has had to finance all printing of his writing. His major work, *Memorias del PAN,* was an important source for this study. The collected writings of Gómez Morín and other PAN luminaries, such as Efraín González Luna, Adolfo Christlieb Ibarrola, José González Torres, and Efraín González Morfín, have either been published under the auspices of Editorial Jus, whose editor was a member of PAN, or by the party's own press. In fact, in earlier years many Mexican writers sympathetic to PAN or critical of the government party often published their works outside Mexico and some even used pen names. This was true of the important work, *La educación socialista en México,* published in Rosario, Argentina, and written by a certain Sebastián Mayo. Only very recently have a few Mexican scholars written more extensive and analytical studies on the role of minority parties.

Perhaps the most important study was under the direction of Antonio Delhumeau of the Instituto Mexicano de Investigaciones Políticas (*México: realidad política de sus partidos,* 1970).

North American scholars of Mexican politics have been even more neglectful of minority parties in Mexico, since their writings merely include token discussions of a paragraph or two. Still, I should mention two noteworthy Ph.D. dissertations: William Robert Lux's *PAN: The Conservative Political Party of Mexico* (University of Southern California, 1967), and James F. Creagan's *Minority Political Parties in Mexico: Their Role in a One-Party Dominant System* (University of Virginia, 1965). I also wish to note that after the research for this book was completed, I came across a recently published study of PAN: Donald J. Mabry's *Mexico's Acción Nacional: A Catholic Alternative to Revolution* (Syracuse, N.Y.: Syracuse University Press, 1973).

There are many whose inspiration, valuable assistance, and criticisms I would like to acknowledge. I want to express my gratitude to Professor William Manger of Georgetown University, Washington, D.C., whose exemplary scholarship and love for Latin America have been major sources of inspiration to all his students. His numerous and constructive comments, as well as those of his distinguished colleagues, Professors Howard Penniman, Jeanne Kirkpatrick, and Luis Aguilar, were most helpful. To James W. Wilkie, of the University of California at Los Angeles, very special thanks for the many suggestions he advanced. I can only hope that I have done them some justice.

A special word of recognition is also due to the Earhart Foundation of Ann Arbor, Michigan; their grants awarded to me in 1967 and 1968 helped in part to cover the expenses of my research in Mexico.

I am particularly saddened to be unable to convey my appreciation to Manuel Gómez Morín and Adolfo Christlieb. Their deaths have left a void; their intellectual contribution is unmatched. But among those who are still active in the ranks of PAN, I owe a special debt of gratitude to Juan Manuel Gómez Morín and Fernando Ayala Carrión.

I also want to thank Ms. Emma Tusing of Stillwater, Oklahoma, for many hours of fine clerical assistance. Of course, I alone take full responsibility for the interpretations contained in this study.

Those persons whose positive contributions I have not acknowledged wished to remain anonymous.

Introduction

> With a larger percentage of the vote than that obtained in previous national elections, the PAN, which is the strongest opposition party, receives in some measure public recognition that its life is not sterile, and that its efforts are not in vain. Its members know, and we all know, that, in a democratic system, the only expression of unanimity is that which coincides with our recognition that we are entitled to hold divergent opinions. PAN has exercised this right, and its members can be certain, that they have acted in the benefit of the civic and political conscience of our citizens.
>
> "The Indispensable Opposition" (Editorial)
> *Excélsior* (Mexico City), July 7, 1970

The growing literature on modern party politics in Mexico has addressed itself almost exclusively to the dominant revolutionary coalition which has monopolized the political system's decision-making process since 1929. Studies of minority opposition parties have been, as a rule, fragmentary. Notable contemporary contributions written by American scholars are markedly concerned with projecting a favorable analysis of the current political scene in Mexico.[1] Indeed, American scholars tend to explain the Mexican political system's shortcomings under a one-party dominant pattern as natural symptoms of a developing political system. At the same time, they often tacitly accept the political elite's contention that the Revolutionary Party has genuinely represented the aspirations of most Mexicans. Also, American scholars echo the facile thesis, often heard in Mexican official circles, that under the tutelage of a single "nationally oriented" party, Mexico has successfully experimented with its own unique brand of democracy. They dismiss minority political movements as the product of a handful of fanatics. At best, they characterize such parties as ideological remnants of forces no longer viable in the contemporary Mexican political scene. They refer to "bankers' clubs," to a "satellite system of opposition parties and out-groups," or to associations which stand either on the right or on the left of the Mexican ideological spectrum. The success and stability of the dominant one-party experience in Mexico they attribute to the growing pragmatism which they see as having been steadily adopted by the ruling cadres, or, to borrow Otto Kirchheimer's phrase, to the cadres' ability to shape their "family" into a "catch-all-people's" party.[2] Conversely, the failure of minority groups to capture the imagination of Mexicans they explain in terms of the groups' rigid, inflexible approach to political issues, which in turn sharply reduces their electoral potential and appeal.

An implicit bias exists, then, in American literature which equates pragmatic belief patterns with a healthy type of democracy and often regards ideological commitments as inflexible and dogmatic.[3] This study does not propose to challenge the view that political parties operating within modern Western democracies are becoming progressively more pragmatic, but it does question the proposition that the Mexican political system has experienced anything that approximates the Western pragmatic approach as defined in recent studies.[4] This study suggests, instead, that modern Mexican society remains sharply divided despite over sixty years of one-party rule. Comprehensive interviews with seven prominent Mexican political figures, conducted by James and Edna Wilkie, have disclosed that the Revolution of 1910 is still subject to sharply divergent interpretations, and that ideological issues continue to play a major role in political discussion among Mexicans. These interviews indicate, further, that such discussion is not found exclusively among irrelevant groups of fanatics bent upon the destruction of those national foundations which the ruling party is said to have established.[5] As Andrew Milnor has suggested, ideological politics and a sharply divided society often go hand in hand.[6] Mexico seems to be no exception, as developments over the past few years indicate. The student disturbances that occurred in Mexico City in October 1968 and the ensuing state of fluctuation in the political scene serve to underscore the fact that the system's often taken for granted stability is precarious at best. The returns of the 1970 presidential elections are significant because they irrevocably revealed that the majorities claimed by the governing party are artificial. For despite the impressive 8-million vote margin of Luis Echeverría of the Partido Revolucionario Institucional (PRI) over his sole opponent, Efraín González Morfín of PAN, with which the ruling coalition substantiates its usual 80 percent-plus victory, PRI had to admit that approximately 43 percent of the electorate chose to remain away from the polls (even though voting in Mexico is compulsory and suffrage was granted to eighteen-year-olds for the first time). PRI also had to admit that the presidential candidate of PAN secured an unprecedented 2 million votes, or twice the number accorded to the opposition in 1964, so that the vote of nearly 20 percent won by all opposition parties combined with voter absenteeism totaled over 63 percent of the registered Mexican electorate.[7]

In fact, these trends continue perhaps even stronger today than before. In 1973, PRI congressional candidates managed to poll a combined majority of only 52 percent in Mexico City, while PAN secured 38.4 percent and other minority parties split the remaining 10 percent. Out of nearly 25 million registered Mexican voters, nearly 46 percent did not vote.[8]

These data suggest that potential dissatisfaction with or alienation from current political practices in Mexico is greater than is generally acknowledged.

To be sure, the ruling party, which today is called PRI, has shown through the years a certain ability to democratize itself internally (bitter opponents would call it opportunism), but the two principal opposition parties, PAN and the Partido Popular Socialista (PPS), have shown the same ability. A limited degree of intraparty democratization, however, should not be automatically construed as a shift toward systemic pragmatism. Communication channels among the various parties remain essentially closed, so that the give-and-take which often characterizes Western-styled pragmatic party systems is far from a reality in Mexico.

This study contends, therefore, that many writers have been so impressed by the "official" version of Mexican politics that they have turned their backs on the possible impact of large-scale organized alienation in Mexico. There is a need for more comprehensive studies which will consider the political alienation of minority opposition parties as a potentially unifying contemporary ideology for Mexicans. This need is particularly felt now that the Mexican electorate is increasingly urbanized and politically conscious.

The choice of PAN as a study in political alienation is based on several considerations. First, PAN is the oldest and most persistent opposition party in postrevolutionary Mexico. Second, PAN is the only opposition party that has shown a steady increase in electoral appeal, winning almost 14 percent of the presidential vote in 1970, 16.5 percent in the congressional elections of 1973, and over 35 percent in both elections in several of the more urbanized areas such as the Federal District.[9] Finally, little is known of the real extent of PAN's efforts and activities. At the time of this writing, I was aware of only one other study devoted exclusively to PAN.[10] It has merit as a pioneer study but shows certain shortcomings. In his crusade against the generalizations on PAN provided by Scott, Brandenburg, Cline, and others, the author goes to extremes in depicting Acción Nacional as a wronged majority, a sort of political bride jilted by the corrupt and fraudulent tactics of her omnipotent partner. Such a defense, although well meant, is certain to embarrass even the most fanatic of contemporary Panistas, who readily admit PAN is a minority party. The late Adolfo Christlieb Ibarrola, former PAN president, said that it was time for PAN to stop playing the role of a deprived national majority: "The tactic of repeated charges of electoral fraud has had adverse psychological effects for our citizens. It is far more logical and practical for us to admit that we are a minority, and to tell the electorate that, as a minority, we still have been able to pressure successfully for this or that goal."[11]

This study, therefore, accepts PAN as a legitimate political party, but it also acknowledges that its national appeal is limited to a minority of the electorate. As a legitimate minority party, PAN is not the political vehicle of a group of discredited individuals, but the end product of political and intellectual forces which have been an integral part of the experience of postrevolutionary Mexico. Chapter 1 sets the stage by postulating that PAN is a significant representative of pervasive belief patterns which I have labeled "ideology of political alienation." Chapter 1 suggests, further, that even though PAN continues to stress ideology, the other political parties, including PRI, also have failed to encourage a pragmatic political dialogue among Mexicans. In fact, ideologisms and irreconcilable slogans seem to prevail to this day, despite impressive steps toward modernization in other spheres of government.

Chapter 2 attempts to show that the political and intellectual origins of PAN are not representative of "antinational" forces as claimed by members of the revolutionary family and some of their publicists. Slogans and labels are, of course, the natural by-product of the one party authoritarian mentality which does not accept the prospect of large-scale opposition to its rule. Indeed, Chapter 2 submits that all the movements which served as political and ideological foundations for PAN were an integral part and a necessary consequence of the destructive phase of the Revolution of 1910, which created severe cultural fragmentation not only within the society but also within revolutionary circles themselves.

This study challenges the commonly held view that PAN has lost most of its initial momentum and political relevance as a result of its uncompromising brand of traditional conservatism. The party has never been representative of what Brandenburg terms "traditional conservatism." Such a label would necessarily imply an affinity with nineteenth-century conservative groups in Mexico, an affinity which cannot be found in Panista ideology.[12] PAN's earlier conservatism was in response to issues arising directly out of the years following the Revolution. Chapter 3 shows, therefore, that PAN's ideology actually incorporated many of the political and social programs advanced by the father of the Revolution, Francisco I. Madero. In fact, prominent members of the Madero family eventually joined the ranks of PAN and actively sought political office under the party's banner. Any investigator would be hard put to label the Maderos as traditional conservatives. As one of the party's original hard-core ideologues, Efraín González Luna, remarked, PAN's aim was not to weep over ancient tombs since the party had little respect for the men buried in them.[13]

Chapters 4 and 5 investigate PAN's continuity as an opposition movement for over thirty years, both as a strictly ideological movement with limited potential to influence policy-making in the early years of its existence (1939–52) and as a party with increased electoral potential since 1952. The relevance of PAN to the contemporary Mexican political scene has been, to no small extent, due to its adaptability to changing conditions. I do not contend, however, that PAN and other minority parties have matured by achieving a pragmatic outlook. Just as the PRI adamantly defends its prerogative to represent the majority, PAN persists to this day in its adamant expression of alienation and in its fixed demands that the PRI, as a party-turned-government, be abolished. But again, as with PRI, the social basis of PAN's ideology has become less identifiable and is often veiled by slogans, so that the Mexican voter today may actually reject folklore such as "a vote for PAN is a clear vote for the Church and regression," and may instead come to regard opposition parties actively engaged in the political life of communities as a viable and legitimate alternative to what he has been used to. This seems likely in states such as Baja California, Sonora, Michoacán, Nuevo León, Chihuahua, Oaxaca, and Yucatán, where PAN has secured surprising majorities in key municipal contests during the past years. If the present trend of regarding opposition parties as legitimate alternatives continues at the local voter level, it is probable that the national significance of opposition parties will increase in time, especially if the parties agree to place unity of purpose above those particular interests to which they appealed in the past.

1

Ideological Politics in Mexico

> JUAN—How was election day for you?
> PEDRO—What elections?
> JUAN—Why, the ones held on Sunday, July 5th, to elect the president, senators and deputies, of course!
> PEDRO—Oh, I stayed home and read *Don Quijote.*

The brilliant pen of Mexico's Antonio Castro Leal relates the imaginary dialogue of two Mexicans on the day after the presidential elections.[1] Juan and Pedro characterize the differences in political viewpoints. Their conversation continues.

JUAN—How awful!

PEDRO—Why awful? Don't you like *Don Quijote?*

JUAN—Of course I do! I meant how awful that you didn't vote. That's the only way to strengthen our democracy.

PEDRO—Well, as far as I am concerned, our elections are like wedding rehearsals, where the bride and groom practice out their entrance procession and how they are going to kneel in Church.

JUAN—A poor comparison, Pedro. When we vote, we are engaged in a civic lesson.

PEDRO—A civic lesson every six years, indeed! The person who begins to vote at the age of eighteen will have received six such lessons by the time he turns sixty-six. What we need is a constant preparation of the citizenry for democracy.

JUAN—Don't be a sophist, Pedro. It is through elections that the people ratifies its will every six years that the present regime remain in power.

PEDRO—Why bother to ratify it?

JUAN—What's the matter? Don't you like the PRI?

PEDRO—I don't like its role as an official party. I would like for it to become a populist party. A political party should always look ahead, and plan a development which will satisfy the needs of our country. It should have a dynamic program, so that each attained goal will serve toward the formulation of new goals.

JUAN—But can't an official party do the same thing?

PEDRO—No. Because no government in any country achieves all it proposes. By its very nature, an official party must show satisfaction with governmental policies, and must celebrate every effort made by the government. Such a party cannot, therefore, be critical, and being critical—that is, recognizing the need for constant progress—is the very soul and essence of a political party. An official party is like the husband after thirty years of marriage, who is respected out of deference, who has already a pot belly, and who has many sons, some good, some bad, and some thieves. He and his wife grow old in a bourgeois atmosphere, and he has come to enjoy his slippers more than his riding boots.

JUAN—What's the matter with that? Don't you like this noble tranquillity, this security of the home, this consoling bliss?

PEDRO—No, Juan. A political party must be a lover, it must have passion, it must dream of a better world, it must take off those slippers and put on the riding boots so that it may continue its restless ride toward the promised land . . .

This conversation vividly summarizes the disenchantment of many Mexicans with the political style which pervades their country. It suggests that the system has failed to give many parts of society a sense of participation and has failed to encourage civic responsibility in the citizenry. It further suggests that sterile political exchange has stifled prospects of meaningful lessons in democratic government. Finally, it suggests that a system of self-congratulatory debate exists and that various political actors choose to subordinate clearly defined social theses, platforms, and programs to a fistful of catch phrases and slogans they often abandon in practice. Thus, the PRI continues to splash its campaign literature with the old revolutionary slogan "Effective Suffrage, No Reelection," while it sits back awaiting the preordained reelection of PRI candidates in every corner of the country. Similarly, other parties try to convince the electorate that action promised by their own slogans would eradicate Mexico's ills once and for all.[2] But whereas genuine ideological commitments have gradually eroded, the system has failed to come up with a pragmatic style of politics. Coined phrases and slogans have brought forth new manifestations of quasiideologisms and have postponed what seems to many Mexicans the impossible dream—open political dialogue in Mexico.

IDEOLOGY AND PRAGMATISM DEFINED

I have referred to the ideological as opposed to the pragmatic style of party politics. I noted that several theorists maintain that the gradual disappearance of ideological parties in traditional Western democracies and the corresponding growth of populist parties have resulted in a healthier form of democratic government in which the citizenry has greater and more meaningful participation. Giovanni Sartori, for example, suggests that ideology is in effect the opposite of pragmatism, so that a definition of pragmatism would qualify the notion of ideology. He writes, "For this purpose 'ideological politics' will be opposed . . . to 'pragmatic politics,' i.e. pragmatism will be used as a designation for non-ideology."[3]

Sartori proceeds to characterize ideology as "a political belief system (which consists of the set of beliefs according to which individuals navigate and orient themselves in the sea of politics)," but he warns that "pragmatism is also a state of belief systems [and that] to contrast ideologism and pragmatism as representing, respectively, a belief versus a beliefless orientation is to preempt the issue from the outset."[4] And yet, while both ideologism and pragmatism represent possible political belief systems, there does exist a discriminating element between the mentality of ideological and pragmatic belief structures. This element Sartori terms the cognitive dimension:

> It appears that the crucial single factor resides in so-called "authority beliefs" and more precisely in the beliefs concerning cognitive authority: the beliefs that tip us off to what is true or false about the world and its events. More concretely, one may say that the crucial factor is "the authorities," those on whom we rely for information.[5]

At this point, Sartori draws a distinction between the closed and the open mind. "A person's [belief] system is open or closed . . . [to] the extent to which the person can receive, evaluate, and act on relevant information on its own intrinsic merits."[6] Correspondingly, the less able one is to evaluate data objectively, the more one's political belief system is closed. It would seem, therefore, that PRI's unwillingness to criticize policies adopted by the Mexican government, of which Castro Leal's Pedro speaks, relates to its inability to question the authorities (in this case the ruling elite) on whom PRI relies for information and, indeed, for its existence. Sartori concludes that "the ideological mentality represents a typically dogmatic, i.e. rigid, and impermeable approach to politics."[7]

Summarized, the cognitive dimension of the ideological mentality is characterized by (a) deductive argumentation over evidence and testing; (b) doctrine over practice; (c) principle over precedent; and (d) ends over means. Thus its perceptions tend to be covered up, doctrine loaded, and indirect. In contrast, the pragmatist's cognitive dimension emphasizes (a) evidence and testing over deductive argumentation; (b) practice over doctrine; (c) precedent over principle; and (d) means over ends. Thus its perceptions tend to be direct.

To this cognitive dimension, which differentiates ideology from pragmatism according to a closed-open mind formula, Sartori adds still another, which he labels the emotive dimension:

> Along the emotive dimension, beliefs can be intense or feeble, passionately or weakly felt. Possibly in each indi-

> vidual cognition and affect are tightly interlinked, but with reference to mass phenomena—e.g. abrupt transitions from "hot politics" to "cool politics," and vice-versa —cognition and affect seem to vary interdependently. Assuming cognition to be constant, we can still have formidable oscillations of emotional intensity.[8]

This added dimension suggests that there are two varying conceptions of ideology: ideologism, which does not necessarily lead to active ideological involvement, and ideological passion, which determines the capacity for activation of a given ideology. The effectiveness of the ideology, therefore, "does not reside in the ideological mentality as such, but requires, in addition, 'ideological heating.' "[9] Manifestations of the emotive dimension may range from strong to weak. Therefore, the closed cognitive status characteristic of ideological mentality may adhere either to belief elements that are adamant, that is, elements that are "rigid, dogmatic, impermeable to argument and evidence," with a high potential for political activism; or, at the other extreme, it may adhere to weak or resilient elements which "are still impermeable to argument and evidence, but which display a low dynamic potential, for they are not passionately felt."[10] In similar terms, the open cognitive status characteristic of the pragmatic mentality may have an emotive dimension anywhere from strong to weak. It may either assume firm belief elements, that is, beliefs which are firmly held, but are "open to evidence and/or to argument, [and] even though they have a tendency to be persistent . . . are not impermeable and are, therefore, changeable, at least in principle"; or it may assume flexible elements, that is, beliefs that are feebly held, "open to argument and/or to evidence, and furthermore, to convenience."

Sartori concludes that ideological politics are generally characterized by a closed cognitive dimension and by fixed (ranging from adamant to resilient) belief patterns. Conversely, pragmatic politics tend to reflect an open cognitive structure and a permeable set of belief patterns that have anywhere from firm to flexible manifestations.[11]

Political scientists have often mistaken shifts from adamant to resilient belief patterns to be manifestations of an end of ideology; in fact, the possibility always exists for ideological passion to revert to a high emotive dimension, so long as the political system does not change from a closed to an open cognitive structure. Several studies of Mexico's one-party democracy have made this mistake. A transition to an open cognitive structure has yet to be made in the politics of every major party active in Mexico today, and Mexican politics have not yet experienced an end of ideology.

CONTEMPORARY IDEOLOGIES IN MEXICO: IDEOLOGY OF ONE-PARTY AUTHORITARIANISM VERSUS IDEOLOGY OF ALIENATION

More than other Latin American republics, Mexico has had a wealth of ideological experience and commitment. The liberal and conservative parties of the nineteenth century produced prominent ideologues such as Juárez and Lucas Alamán. Indeed, the political history of Mexico in that century attests to deep-seated and passionately felt ideological differences which often resulted in the hot politics of which Sartori speaks. The Revolution in the first decade of the twentieth century was perhaps the last of the great battles of ideology, and, at least during the Madero presidency, which not only tolerated opposition but openly welcomed it, political parties went in search of ideals. Postrevolutionary political dialogue in Mexico has also revealed an extraordinary variety of ideologisms. In more recent years, however, political groups have increasingly divorced themselves from the particularistic interests which they had previously espoused. PRI, for example, has on occasion been adamantly committed to large-scale expropriations of large landholdings, as in the years 1934 to 1940, but today those commitments are resilient. PAN, although in its earlier years as an opposition party was a vigorous crusader for the rights of the Mexican Church in such areas as education (see Chapter 4), has become progressively more preoccupied with the prospects of victories at the polls. The Marxist-Leninist commitment which kindled the spirit of Vicente Lombardo Toledano and his associates when they originally formed the Partido Popular has all but vanished, in spite of unconvincing statements to the contrary by Lombardo's successor, Jorge Cruickshank García.[12]

What kinds of ideologies prevail, then, in Mexico today? The ideological diversity of past years has now two central manifestations. I shall refer to them as the ideology of one-party authoritarianism and the ideology of alienation.

The ideology of one-party authoritarianism has replaced, or at least neutralized, the earlier social aspirations and commitments of the dominant party. The presidency of Lázaro Cárdenas (1934–40) represented the last clear attempt to commit the party to an ideology of social content. It was an era of Soviet-patterned six-year plans and of marked socialist overtones. It was also the era in which the ideological battle in Mexico was reawakened, and which, significantly, saw in September 1939 the emergence of the first permanent counter-ideological movement, the Partido Acción Nacional. Following the Cárdenas era, however, the old revolutionary commitments lost momentum, as Cardenistas gave way to supporters of more enigmatic administrations. To be sure, PRI still supports the purpose, aims, and objectives of the social revolution, but so do PAN and other minority parties. Each, however, reserves for itself the right to interpret just what the purpose, aims, and objectives really are, and to correct the misinterpretations by former colleagues. Within PRI, it is still possible today to speak of the left and right wings; very often differences between Cardenistas and Alemanistas go deeper and are far more bitter than those between Democratic and Republican candidates in this country. Still, it is no secret that the overall governmental policies subscribed to by presidents since Cárdenas have been characterized by a growing resilience in belief patterns. "Hot politics" have tended to cool as ideological passion is no longer shown by parties but only—at least in recent years—by students of the National University and by other out-groups. In effect, what has taken place within the ranks of the PRI has been an accommodation of diverse ideologies, some adamantly held. Such accommodation was a prerequisite to preservation of the coalition's artificial unity.

It is a serious error, however, to interpret this kind of accommodation or neutralization as a shift toward pragmatism. Even though PRI has steadily shown its reluctance to adopt the kind of messianic ideologism evidenced in the 1930s, opting instead for greater doctrinal moderation, the hegemonic pattern of the system has remained authoritarian; that is, the cognitive structure of the ruling party continues to be closed. As Joseph La Palombara and Myron Weiner suggest, a dominant party need not subscribe to an ideology of the right or of the left in order to remain an ideological party: "The ideology of the dominant party may actually be *that of defending the status-quo and of impeding changes that are inconsistent with its maintenance.*"[13] They note, further, "It is typical of this pattern that members of the opposition are defined as traitors to revolutionary causes and as threats to security. The developmental aspirations and mission of the nation . . . are identified with a single party."[14] Therefore, while administrations since Cárdenas chose not to commit themselves to far-reaching solutions of specific social problems, there has been no corresponding loss in the intensity of PRI's desire for *continuismo* and *imposición.*[15]

This pattern, which I call the ideology of one-party authoritarianism, has proved relatively successful in placating certain members of the coalition that would have preferred a more definitive commitment in PRI's ideological position. In most of these cases, however, the offer of political self-enhancement through guaranteed electoral victories showed that ideas can often be sacrificed for spoils. At the same time, there have been recurrent indications that an ideology based solely on authoritarian principles may, in the end, provide insufficient motivation to preserve the unity of the revolutionary sectors. Ex-President Lázaro Cárdenas warned against the *continuista* orientation of PRI, urging his revolutionary colleagues to revert to a "systematic analysis" of current social problems in the country.[16] Over 40 percent absenteeism in both the last presidential contest and 1973 congressional elections also indicates a decrease in motivation to preserve unity.

I suggest, therefore, that the neutralization of ideologies which has occurred within PRI is far from the open, flexible, and empirical character which so many contemporary Western scholars attribute to the pragmatic mind, because the party persists to this day in its authoritarian approach to politics. In a statement to the Mexican press, former PRI president

Alfonso Martínez Domínguez again gave evidence of his party's limited interpretation of open political dialogue; he said, "Minorities only have the right to offer opinions; they may not decide. The PRI will never be willing to share the responsibilities of government."[17]

Hence, if one accepts the distinction between ideology and pragmatism suggested by Sartori (that is, if one differentiates pragmatic political parties from ideological parties in terms of the kind of cognition and the degree of intensity which characterize their political belief patterns); and if one regards pragmatism as a sign of healthier democratic systems, then one must challenge the often unqualified optimism some reveal when they refer to Mexico's "one-party democracy," or to "popular participation" within such a system.[18] Moderation in the social content of a party's program does not automatically introduce a system of open politics, and it almost certainly never will, so long as the hegemonic-authoritarian pattern persists. As Sartori has suggested, ideological politics become pragmatic only when the cognitive dimension of the given system makes the transition from closed to open, and when the emotive dimension substitutes adamant-to-resilient for firm-to-flexible belief patterns.[19] PRI may have shifted toward greater resiliency (still a dimension within the closed cognitive structure) where ideology of social content is concerned, but it has persevered in its adamant commitment to the political status quo.

The ideology of alienation is the second ideology in post-revolutionary Mexico. This ideology characterizes all those political movements which have shown a marked distaste for the existing system and have chosen to operate either along the fringes or outside the revolutionary coalition. It incorporates a number of groups with class commitments ranging from the extreme left to the extreme right, as well as transient movements which at election time choose to split away from the ruling coalition and to challenge the authoritarian practices of the government party. Despite their diversity, these groups have all challenged in one way or another the ideology of one-party authoritarianism, and they have all maintained a pessimistic, highly critical outlook toward contemporary political trends in Mexico. Because this ideology of alienation has tended to be the ideology of a variety of political groups, it deserves careful examination.

While it is obvious that the social commitment of the individual ideologies advocated by these minority groups has prevented the kind of coalition which exists within PRI, there are some signs today that individual ideologies are progressively less adamant and are uniting under the general bond of ideological alienation. For example, the system of proportional representation for minority parties introduced in the Federal Chamber of Deputies through the 1962 and 1973 electoral reforms was in large measure a concession which PRI made to organized and persistent pressure from such unlikely allies as the Partido Popular Socialista (PPS) and the PAN. These joint efforts, heretofore unimaginable, could become the rule rather than the exception in the foreseeable future. The PPS, formerly a haven for the committed left, has been busy purging some of its most avowed Marxists; the party expelled three of its deputies because they were not following a more moderate line. Jorge Cruickshank García, who succeeded to the post of PPS president after the death of Vicente Lombardo Toledano, was described by political observers as considerably more conservative than Lombardo Toledano.[20] While the PPS has been shifting to the right, PAN also has adopted a more resilient set of beliefs. Indeed, PAN has veered sharply to the left in recent years, and in so doing won a pair of important municipal contests in the capital cities of Sonora (Hermosillo) and Yucatán (Mérida) in 1968.[21] These shifts toward the center may be creating opposition parties that show less diversity in class commitment and greater affinity in a shared sense of political alienation. The dialogue among alienated political groups now reflects paranoia. Name calling is still common between leaders of PAN and PPS. However, parties of alienation may be better equipped to make the transition to Western-style pragmatism than is PRI, because PRI is of necessity committed to perpetuate itself in power and is likely to continue to oppose any changes which might upset present patterns of power. The alienated, however, might create a more conciliatory dialogue to use as a common denominator against the static conditions that prevail under PRI rule. The former PAN president, Manuel González Hinojosa, suggested such a move when he stated that the national administration should be integrated by men of diverse ideological commitment, even by communists, in order to end political sterility in Mexico.[22]

Together, the minorities with ideologies of alienation could become a majority. Studies of election returns in the Federal District—certainly the most sophisticated political center in the country—indicate that minority party vote totals have nearly equaled PRI totals.[23] In 1970, a new manifestation of alienation—voter absenteeism—threatened to create, when coupled with percentages polled by opposition parties, a majority of national proprotions. Had the 43 percent of the voters who were absentees and the opposition parties (who polled 20 percent of the vote) selected a mutually acceptable candidate for the presidency, PRI and Echeverría might have found themselves unoccupied. Indeed, increased absenteeism in 1973 jeopardized any claims which PRI's congressional delegation had to majority support from citizens in Mexico City.

2

Political Alienation of the Right: The Intellectual Origins of Accion Nacional

> In a democracy, the opposition is not a negative force. On the contrary, the opposition in a democracy represents a force which prevents governments from pursuing narrow horizons that eventually lead them to a fatal dependency on one single party. When a government takes into account the demands of the opposition, it opens itself to the aspirations of the country, gathers the maximum number of elements for unity, and strengthens the foundations of its very existence.
>
> Adolfo Christlieb Ibarrola

One salient problem which developing systems have had to face is political and cultural fragmentation. As L. Vincent Padgett suggests, "Mexican history has generated a legacy which raises a number of problems for political socialization."[1] He notes, further:

> The Mexican political culture is a fragmented one in which the violence of internecine struggle has appeared again and again in the absence of consensus on fundamentals as to the way government should operate. . . . These matters have been much disputed, leaving in various sectors of society residues of commitments to values regarding proper uses of governmental power and reasons for existence of government which are at variance with major characteristics of the present system. These residues of allegiance to values of other periods have raised more

> questions of social adjustment because the dominant groups in the present situation cannot fall back upon some distinct philosophical system, such as Marxism, which can be treated as revealed truth for justification of the present political arrangements. Fragmentation of political culture is related to many questions over which Mexicans have shed each other's blood in the past. . . .[2]

Although the residues of allegiance of which Padgett speaks have been present since the early years of Mexico's quest for independence[3] and on both ends of the ideological spectrum, I shall in this chapter investigate the politics of alienation in postrevolutionary Mexico, specifically those movements representing the conservative position regarding the birth and formation of modern Mexico. Gastón García Cantú, a noted Mexican historian, has aptly defended the thesis that recent conservative manifestations in Mexico tend to differ from conservative movements of the nineteenth century in at least one significant area: the acceptance of juridical avenues of protest as opposed to the armed offensive, or *cuartelazo,* of yesteryear. As he notes, "certainly, the reaction's shift from the barracks to the legislature exemplifies the difference between past and present."[4]

This shift on the part of Mexican conservative groups and church elites[5] was not solely due to pressures within such groups. To be sure, the Mexican Church and some of her political allies were gradually sensing the need to elaborate theses on social justice, and to deemphasize the individualistic orientation that had marked Catholicism in Mexico since her independence from Spain. Equally important, however, were the transformative pressures brought about by the Mexican Revolution itself. As Ivan Vallier suggests, "Because of the special historical and institutional conditions that prevailed from the time of the conquest in the sixteenth century up to the independence period, the Church had not consistently pursued policies aimed toward building religious solidarity or the deepening of lay spirituality. Consequently, when basic changes occurred in the political sphere, the Church . . . could not resist the strategy of realigning itself with political power, and turned energetically to the task of securing both the legal bases of privilege and the support of political elites."[6] I shall show that Madero's desire to put an end to religious conflict in Mexico, despite the anticlerical tradition of Mexican liberalism, and the guarantees he was able to secure for the legitimacy of Catholic political action during his short-lived administration, contributed greatly to the adoption of a new political style by the conservatives. Subsequent administrations committed to anticlericalism eventually reawakened the militancy characteristic of nineteenth century conservatism in certain groups, such as the Cristeros and Sinarquistas. However, in spite of the anticlerical tone of the 1917 Constitution, other conservative groups such as the Asociación Católica de la Juventud Mexicana and PAN insist to this day that changes and remedies can be secured only through legitimate political action.

PAN does not regard itself as the successor of traditional conservatism, as prominent Panistas make clear. Juan Manuel Gómez Morín, son of the party's founder, observes, "The movements of the nineteenth century had many heroes. Perhaps these movements were the product of inevitable confrontations in the integrative phase of a nation; but one can certainly not characterize them as manifestations of institutionalization. In contrast, the new era is based on conviction, on a rational study of problems and solutions, on voluntary adherence to principles and platforms, on the permanent and free organization of the citizenry, and, consequently, on political action through genuine political parties."[7] The more immediate political and intellectual origins of PAN are to be found in this newer Mexican approach to conservatism, which began to manifest itself during the presidency of Francisco I. Madero.

THE MEXICAN REVOLUTION OF 1910 AND CATHOLIC CONSERVATISM

The real meaning of Mexico's 1910 Revolution has been much debated, and it is clear by now that no single study has offered the solution that will end the debate. The problem of interpretation is perhaps best explained by Mexican historians' common insistence on attributing to the original intent of the

Revolution goals and programs pursued and implemented only later. Therefore, attempts at defining and determining intent have given way to a less ambitious proposition, namely, that the Mexican Revolution never had a definite ideology or program. Certain goals and ideals were established, to be sure, from the start; the most notable was the condemnation of indefinite retention of power by one man or one group. But, as Daniel Cosío Villegas observes:

> Not all the initial aims were preserved to the end. On the contrary, some of the original goals lost their force and finally gave way to new ones. By these juxtapositions the ideological trend of the Revolution became even more confused, for these new propositions did not replace the old; rather, both old and new coexisted, superficially at least.[8]

This view is echoed by Antonio Roa Hernández, who notes that "the Mexican Revolution undoubtedly lacked an economic, political, and social platform planned in advance. It did not have theorists or ideologues to project and shape the movement. The Revolution was but a spontaneous uprising that was eventually able to develop a program through its own experience and the passage of time."[9]

If Madero's slogan, "Effective Suffrage, No Reelection," were accepted at face value, that is, if it meant that "political life, liberty, and democracy were of greater value even than material progress and that because of this it did not matter if this last were compromised in order to achieve the former,"[10] then one might guess that many Mexicans, regardless of ideological orientation, clung to Madero's movement, although admittedly in varying degrees of intensity.[11] After all, most groups with strong political aspirations had come to recognize by 1910 that the Díaz years had denied them all access to meaningful political participation, so that Madero's democratic message, which from the beginning was stated in abstract terms, was a welcomed alternative. I will show in the following pages that many leading Catholic groups, particularly the Partido Católico Nacional (PCN), founded on May 3, 1911, were among those who rallied in support of the Madero government.

After a period of intellectual dormancy which extended over almost half a century following the defeat of Mexican conservative theories and the implementation of the liberal 1857 Constitution, Catholic political thought tried to stage a comeback from 1903 to 1913, by identifying itself more closely with the growing social aspirations of the Mexican people. This liberal shift in the Church's position became particularly evident as a result of four Catholic Congresses, four Catholic-Agriculture Conventions, four Social-Catholic Seminars, and two Diets. These meetings investigated the problems of alcoholism, plagues affecting crops and cattle, and postulated programs to establish minimum family wages, to secure social benefits for labor and agriculture, and to combat communism. Still, the most salient feature of these Catholic gatherings was a new spirit of realism. The discovery of Catholic social theses, then, began to introduce new religious sentiments throughout the country, sentiments motivated by the conviction that these theses could indeed be applied to the solution of basic temporal problems within Mexico. Unlike those Catholic movements that had traditionally allied themselves with nineteenth century Mexican conservatism, and that had stressed the realms of the individual and of the liturgy, these meetings reoriented their thought toward man and society, and toward the social and temporal realms.[12]

Three factors were responsible for the failure of this new Catholic movement to create a general national conscience in Mexico. First, the Revolution itself supplanted many of the efforts of these meetings, since it had opted for violent change whereas the Catholics believed in a natural and peaceful evolution of society. Second, the assemblies themselves reached only select minorities and organized associations in the center of the country. Finally, the movement was late, slow, and fearful of reprisals by politicians averse to any form of organized Catholic participation in political affairs. In sum, "it was a period of faith, of religious life; yet, at the same time, it was marked by lack of organization, inertia, and apathy. The Church knew how to reawaken the religious spirit of the Mexican people. But circumstances, perhaps, prevented the Church from defending its social and political rights, as well as those of Catholic citizens."[13]

However, with Madero's victory over Porfirio Díaz and with his message of political democracy and liberty for all Mexicans, these Catholic groups were at long last able to move from mere statements of principle in a direction of active participation in the political arena. In May 1911, they grouped together to form PCN.[14] In the presidential elections held that year, PCN supported the Madero and de la Barra ticket, explaining:

> The Catholic Party has agreed to support Mr. Madero, not because it believes that this gentleman will try to favor Catholics in any way, outside of what the Constitution and other laws of the Republic prescribe, but because it believes to have found in him a true liberal who, wanting liberty for his own followers, does not propose to deny it to others.[15]

Madero, who had in his earlier writings emphasized the necessity of strong opposition parties for effective good government, welcomed the participation of the Catholic Party in the electoral contest.[16] In a public statement he observed "I consider the organization of the Catholic Party of Mexico as the first triumph of the liberties which we have conquered. Its platform *reveals advanced ideas and a desire to collaborate in our country's progress,* in a serious manner and within constitutional prescriptions."[17]

Other liberal elements, however, were less convinced of the wisdom of permitting conservative parties to operate in the newly won revolutionary system. Even within Madero's own party, the Constitucional Progresista, such a leading figure as Díaz Soto y Gama openly condemned the president for his conciliatory policies.

> Since Mr. Madero is a conciliator, we, his partisans, must guide him, lest we leave the country in the hands of the clergy to turn it into a Portugal or a Spain. We have the duty to demand adherence to the Laws of the Reform.[18]

Similarly, members of the Partido Liberal charged that Madero's program "reeked of sacristy." Still, the liberals as a group found it most difficult publicly to justify the persecution of conservatives while talking of political freedoms that should now guide Mexico. Horacio Barreda of the Partido Liberal declared that the existence of the PCN as a political force was justified, since its source of support was derived from a social group which had not lost its voice in Mexican society. He proceeded to observe: "The new name of 'National Catholic Party' . . . indicates that its ideals *have been modified,* and that it no longer pretends to be the conservative party of *fueros* and privileges. . . ."[19]

The debate among the liberal factions centered on the necessity of implementing the anticlerical provisions of the Laws of the Reform, particularly the Juárez and Lerdo Laws, and risked thereby the revival of old antagonisms. At least during the Madero years, it was the president himself who put an end to the debate. He emphatically declared that the reform laws could only be viewed from historical perspective, and that once the temporal powers of the Church had been destroyed, as he believed they already had been, old divisive issues and hatreds between conservatives and liberals should give way to a united effort on the part of all sectors of society. Madero warned: "We must treat all Mexicans as brothers and . . . we must not forget that we are no longer foes, that we are friends, and that united we fought against dictatorship. Just as we were allied and united during the struggle, so too, after having secured victory, we must unite now, and not argue over the spoils we have won. I am speaking of those legitimate spoils which consist of the attainment of our basic freedoms."[20]

For its part, PCN advanced a program in defense of national sovereignty, religious and educational liberties, an independent judiciary, credit for agriculture and industry, effective suffrage, and no reelection.[21] In addition to its platforms and public pronouncements, evidence of this program appeared in the party's press organ, *La Nación,* and in other pro-PCN newspapers throughout Mexico.[22]

This suggests that the intransigent Catholic groups of the past had largely given way to a new, more moderate breed of Catholic activists in the postrevolutionary Mexican political scene. Although many Catholics did advocate a return to pre-1857 conditions,[23] the early revolutionary period saw the emergence of tolerant organized groups, many of which PAN would later embody. The motto of the tolerants became:

"Catholics in Religion, but Mexicans in Politics." Thus, unlike traditional nineteenth century conservatives whose principal aims included the defense of the Catholic Church's property and temporal powers and the preservation of religious unity in Mexico, the PCN had to confront new issues, such as religious and educational liberties to which the Constitution of 1857, valid until 1917, was committed. The PCN's willingness, in spite of its sentiments of alienation, to operate within the system's legal framework cannot be overemphasized. It would suffer existing conditions rather than resort to force, but it would defend the sectors it represented by legal means such as advancing candidates for municipal elections and for election to local and national legislatures.[24]

The Catholic Party was active in the federal elections of September 1912—a contest which Brandenburg characterizes as the one which observed the principle of effective suffrage most carefully of all contests in Mexican political history.[25] PCN, one of eight major parties to present candidates during the campaign, won four senate seats and twenty-nine deputy seats.[26] More significantly—and unprecedented in Mexican politics—Madero's own Partido Constitucional Progresista (PCP) could not win a majority of deputy seats.[27]

In 1913, PCN obtained two addititional deputies in run-off elections, but the most striking victories came at the local level. PCN secured majorities in the state legislatures of Jalisco and México, a total of twenty-six *ayuntamientos* (precincts) in Michoacán, and *ayuntamientos* in Guanajuato, Aguascalientes, Oaxaca, Puebla, Querétaro, and Veracruz; PCN also won the governorships of Querétaro, Jalisco, México, and Zacatecas.[28]

PCN exerted legislative influence proportional to its numerical strength. In Michoacán, for example, with only two deputies in the state legislature, PCN was able only to press for a new electoral law. In Jalisco, however, with a majority of seats in the state legislature, the party was able to enact into law a substantial part of its program. This included a law on public education, which required liberty of instruction and the recognition of the competency of private schools, a law prescribing electoral reforms, and laws in defense of small property and of municipal autonomy. And, as I shall show in following chapters, the pursuit of these same objectives became a fundamental reason for the existence of PAN.

PCN's accomplishments in the National Congress were modest, since its proportional representation there was smaller than in some state legislatures. The most important laws enacted on the initiative of PCN were a law on lands (December 6, 1912), Sunday rest (April 7, 1913), and a law on unions (May 18, 1913).

In not quite three years, the party acquired 783 centers and almost a half-million members throughout the Republic, but the 1913 coup which ousted Madero destroyed these achievements. If Madero had survived, or if his views had prevailed after his assassination, perhaps the history of revolutionary Mexico would have been quite different, at least insofar as its internal political organization and structure was concerned.

Victoriano Huerta's attempt to secure the support of the PCN in the November 26, 1913 elections proved futile; the party threw its weight behind the candidacy of Federico Gamboa. In those elections, the Electoral College conceded only five congressional seats to PCN, but the party had the satisfaction of depriving Huerta of the possibility of legalizing his betrayal of Madero; PCN pressed for the nullification of the elections, thereby compelling Huerta to resort to an armed revolt to seize power. The PCN was the first organized group to feel the effects of the new dictator's wrath. He banned its paper, *La Nación,* on January 14, 1914. He imprisoned Fernández Somellera, the president of PCN, and Enrique M. Zepeda, the director of *La Nación,* in the fortress of San Juan de Ulúa and eventually exiled them on February 2, 1914.[29]

Although separated by two decades from PCN, PAN's intellectual and political debts to it are readily apparent. Like PCN, PAN has sought to dissociate itself from traditional conservative movements and to project a more tolerant image. Both parties were willing to reject solutions by arms and to operate within the existing legal and institutional framework of the system. But most important, PAN has crusaded for programs such as electoral reform, municipal autonomy, and educational liberties, programs remarkably similar to PCN's programs. In the truest sense it was PCN that gave birth to modern conservatism in Mexico. Because Madero recognized the legitimacy of this movement and its right to be heard openly, he has become, among contemporary conservative circles, the most respected figure of the 1910 Revolution.

THE CONSTITUCIONALISTA PERIOD AND THE POLITICS OF THE CATHOLIC STUDENT MOVEMENT

The "glorious" Revolution initiated by Francisco Madero—the revolution which had aroused general sympathy in Mexico—came to an end in 1913. According to the new breed of conservatives, that year marked the beginning of the "ugly" revolution. It was then that the peasants of the state of Morelos took the movement into their own hands, creating devastation and confusion, and replacing those values initially espoused by Madero. Following the Huerta coup, guerrilla forces throughout the country lashed out against Catholics and the Church. This resurgence in anti-Catholic sentiment was brought about chiefly by the perennial animosities between liberal and conservative camps in Mexico; Madero, during his short-lived administration, was the only man ever able to tone down these animosities.

Despite this undeclared persecution and the disappearance of PCN as an organized political group, the Church continued to exercise considerable influence on Mexican society. With no immediate prospects for a return to a climate in which opposition parties could operate effectively, the Church and her allies chose to try to create powerful interest groups. During a period which lasted approximately from 1913 until the Cristero uprising of 1926—including the immediate post-1917, or constitutional, stage of the Mexican Revolution—outspoken student and Catholic youth organizations carried on the politics of political alienation of the right. The most notable organizations were the National League of Catholic Students (Liga Nacional de Estudiantes Católicos), composed principally of university students and students of private institutions and organized by the Jesuit Carlos M. Heredia,[30] and the Asociación Católica de la Juventud Mexicana (ACJM), founded by Father Bernardo Bergoënd, S. J. These organizations shaped leaders for future conservative movements. Pedro Durán, Manuel Herrera y Lasso, Jorge Prieto Laurens, and Capistrán Garza played chief roles during the Catholic revolt against President Plutarco Elías Calles. Still more significant, PAN has attracted, to this day, a large number of former ACJM militants.[31]

The major objective of these organizations, particularly of ACJM, was to propagate the social teachings of the Church as expressed in such papal encyclicals as *Rerum Novarum.* But ACJM went beyond the mere study and propagation of this doctrine; it promoted the creation of services and of economic and syndical organizations. In this way, the Catholic student movement in these years took over that new spirit of conservatism which PCN had initiated. However, unlike PCN, ACJM had to operate in a climate marked by violence and open hostility toward the Catholic Church. The constitutional convention at Querétaro and the resulting Constitution of 1917, which in effect legitimized anticlerical sentiments in the country, contributed greatly to the right's deepening sense of alienation from the political process. In brief, the anticlerical provisions of the Constitution of 1917 closely followed the text and the spirit of the Laws of the Reform, promulgated by Benito Juárez. They denied the Church its temporal possessions, placed religious orders on an equal footing with other professions, and removed the Church from the field of education.

When the new Constitution was declared, the clergy was quick to respond. The Pastoral Letter of Mexican Prelates of February 24, 1917 incorporated most of the conservatives' case against the Consititution. Not only did it protest against the anticlerical provisions themselves, but the letter also condemned the Constitution for its alleged attack on the individual and social liberties of the Mexican people. In defense of the position taken by the Mexican clergy, protests against the Constitution were also voiced by Catholic leaders throughout Latin America, the United States, and the Holy See, as well as by some members of the propertied class in Mexico.[32] These protests contributed to reinforce the liberals' conviction that the Mexican Church of the 1920s was still the same Church of the past, sympathetic as ever toward individualistic, liberal-capitalist regimes, and that the social message issued by the Roman Church was either insincere or had failed to become a source of inspiration for Catholic elites in Mexico. To complicate matters, many of the Mexican clergy did little to mitigate this conviction, because most parish priests had been educated in another century and lacked the necessary preparation to fully understand the new conservatives' insistence in spreading the social teachings of the Church.

Convinced of the impossibility of active participation in the political process, ACJM and other organizations substituted for their original enthusiasm a gradual withdrawal. They decided to remove themselves totally from politics, looking upon politics as a repulsive profession, and to work instead for the integration of Christian thought in revolutionary Mexico.[33]

The undeclared persecution against the Mexican Church which had been rekindled under Venustiano Carranza and the Constitucionalistas was continued by the Alvaro Obregón Administration (1920–24). Yet the constitutional provisions which could have turned the undeclared resistance into open resistance were never invoked or enforced. Indeed, one of the keys to the success of the Mexican constitutional system has been and continues to be the willingness on the part of political leaders to differentiate between constitutional theory and practice, that is, the willingness not to press for the implementation of laws which could have serious divisive effects on society. Thus, laws often function as warnings, as omnipresent testimonies that, if seriously challenged, the system is indeed capable of meeting the challenge. Both Carranza and Obregón, while avowedly opposed to Church interests, demonstrated this flexible attitude. Obregón's successor, however, refused to play with the Church according to this tacit rule of the constitutional game. His refusal was largely responsible for the three-year Cristero uprising (1926–29). When Plutarco Elías Calles became president in 1924, he placed the Church on the firing line of legality and sparked a confrontation with Church forces that temporarily interrupted the way of life which postrevolutionary conservatism had come to expect. Calles drove the Church and her sympathizers to traditional means of arms and violence and created an irreparable division within post-1910 circles of the right.

THE CALLES ADMINISTRATION AND THE REVOLT OF THE CRISTEROS

The declared persecution of the Catholic Church in Mexico commenced on January 2, 1926, when President Calles requested a reform of the penal code from Congress. Five days later, the legislature granted the president the faculties necessary to put the reform into effect. It called for the regulation and implementation of the provisions of the Constitution's Article 130 which curtailed the Church's temporal privileges. Amid increasing rumors that Mexican Catholics were about to begin an active campaign against the Constitution's anticlerical provisions and aggravated by an interview in one of the leading Mexico City dailies which quoted Archbishop José Mora y del Río using the phrase "combat the laws," Calles formally put the controversial regulative law into effect on February 10.[34] Archbishop Mora emphatically denied having used the controversial phrase, and the charges which the government had brought against him were eventually dropped.

The Catholic opposition centered around the federal authority's claim (supported by Article 130) that it had rights in the regulation of Church discipline. According to the law, the Church had no claim to any juridical personality whatsoever, priests were classified as simple professionals, state legislatures could determine the maximum number of priests in their localities, priests had to be Mexican-born, and no churches could be opened without prior authorization from the Secretaría de Gobernación.[35]

The ACJM, whose own active interest in the political process had been rekindled by Calles's war of laws, delivered a message to the nation on February 25, charging that a law contrary to natural law was no law at all, and adding that it would exhaust every available legal avenue to press for constitutional reform.[36] New ACJM groups grew rapidly throughout the country, even in areas where it had not previously been active.[37]

Unimpressed, President Calles ordered the state governors to waste no time in enforcing the provisions of Article 130.[38] At the same time, he introduced additional legal provisions outlawing opposition to the Constitution. On July 22, 1926, the president and his Secretary of Public Education, Juan Manuel Puig, decreed the compulsory inspection by the federal government of all private grade schools, and the Calles law of July 31 proposed rigorous sanctions against any violator of constitutional Articles 3, 5, 24, 27, and 130.[39]

The reaction of the right to these new provisions was almost immediate. On the same day that the Calles law went into effect, the Mexican bishops suspended public worship and discontinued all church services in an effort to arouse the indignation of the Mexican people. A week later, the general committee of the ACJM declared an economic boycott aimed principally against all theaters and cinemas (fifteen had to close down within days); against businesses selling luxury items; and, most significantly, against the Banco de México, which was the bank of the nation and President Calles's pet project. Although a total of 7 million pesos were withdrawn from the bank, a large sum considering the bank's small reserves, the lives of most Mexicans were not affected.[40] If anything, these actions served to unite a small number of conservative forces who wished to take up arms against the Calles regime in defense of the Church.

In his State of the Union Message of September 1, 1926, President Calles defended his actions, insisting that the Church had not been deprived of any rights, since all he had done was to enforce constitutional provisions.[41] On September 24, in what was to be the last peaceful effort in the controversy, the National League for the Defense of Religious Liberty (Liga Nacional Defensora de la Libertad Religiosa) submitted to Congress a petition signed by 2 million people demanding the immediate reform of Articles 3, 5, 24, 27, and 130. After due consideration, the Chamber of Deputies discarded the petition and threw its full support behind the president.[42]

Already as the result of some scattered incidents in which the authorities confronted, and often shot, individual citizens, and with declared support from Rome, the Cristero resistance with its slogan "¡Viva Cristo Rey!" made itself felt during late summer 1926.[43] On October 29, however, the resistance became a rebellion with the armed movements led by Rodolfo Gallegos in Guanajuato and by Enrique Gorostieta in Jalisco. I shall not present a detailed account of this civil war, since the

Cristeros' violent approach to politics represented a clear departure from the tradition of legitimate and peaceful participation which postrevolutionary conservative groupings had tried to advance.[44] The actions of the Cristeros were more like actions undertaken by nineteenth century conservative movements. Their intellectual program, however, is more important here since PAN was to incorporate a large part of it a decade later.

The two most important spokesmen for the Cristero movement were René Capistrán Garza, who had been designated by the Executive Committee of the National League for the Defense of Religious Liberty as titular head of the Catholic armies, and Anacleto González Flores, the chief engineer of the rebellion.[45] Early in 1927, Capistrán Garza presented a written manifesto to the Mexican people, which in effect became the ideological platform of the movement. A review of its major theses presents a striking testimony of the parentage of the Cristeros to PAN. The manifesto included freedom of religion and conscience; separation of church and state; freedom of education; political liberties; freedom of association; effective guarantees for the worker; protection of national and foreign capital; prohibition of retroactive laws; respect for private property; equitable land distribution; and creation of a small propertied class.[46]

This program of action, the imprint of the more progressive brand of Mexican conservatism, was intellectualized by Anacleto González Flores whose writings give the most concise philosophical statement of the Cristero position.[47] To the revolutionary family, as Brandenburg calls the ruling coalition, these writings were clearly subversive, since they contained lucid attacks on the developing political system. González Flores mercilessly lashed out against the Revolution and the Constitution of 1917 as responsible for a divided nation, and recognized—as indeed did the revolutionaries—that the ideological battle for the sympathies of the Mexican people could be won only through the educative process. This recognition of the influence of education on societal values was to become, under President Lázaro Cárdenas (1934–40), a vital issue in the revolutionary-conservative struggle (see Chapter 4) but it was considered prophetically in one of González Flores' best known articles, "The Three Crusades": crusades of the good (that is Catholic) press, of the catechism, and of the book.[48]

The Cristero episode was terminated in mid-1929 by provisional President Emilio Portes Gil. Any evaluation of the movement must credit it with compelling the government to admit, tacitly of course, that an inflexible pursuit of constitutional ideals was impractical if the unity of the nation was to be preserved. An end of the civil war had not been possible under Calles, since he had clearly committed himself to a position which, although legally tenable (he was, after all, merely enforcing the law of the land, as he had stated), had very serious practical consequences. Calles' hand-picked successors, Portes Gil, Pascual Ortíz Rubio, and Abelardo Rodríguez, who successively occupied the presidency from 1929 to 1934, chose not to follow the pattern introduced by their mentor, preferring instead to pursue the extralegal avenues of coexistence with the Catholic Church and her allies. Thus, as the result of a series of conciliatory talks which took place on 12, 14, and 21 June 1929, between Portes Gil and Church representatives Monsignors Ruiz y Flores and Pascual Díaz, with the good offices of United States Ambassador Dwight Morrow, the clergy was induced to reopen all churches in Mexico on June 30.[49]

This victory should, however, not obscure the negative effects of the Cristero revolt on the postrevolutionary conservative movement in Mexico since it seriously divided the movement itself. On one hand, militants regarded the political system as irreconcilable with their own aspirations and considered the Church's willingness to negotiate a major sign of weakness. The principal representative of this position was to become the Sinarquista movement. On the other hand, the tolerants accepted the realities of the Revolution and were willing to operate within the system in an effort to improve it. PAN eventually came to represent the tolerants.

The return to politics of violence thus undermined the unified conservative front even though a consolidation of forces has taken place from time to time on certain common issues. Also, the Cristeros strengthened liberal opposition to the Church and her allied forces. Having chosen violence as their weapon, they obscured the conscious pacific and social efforts of other conservative elements in Mexico, and they thereby provided liberals with the needed ammunition to attack all conservatives as subversives bent upon the complete destruction of Mexican society.

Finally, the revolt was partly responsible for President Calles' efforts toward the creation of a unified party of the Revolution. For, with the introduction of a structure which would incorporate the various sectors of society into a revolutionary family of sorts, a structure with the potential of legitimizing once and for all the goals of the Revolution, however these might be defined, and capable of dominating the process, Calles clearly hoped to reduce the ambitions of alienates of the right to participate in the system.[50]

THE REVOLUTIONARY PARTY AND THE POLITICAL AND IDEOLOGICAL BATTLES IN MEXICO

With the presidential term of Calles drawing to an end, Mexico was confronted with the delicate issue of succession. The issue was delicate because the Madero tradition had clearly committed the Revolution and its heirs to the inviolability of the no-reelection principle. General Alvaro Obregón's decision to depart from this tradition by announcing his intention to become president for a second time shook the very foundations of the emerging Mexican political and constitutional system. For one thing, the decision called for an immediate reform of the Constitution of 1917 to permit a second term of office. Calles and the Congress promptly carried out this reform, in the face of no small opposition. More important, the decision had divisive effects which the country, already plagued by three years of violent civil strife, could ill afford. Obregón campaigned actively throughout Mexico in 1927, deriving his major support from the Agrarista party, and the popular reception which generally met him increased his confidence and obscured the solid opposition that was developing against him, not only from revolutionary groups, but from conservative elements as well. In 1927, at the height of the presidential campaign, the Executive Committee of the National League for the Defense of Religious Liberty decreed that Obregón had to be eliminated. Whether the decree actually called for the assassination of the candidate or for something short of assassination is not clear, but an unsuccessful attempt on Obregón's life soon followed on November 13, 1927. Manuel Velázquez Morales, Nahúm Lamberto Ruíz, and Juan Antonio Tirado Arias were involved in the plot. The three were seriously wounded before their arrest and died before the authorities could conduct further investigation. It was suspected, though never proved, that all had been active members of the League.[51]

The remainder of the Obregón episode is well known to students of Mexican history. Obregón won handily his second bid for the nation's highest office, but on July 17, 1928 when he was still president-elect, he was assassinated by José de León Toral, a religious fanatic. As in the earlier attempt on Obregón's life, the authorities were either unable or unwilling to link the assassination to any organized conspiracy.[52]

In his last State of the Union Message in September 1928, Calles called for the creation of a revolutionary party. A convention—symbolically held in Querétaro—attended by "groups identified in some way with revolutionary ideals," established the Partido Nacional Revolucionario (PNR) in March 1929, subsequently known as Partido de la Revolución Mexicana (PRM) (as of 1938) and as Partido Revolucionario Institucional (PRI) (since 1946).[53]

Although Calles committed himself to a return to the no-reelection principle (the constitutional provision was restored to its original intent shortly after the death of Alvaro Obregón) by refusing to remain in office, certain circles thought that he intended to use the PNC to perpetuate his political control and promote his own ambitions. His choice of Emilio Portes Gil as the first in what was to be a series of presidents submissive to Callista policies clearly reinforced this suspicion. Calles had ceased to be president in person, but the power of the office was still his. It was against Calles' indirect retention of presidential power that the new conservatives waged the first in a long series of battles against the newly founded Revolutionary Party.

VASCONCELISMO AND THE 1929 PRESIDENTIAL CAMPAIGN

The movement most directly relevant as a political origin of PAN during the decade that preceded its foundation was the 1929 presidential campaign and the Vasconcelista challenge to the emerging monopoly of the PNR. The prominent Panista, Luis Calderón Vega, himself admits to this: "In many respects Vasconcelismo may be regarded as a historical precursor of Acción Nacional."[54]

Named after its inspirer, José Vasconcelos, who was the brilliant first Secretary of Education in the Obregón cabinet and respected philosopher-pedagogue, this movement came to embody the opposition to the political victories won by Calles in 1928–29. As has been noted, these victories included the temporary departure from the principle of no reelection, the defeat of Catholic forces, and the establishment of a monolithic revolutionary party. With Vasconcelos, it was a teacher, not a general, who, for the first time in the aftermath of the Revolution, campaigned for the dignity of public life and for the elimination of corruption in government. Running under the banner of the Antireeleccionista party, he derived his support primarily from the middle class. Intellectuals formed the genetic nucleus of Vasconcelismo, and it was the 1915 and 1929 university student generations that first came out in support of Vasconcelos' bid for the presidency. It is important to note that PAN founder, Manuel Gómez Morín, became actively involved in the Vasconcelos effort by serving as campaign treasurer.[55]

The Calles-controlled PNR had endorsed Pascual Ortíz Rubio as its presidential candidate, a man who was undoubtedly a pale political figure in contrast to the fiery philosopher-*caudillo.* The official election returns which, as expected, declared Ortíz Rubio the winner are considered to have been fraudulent.

Vasconcelos' great relevance to Mexico's political development, therefore, is not to be assessed in terms of his own unsuccessful bid for power. Rather, his movement represented a patent manifestation that alienation from the Mexican political system extended to the ranks of the so-called revolutionary family; that certain prominent revolutionaries did sympathize with the aspirations of these new conservatives;[56] and, most important, that the reemergence of political parties, defunct for all practical purposes from the time of the Huerta coup until the founding of the PNR, once again provided the opposition with organizational avenues to voice their discontent, as the Madero presidency had recognized. The Vasconcelismo of the 1920s was in many respects a direct descendant of the Maderismo of the early revolutionary period. Both movements were aimed at rekindling civic spirit in the country. Both represented struggles on behalf of political freedoms and against political monopoly and dictatorship (this time, the dictatorship was in the form of the PNR and Calles.[57] The issue of no reelection had been a central concern of these two leaders; for Madero it had been Díaz' *continuismo,* whereas for Vasconcelos the concern had resulted from the relative ease with which revolutionaries were able to depart from democratic principles at will, evidenced by the Calles-Obregón manipulations to alter the initial spirit of the Constitution. It was, therefore, no small coincidence that they ran equally under the banner of so-called *antireeleccionista* parties. Vasconcelos had in effect campaigned for a return to Madero's notions of political democracy, which were for the new conservatives the most appealing of all revolutionary tenets.

Panistas today point out that Vasconcelos, like Madero, failed to effectively translate his worthy aspirations, because his movement never really departed from the ills of *personalismo,* or personality-cult, which had traditionally plagued the history of political parties in Mexico. In other words, by failing to translate his own personal appeal into the establishment of a permanent party of opposition, Vasconcelos was unable to challenge the increasing institutionalization within the PNR. In his correspondence with Vasconcelos, Alfonso Taracena notes that, in his exile, Vasconcelos had been attracted to the idea of forming a permanent party under the name of Partido Regenerador. The decision not to pursue the project was probably in part the result of a wounded ego, which was aggravated by the Antireeleccionistas' censure of Vasconcelos as a madman and a coward for his failure to return to the political scene following his defeat. But it was equally the result of his deep-seated conviction that the political battle could only be won by men, not by "theoretical schemes." In fact, the eventual distantiation between PAN and Vasconcelos revolved around the pros and cons of ideology-based parties as opposed to personality-oriented parties. "A political party," Vasconcelos once wrote, "must be given life by men, because it is made for action, not for theory. There can be no contest of parties in Mexico, at least not until an end is put to the conflict between the educated man and the cave man, who, from his barrack, has been polluting a century of our history. The new party must be made up of armed men. I was always very proud to be *personalista* like Madero, for it is he, and no one else, who truly embodied the goals of national regeneration."[58]

Although the Vasconcelista effort was transitional in nature,[59] it did serve to underscore in the minds of many of his followers the fact that the politics of opposition could be effectively waged only through permanent structures. This conviction was strengthened by one of the gravest ideological issues to divide liberals and conservatives, the battle for the minds of the citizens, which Anacleto González Flores had prophesied a decade earlier.

ARTICLE 3 AND THE EDUCATIONAL BATTLE UNDER CARDENAS

In the preceding pages, I observed that the Vasconcelista movement of 1928–29 served to reorient conservative forces in Mexico toward the political process and to emphasize the necessity of permanent political parties in order to challenge effectively the existing structures. The presidency of General Lázaro Cárdenas (1934–40) represents the last important stage in the political consolidation of postrevolutionary conservative groups in Mexico, and it was during his administration that the most powerful contemporary movements of the right were born: the Unión Nacional Sinarquista (UNS) and PAN.

Padgett notes that from the time that Cárdenas assumed the presidency until he left office in 1940, it was "the left wing [of the Revolutionary Party] that dominated Mexican government policy."[60] As a consequence of this, the struggle between revolutionary and conservative forces was characterized mainly by ideological overtones. Of all the issues that aggravated this struggle, it was the reform of Article 3 of the Constitution of 1917, engineered by Cárdenas, that had the most serious consequences.

Article 3 of the Constitution had, since its formulation at the Querétaro convention of 1917, always been opposed by conservative groups, and, as noted earlier in this chapter, conservative constitutional opposition had included this article among others. The obvious and stated intent of the provision had been to combat the influence of the Church and private Catholic schools in the Mexican education process.[61] But the potential opposition to the article had managed to remain silent since very loose implementation was practiced by the authorities. The Calles years, to be sure, had served to revive the issue, and they, in effect, set the stage for the great controversy of 1934, but the Calles "puppets" had been unwilling to press the issue further.

Toward the end of 1933, however, the socialist forces in Mexico began to regroup. With the blessings of candidate Cárdenas, the PNR convention, held in Querétaro that year, set out to formulate the controversial Six-Year Plan, which, among other measures, proposed that the state not only have complete control of education, but that it should give it a social orientation.[62] It is significant to observe here that the wording used at the convention (*orientación social*) was sufficiently obscure to win the support of party leaders and to conceal the real intent of its authors and chief engineers which, besides Cárdenas, included Narciso Bassols, Secretary of Public Education under President Rodríguez, and Federal Deputy Alberto Bremauntz, whose Marxist orientation was secret to no one.

This became clear soon after the PNR convention, when it was learned that a Special Commission of Deputies, appointed by the National Revolutionary Bloc of the Chamber, and headed by Mr. Bremauntz, had met on December 11, 1933 to urge the immediate reform of Article 3 to read "Mexican education shall be *socialist*." This initiative met with a temporary setback, as the result of the direct intervention of out-going President Abelardo Rodríguez. In a letter addressed to Carlos

Riva Palacio, president of the PNR, Rodríguez stated his opposition in the following terms:

> It is my sincere opinion that the modification introduced to the Six-Year Plan, which pretends to establish in our Magna Carta the principle of socialist education, represents one of those errors committed—in good faith, perhaps—with the idea of establishing a progressive system, but one which is clearly unadaptable to our realities and impractical for the life of the Mexican collectivity. If our banner, our objectives and our principles have been geared to the elimination of religious prejudices in education, I believe that we would equally destroy all our accomplishments if we were to substitute socialist sectarianism for religious sectarianism.[63]

Despite this temporary setback, the socialist elements were able to get their way almost immediately after President Cárdenas took office. On 13 December 1934, a decree reforming Article 3 appeared in the *Diario Oficial.* The new constitutional text read:

> The education which the State shall impart will be socialist, and, in addition to excluding all religious doctrine, it will combat fanaticism and prejudices, to which end the school shall organize its teaching and activities in such a way as to be in the position to form in the minds of youth a rational and exact concept of the universe and of social life.[61]

This "rational and exact concept" clause was subjected to much ridicule in certain intellectual circles. Salvador Novo, with his great flair for sarcasm, writes:

> And what happens now to the people's ideology? Well, gentlemen, the matter is quite simple. The humble and uncultured people continue to believe in heaven, in the saints, in God, in the devil and hell, because all these ingredients facilitate a simple interpretation of life and the universe. But the fashionable leaders of the day, who also happen to adhere to a fashionable ideology, predicate socialism and demagoguery, which results in an internal

> conflict for our hapless proletarian comrades. On the one hand, they are instructed to believe that private property must be done away with, yet on the other, they are given *ejidal* property; they are commanded not to worship the saints, but they are encouraged to worship Marx, Engels and Lenin; they are told that the banner of Our Lady of Guadalupe is not sacred, that it is only a piece of cheap cloth, but that the red and black flag is sacred. Thus, we see that demagogic socialism represses the inclinations of a people that is still basically committed to religious principles.[65]

In many ways, the text brought back to mind Calles' "Grito de Guadalajara," in which the ex-President had asserted: "We must penetrate and gain control of the consciences of our children, because the youth and children are and must belong to the Revolution."[66] Although the intent of the new article was directed exclusively to primary education, advocates of socialism aimed ultimately to take possession of all levels of education, including the National University of Mexico (UNAM), whose struggle for autonomy had been recognized and decreed by President Emilio Portes Gil in 1929. The task of infiltrating the university was undertaken by Vicente Lombardo Toledano, with the unreserved support of Education Secretary, Narciso Bassols. And the task of defending the university in the earlier stages of this ideological battle fell upon its rector, Manuel Gómez Morín. The confrontation of these two men, both members of the famous 1915 student generation, both widely acclaimed as among the "Seven Wise Men of Mexico,"[67] and both the eventual founders of the major opposition parties in existence today, PAN and PPS, is a remarkable chapter in the history of Mexican education.

When Gómez Morín was unanimously elected rector of the National University of Mexico on October 23, 1933, the institution had already faced a series of crises related to the autonomy issue. Vicente Lombardo Toledano had attempted during the First Congress of Mexican University Scholars held in Mexico City (September 7–14, 1933) to impose the socialist orientation on the university curriculum, but he encountered stiff opposition from his former teacher, the highly respected Antonio Caso.[68] After a lengthy speech, Caso declared:

> The thesis that I oppose says that the University must have a creed, or a posture, or a declaration of doctrine. I shall always vote against this, because the University, as a moral entity can not give patronage to any thesis, creed, or doctrine . . . If this proposal passes, we are left but with two alternatives: either we engage in collectivism or we abandon the classroom. If it passes, professor Caso ceases to belong to the University; this I swear to all of you with all my heart, with all my soul.[69]

Thus, Caso opposed Lombardo not because the latter was a Marxist, but because his student in effect was pretending to deny him the right to dissent. Having failed to impress Caso, Lombardo set out to woo major socialist leaders and the so-called Cardenista student elements, whose major organ was the Partido Nacional Estudiantil Pro-Cárdenas.[70]

Except for Cardenista students, a small minority, the university students supported Caso and his stand for autonomy and academic freedom. On September 25, 1933, the School of Law and Social Sciences initiated a massive student strike that forced the expulsion of Lombardo Toledano and the resignation of university rector, Roberto Medellín, who had been linked to the infiltration movement. It was at this point that Manuel Gómez Morín appeared on the scene.[71] From the very beginning of his term as rector, he was faced with the wrath of the Lombardistas.

Using the complementary law which granted the National University its autonomy on July 10, 1929, Secretary Bassols handed a severe blow to the very financial bases of the university. He decreed for UNAM a patrimony for life of 10-million pesos (when the budget had in previous years averaged 4 to 5-million pesos annually) and stated that henceforth it was to subsist from the interest that it could draw from that sum. This meant, in effect, that UNAM had to conform to a limited budget of 70,000 pesos per month. When he decreed the financial starvation of the university, Bassols warned in Congress: "Citizens of the University, we give you this money of the people, but keep in mind that this is the last sacrifice; if you don't use it properly, the Revolution will have met its obligations, and shall instead gladly spend its patrimony in the fields of the proletariat."[72]

Gómez Morín met this challenge promptly. He instituted his now famous program of "Austerity and Work" which called for the reduction of faculty salaries and other university programs, and which, "thanks to his talents and example" was seconded by the university community without reservations. He began by alloting himself a token salary of 300 pesos per month, which he never collected. In his two years as rector, 46,000 pesos in salaries was donated by the faculty to the university. The total university budget was reduced from 5 to 1.5 million pesos, this despite the fact that the Lombardistas had left a deficit of over 200,000 pesos.[73]

By November 1934, the university had successfully frustrated all efforts to include it in the reform of Article 3. I should note that UNAM did not join the antisocialist movement and demonstrations. It was the opinion of university officials that so long as it authentically met with its proper mission, UNAM would continue to cleanse the political life in Mexico.[74]

THE CONSERVATIVE CONSOLIDATION AGAINST CARDENAS: SINARQUISTAS AND PANISTAS

When Gómez Morín stepped down from the Rectory in 1934, Cárdenas and the PNR had just begun to implement fully the Six-Year Plan. In the educational sphere they had successfully reformed Article 3 to conform to their ideologies, despite some organized popular opposition.[75] The new administration moved swiftly into other areas by calling for the increased collectivization and socialization of the national economy and of agriculture. Article 27 of the 1917 Constitution, which had established the bases for agricultural reform in Mexico, was to become under Cárdenas a major weapon against conservative forces. Article 27 was used sparingly in the earlier decades of the Revolution—in five years, Carranza had redistributed only 224,000 hectares, and the successive administrations from Obregón to Cárdenas, 10 million—Cárdenas was eventually to distribute 18 million hectares in his six years in office; he placed major emphasis on the development of communal *ejidos.*[76]

The thesis has been advanced that in Mexico the cycle for the gestation of political crises is three years. Whenever a new administration comes into power, the struggle of the social classes for the control of the policy-making process is renewed. Interest groups clash among themselves, forcing alignment with or against the new administration. Thus, it is during the first three years of the government that a regime is best able to develop its program. In the first half of his term the president reveals his capability for offensive action. Then comes the period of decadence. The second half of the presidential term is characterized by a constant strategic retreat, by an elastic resistance against new political forces which no longer think in the present but in the future.[77]

This thesis is particularly applicable to the Cárdenas years. Except for sporadic opposition, mostly by the university community, Cárdenas was able to obtain support for most of his programs; and according to the thesis above, the most intense year of Cardenismo was 1937. Attempts at establishing a permanently organized opposition to the president had met with little if any success before that date.[78] But toward mid-1937, the Mexican political scene witnessed the growth of some significant conservative opposition movements. On May 23, 1937, the first of these movements, the Unión Nacional Sinarquista (UNS), was founded in León, Guanajuato.[79] It was intended as an order of Christian democracy, first under God, then under a God-fearing state, and the UNS was most directly descended from the earlier Cristero movement. Like the Cristeros, the Sinarquistas were not only ardent Catholics but also disciplined soldiers of a militant theocratic faith.[80] Again, like the Cristeros, they directed their efforts toward the forgotten peasant masses—those who had benefitted little from the Revolution. Both movements eventually gained their greatest strength in the *Bajío* region of Mexico, where 70 percent of the peasants did not own their land.[81] In contrast to the policies of President Cárdenas, whose objective was the communization of land, the two movements urged the development of the small private property.

Appealing primarily to the humble, the Sinarquistas were markedly anti-intellectual, as the Cristeros had been a decade earlier. Their militancy was in direct line with the intransigent position taken by prerevolutionary conservatives, and it reflected a strong sense of alienation from the entire revolutionary tradition, perhaps more so than any other single conservative group. In effect, the Sinarquistas were heirs to that extralegal approach which, as already noted, the Cristeros had helped to revive, and they weakened the more tolerant forces which had attempted to take full command of the conservative movement in the postrevolutionary period. Unwilling to take any part in the existing system, the Sinarquistas moved with missionary zeal into the countryside, often living, working, and eating with the peasants. In confrontations with the authorities, Sinarquistas placed major emphasis on martyrdom. "God demands the blood of martyrs to save Mexico," became an instant battle cry. As one author puts it, "within the ranks of the UNS there emerged a sort of ode dedicated to blood, and a literature that was both morbid in content, and destined to weaken the spirit."[83] Guanajuato was the state that gave the movement its greatest number of martyrs—fifty-seven in 1939 alone.

If the politics of Sinarquismo are not of direct relevance to those later adopted by PAN, their doctrine and program certainly are. The Pentágolo Sinarquista and the Sixteen-Point Program represent the two most complete statements of the Sinarquista position, which incorporated many of the aspirations of post-1910 Mexican conservatism.[84] For example, their doctrine spoke of a common good—*Bien Común*—a concept which for them represented the exact antithesis of the class struggle which Cárdenas had encouraged in Mexico. The idea of *Bien Común,* which will be developed in the following chapter, was to become the foundation stone of Panista ideology.

Although the influence of the Sinarquista movement centered primarily in the states of Guanajuato, Jalisco, Querétaro and Michoacán, it managed to grow to national proportions in the last part of the Cárdenas administration. The exact number of adherents cannot be determined, but it was estimated that by 1940 there were over one half million hard-core Sinarquistas throughout Mexico.[85]

During its early years, the UNS never intended to become a political party, and its lack of structural orientation was provided eventually by PAN. There is much accuracy in the statement, "PAN is the brain, cold, calculating, and proud; UNS is the heart, burning, blind, fanatical, and willing to shed its blood to the very last drop."[86]

The efforts of providing Mexican postrevolutionary conservatism with an organized, permanent party of opposition—efforts which date back to the Madero years—resulted in the birth of PAN in September 1939. In subsequent chapters, I will discuss the ideology, organization, policy influence, and electoral activities of PAN.

3

Maderismo Revisited: The Political Ideology of PAN

> The guiding principle of a party is its ideology or doctrine; it is the compass or polar star which permits the navigator to fix and verify his course any time during the cruise. The political ideology of our party is national in scope, because it proposes to strengthen and perfect the natural and cultural roots that are the basis of the historical unity of the Mexican people, of what has made it into a nation. *Acción Nacional* maintains that the common good of the Mexican people cannot ever be attained by ignoring its history and depreciating its national roots.
>
> Rafael Preciado Hernández

On March 1, 1940, Acción Nacional was formally registered with the Secretariat of Gobernación as a national party of the opposition.[1] This date marked the first time since the short-lived efforts of the Partido Católico Nacional (PCN) during the Madero administration that alienated groups within the Mexican political right were given the opportunity of consolidating their political efforts in line with the constitutional framework of postrevolutionary Mexico. As noted in the preceding chapter, the Sinarquista movement of the 1930s had unmistakably committed itself to extralegal procedures (that is, the violent overthrow of the existing system). These political tactics were used frequently in the nineteenth century. But PAN, like the PCN, was originally founded to function as a permanent opposition party, sanctioned by the existing system yet wanting to introduce significant changes which would, in turn, reduce discrimination against those sectors that the party initially represented. This discrimination, so PAN felt, had become statutory through the Constitution of 1917.

Through his correspondence with PAN deputy Federico Estrada Valera, Lux concludes that PAN was from the beginning a party of wide popular appeal. Estrada contended that "from the very beginning, workers, farmers, employees, professionals, businessmen, industrialists and artists joined Acción Nacional."[2] The evidence, however, suggests that the original membership of the party was derived principally from a very reduced number of professionals, businessmen, and industrialists. Luis Calderón Vega readily admits to this fact, and advances two reasons for it. First, he suggests that intellectuals were the most likely to understand the party's original message of political permanence above electoral episodes and charismatic personalities. The Mexican masses, long drilled to perceive politics in terms of confrontations among *caudillos*, were not, in those early years, ready to align themselves with a party which emphasized permanent political action and depersonalization in Mexican politics. Permanent and depersonalized politics, in turn, represented a call to a battle of words and ideologies, not a battle of arms, which so often in the past had enkindled the *machista* spirit of the masses. The risks of an ideological, idealistic struggle were ones which only young university students were prepared and willing to take. Second, the original membership directly reflected the party founder's own spheres of influence. It was quite natural for the young men in the university community, especially those who had lived when Manuel Gómez Morín as rector of the National University had fought for academic freedom and university autonomy and those who had known him as Dean of the School of Law, to see in him a man of singular prestige and unquestionable integrity. It was also quite natural for certain businessmen and industrialists to answer Gómez Morín's call to political action, because Gómez Morín himself was known as one of Mexico's most respected legal advisors to banks and other financial groups.[3]

At first glance, these two explanations of the nature of PAN's original membership advanced by Calderón Vega may seem conflicting, since he suggests that the kind of depersonalized politics envisioned by PAN could only attract a certain kind of citizen, and yet he emphasizes that many of the early members of the party joined out of respect and previous association with one man, Manuel Gómez Morín. Indeed, Calderón suggests that the first Panistas "were confident that his personality would protect them from the perils of a struggle which many would have otherwise assessed as 'suicidal' without his presence."[4] While it seems evident that Gómez Morín always enjoyed the great esteem and respect of all Panistas it should be noted that his own personal magnetism never bordered on the vulgar, aggressive *caudillismo* so common in prominent Mexican political figures. Even an intellectual of the stature of José Vasconcelos had been representative of this type of incendiary personality. Instead, Gómez Morín was and remained the thinking-man's politician, suave, highly cultured, soft-spoken, and academic in orientation. An indication of this is that, despite the dominant role which he played in the creation of PAN, the party's identifying initials have not substituted for or become subservient to personality "ismos" which have invariably characterized transient opposition movements in Mexico. Thus, one does not speak today of a Gomezmorinista movement or of Gomezmorinistas, but one does recall Vasconcelistas, Almazanistas, and Padillistas. Even within the PRI, the presidential candidates have created their own cliques, in the form of Cardenistas, Alemanistas, and, more recently, Díazordazistas; but within PAN, there is no talk of Gonzalezlunistas, or of Gonzaleztorristas. For PAN it has always been PAN or Acción Nacional. PAN has (perhaps more so than any other party in Mexican postrevolutionary history) been the foremost exponent of depersonalized politics in Mexico.

As will be shown in subsequent chapters, PAN's original reason for existence had little to do with direct electoral participation. In the words of Gómez Morín, "it is an organization established not to seek immediate success at the polls, which does not cater to the appetites of a forthcoming electoral victory, since it is not even prepared to cope with the responsibilities of such a victory."[5]

Gómez Morín proceeds to characterize the Panista as follows:

> He is a professional man who has not engaged in the past, nor will he constantly engage in the future, in 'politicking', but who will instead work within the political system out of a sense of civic responsibility which is primordial and preferential, to be sure, but which will not prevent and distract him from compliance with other everyday responsibilities.[6]

From this statement it is clear that, for the Panista, working "within the political system" did not necessarily entail active participation in the electoral process. Rather, it indicates that the party's principal concern should be to offer Mexicans an ideology that would serve as a meaningful alternative to the primitive ideologisms introduced by the various sectors of the revolutionary family. The responsibility for the formulation of Panista ideology fell upon Manuel Gómez Morín, Efraín González Luna, and Manuel Herrera y Lasso, among others. If one were called upon to identify the bible of early PAN ideology, one would have to select González Luna's *Humanismo polítíco.*[7] I feel that this chapter shows that any objective survey of the party's basic ideology negates Frank Brandenburg's thesis that PAN is "the political embodiment of Traditional Conservatism."[8] Brandenburg identifies traditional conservatives as advocates of "a concoction of Spanish colonial values intermixed with corporate state designs. Its elite . . . still view society as founded on castelike racial distinctions and composed of inferiors and superiors . . ."[9] He dismisses entirely the possibility of including PAN under his more radical category of conservative, which he terms "New Conservatives" or "Revolutionary Right," presumably on the basis, inferred in his study, that in order to be revolutionary, whether a conservative or liberal one, one must in effect be a member of the dominant party. I suggest, instead, that PAN's ideological commitments seem to be more consonant with values which Brandenburg attributes to the "New Conservatives"; that PAN is actually representative of the "Revolutionary Right" in its most adamant expression; that rightist elements within the PRI (those which Brandenburg labels "New Conservatives," such as the Alemanistas) have been much less adamant in their ideological position, even though they can be said to have been more influential because of their privileged role in the system and their success at the polls. Indeed, as will be shown in the next chapter, the moderate conservatives within the revolutionary family have often allied themselves indirectly with many of PAN's own reform initiatives. This is because most of these initiatives have been consonant with values held by moderates within PRI. For Brandenburg's identifying label of PAN to have validity, he would have had to establish convincingly that PAN was, from the very beginning, openly committed to counterrevolutionary goals. This investigator finds no such evidence. On the contrary, the evidence suggests that PAN's political ideology often resembled the stated objectives of Francisco I. Madero, the instigator of Mexico's revolution. PAN's doctrine, which members of the party often label political humanism, appears to be essentially a restatement of Maderista values of effective political democracy and rationalized reform, values which PAN feels have been abandoned by subsequent regimes, particulary from the time that the single-party system became an institutionalized reality in Mexico. Today Maderismo might well be interpreted by the more radical elements within the official party as reactionary, but commitment to basic Maderista principles is not necessarily tantamount to commitment to traditional conservatism. The extent of commitments shared by Maderismo and Panismo is given through a comparative analysis of pronouncements made by Madero and his close associates and by leading PAN figures.

It is a generally accepted thesis that Madero's revolution was primarily a reaction to political monopoly in Mexico. Porfirio Díaz, the liberal and the political associate of reformist-bent Benito Juárez, became president of Mexico in 1876 and, except for a brief period (1880–84), he remained in office until 1911.[10] The Liberal Party's slogan on which Díaz had originally run his campaign (no reelection) was promptly discarded in favor of *imposición,* and the conservation of the political status quo. By 1908, Madero had written:

> The Mexican republic is presently governed by a military dictatorship, which exercises absolute power, although in

> a moderate way. Indications of this include: the unanimity of votes in the selection of all public officials; the servile conformism of the Legislature, as attested by its prompt acquiescence to all governmental initiatives; the immobility of officers, whose power in all instances is directly derived from the Administration; the very scant liberty of press, etc., etc.[11]

To Panistas, the situation depicted by Madero applied exactly to the one which prevailed in 1939 after ten years of monopoly exercised by the PNR. In his address to the Constituent Assembly of PAN on 14 September 1939, Gómez Morín asserted:

> The entire country feels the awakening of citizen conscience, in the same way it felt this awakening in 1909. During the past years, public life has so frequently been a mere exploitation of power, a mere succession of battles and treachery among the engineers of that exploitation. The group of men who are now in possession of the government—a government which is progressively more distantiated from the national interest—is preoccupied exclusively with the retention of that power by means of corruption and deceit.[12]

Efraín González Luna, also a founding father of PAN, characterized the Cárdenas administration as that "military-demagogic dictatorship which typifies a factional regime."[13]

Madero and PAN leaders, therefore, both emphasized the need for the effective elimination of political monopoly in Mexico and the establishment of a governmental arrangement which would reflect the pluralist interests in Mexican society. For Madero, the monopoly had been in the hands of General Díaz; for PAN, that same monopoly was being enjoyed by the Revolutionary Party. As the well-known Maderista, Juan Sánchez Azcona,[14] has suggested:

> When the Maderista movement began, the capital problem, that which took precedence over all others, was clearly of a political nature. Madero's motto, "Effective Suffrage, No Reelection," was aimed at the dictatorship.

> For Madero, "Effective Suffrage" means free elections, but also citizen freedom of conscience in the expression of the popular will; and "No Reelection" also means "no *imposición*" and *"no continuismo."*[15]

Sánchez Azcona's interpretation finds support in Madero's own words: "In order to avoid any impediments to freedom of suffrage, and to secure the legitimate participation of the people in the selection of public officials, we shall refrain from lending our support to so-called 'official' candidates."[16]

Madero's vigorous protest against political monopoly and against the corresponding Mexicanismos of *imposición* and *continuismo,* coupled with his desire to promote the establishment of legitimate institutions which might enable unobstructed citizen participation in government, represent the very core of Panista doctrine. Madero and PAN leaders agree that the ultimate key to effective democratic government rests in the awakening of a sense of civic duty in the perennially stifled Mexican electorate. Gómez Morín's famous slogan, *"Hay que mover las almas!"* (We must move the spirits of the citizens!), expresses exactly that. Perhaps the only difference between the two positions is that Madero was convinced that the Mexican people were indeed ready for democracy at the time he made his call for action,[17] whereas the major figures in PAN placed the blame for Mexico's "primitive democracy" on citizen apathy.[18] In the words of Adolfo Christlieb, the late past-president of PAN, "there will be free elections as soon as the moral environment allows them to take place; as soon as the citizen is prepared to read the lists of candidates, placing priority on a good platform, and not on possible 'influences.'"[19] These pronouncements, however, should be read against the background of electoral frustrations and defeats which perennially plague PAN. The fact remains that PAN has offered candidates and alternative solutions to the "unprepared" Mexican electorate for every type of election held since the party first came into existence, and if it really believed that Mexico was unprepared for democracy, PAN would certainly have desisted in its electoral efforts. Thus, despite this difference in their respective evaluations of the Mexican electorate, both Madero and PAN are unequivocally committed to what Gómez Morín termed "the three pillars of democracy": civic education, civic organization, and the establishment of legitimate institutions.[20] Furthermore, neither Madero nor PAN in declaring itself democratic, views democracy in the traditional sense: that is, the end-product of a collection of individual wills. Madero called for corporate units, formed out of an affinity of group interests and needs. Maderismo was, therefore, a social-democratic movement, fully cognizant of the organic nature of politics and government, and of pluralism in society. The same may be said of PAN, which has always claimed that PRI's gravest error is to regard Mexican society as an undifferentiated mass. Sector politics within PRI, PAN suggests, represents but a token concession of pluralist interests, and such a concession is apt to be granted only to those "differentiated" groups that are willing to bow to the uniform demands formulated by PRI. As Rafael Preciado Hernández once observed:

> When we speak of society, we are not alluding to a composite of individuals, who live in a territory as a 'mass.' Society is integrated by human beings who possess a common essential nature, but which places each human being within a concrete set of social relations. We are not speaking of abstract man, of an individualistic liberal State, but of man as he forms part of a family, of a county, of a union or of a professional organization, of a religious or a cultural institution, and who, through these various intermediate social organizations, is incorporated into the State.[22]

Both movements accept the legitimacy of intermediate groups in society under the guidance of some form of leadership, but neither Maderistas nor Panistas will subscribe to anything short of leadership selected independently by the membership of each represented group. Official pressure in the selection of such leadership is unacceptable to both. According to Sánchez Azcona, "the Maderista movement recognizes and respects the legitimate leadership of unions, but it rejects the agitators, those demagogic leaders who, with the pretext of representing the will of their members, seek political influence and rewards."[23] In other words, economic groups should not be subjected to the whims of one man or of one group of men. The different intermediate groups, which jointly form society, are not to be at the mercy of particularistic bosses. For PAN, the Maderista position represents a direct attack on today's so-called sector politics within PRI. Under the existing arrangement, PRI derives its image as a party of national appeal largely through the formal incorporation of government-controlled and government-sponsored syndicates. Thus, the labor sector is said to be fully represented by the leadership of the Confederation of Mexican Workers (CTM), which in turn lends its full support to the ideals of the Revolution by submitting itself to the control of the Revolutionary Party. The same is said to hold true for the other two existing sectors, the National Peasant's Confederation (CNC) and the National Confederation of Popular Organizations (CNOP).[24]

PAN's position on government-controlled sector organizations is based on Madero's own ideals. PAN ideologues refer to sector politics as "that filthy swamp of faction."

> Faction is the egotist determinant of a political conduct which subverts the immutable order of human values, which sacrifices the Common Good for the satisfaction of individual passions, by means of the illegitimate interests of the elites. Faction has its own singular characteristics: it manifests itself through four equally distasteful phases: intolerance, monopoly, corruption, and despotism.[25]

PAN contends that, whereas peasants and workers had been victimized by the landed oligarchs before the Revolution, the present regime has converted them into slaves at the mercy of a small number of hand-picked demagogues. "Formerly, the farmer had to fear his *patrón,* or complain about wages that were insufficient to meet his needs. Today, however, he must fear reprisal, and the whip of the bureaucratic committee."[26] These charges were again formulated by former PAN president, Adolfo Christlieb, during the controversial 1968 state elections in Baja California (see chapter 5).

In a memorandum to the Mexican Supreme Court, Christlieb cited several articles in the constitution of the CTM which he claimed were contrary to the original intent of Madero's Revolution, and to the spirit of the 1917 Constitution, since they, in effect, deny workers the right of effective suffrage. Article 113 of the CTM constitution, for example, characterizes the CTM as a member of the PRI and representative of the labor sector within the party. Article 114 states, further, that all CTM members, individually and collectively, are also members of PRI and derive all rights and duties directly from PRI. Article 115 prescribes that all CTM members are obligated to contribute to the preservation of the Revolution (that is, PRI), and to oppose the counterrevolutionary forces in the country (probably opposition parties).[27]

In the same document, Christlieb noted that similar provisions could be found in the respective constitutions of the CNC and CNOP. Such provisions, he suggested, are invariably interpreted by the bosses of these sectors as a mandate for uniformity in their respective membership's vote at election time. Leaders are prone, therefore, to resort to a variety of methods and threats in order to keep the unions in line with PRI. The following observations by Christlieb illustrate this:

> Workers, peasants, public employees, shop owners, cab drivers, shoeshine boys, public construction workers, and members of other social groups, were pressured especially through the CTM to attend all public acts connected with PRI's electoral campaign, thereby violating their liberties of political organization, guaranteed in Article 8 of the Constitution. Pressure tactics consisted in the threat of imposing syndical and working sanctions against anyone failing to attend such public acts.[28]

On occasion CTM and CNOP memoranda are circulated that urge union members to attend PRI events and which contain succinct threats that individuals not present would be denied certain privileges such as syndicate-sponsored holidays. Another often-voiced claim is that a common type of threat frequently employed for nonattendance is to deprive absentees of their jobs. For example, shoeshine boys, all of whom are unionized, were indirectly forced to attend a welcoming rally for President Gustavo Díaz Ordaz following his tour of friendship to Central America. This was evidently done by announcing that union leaders would distribute at the rally new membership cards, which would, in turn, have to be presented later to secure new uniforms (of a different color). Without the new uniform, members could no longer obtain a permit to shine shoes!

Along with their adamant position against sector politics, Maderistas and Panistas oppose the utilization of unions to engender class conflict and class warfare. Such utilization was especially observable during the Cárdenas years, since the socialist coloration of Cardenista policies fully condoned the demagoguery of sector leaders. In contrast, Maderismo defended, in principle, the destitute against any exploiters and advocated the social betterment of the underprivileged classes in society, not solely by means of state-sponsored handout programs but rather by rewards earned from determinate efforts. Charity, for Maderistas, could lead only to inertia and to the loss of human individualism.

> This is why Maderismo rejects the theory that the poor will invariably improve his condition by despoiling the rich. Similarly, Maderismo obliges the rich to prove himself worthy of his favored status.[29]

The central thesis of Panismo on this same subject is to be found in the concept of common good, or *Bien Común.* Adopting an Aristotelian position, PAN's ideologues contend that a just state is one which promotes the common good of society. Only a society directed to the good of the whole of its members can effectively serve as a bridge between the individual and the state. González Luna notes that "only an absurd, antisocial, suicidal policy has made it possible for Mexicans to regard individual man and social man as irreconcilable enemies."[30] He writes further:

> In reality, the supposed conflict between personal good and the common good does not exist, for it is the same human good which both man and the social community pursue. This is so, because man alone cannot obtain his own personal good, and because human nature has predestined him to coexist with society. The Common

> Good is nothing more than the sum total of conditions inherent in social life which permit the individual to attain his destiny, to comply with his nature, and to perfect his existence.[31]

Echoing the Maderista opposition to factional syndicalism, González Luna charges that sector politics in Mexico do not have the good of the worker in mind:

> They are not primarily interested in correcting his present woes, but in exploiting him politically, in using him as a tool for rebellion, in instilling in him the inevitability of class warfare. This is why the ruling elites guard jealously their control over worker and peasant organizations, and stifle every attempt at creating genuinely free unions.[32]

Since class warfare, waged at the expense of other legitimate sectors of society, is unacceptable to Maderistas and Panistas, the following questions might now be raised: In what manner do they perceive the social betterment of the underprivileged classes? How is social justice to be attained? For both groups the answer lies in a rationalized evolutionary process. In their Manifesto of April 1910, Madero and his vice-presidential candidate, Francisco Vázquez Gómez, declared that it was their aim to improve and sponsor public education, and to remove all barriers to liberty of instruction.[33] Madero and his supporters were convinced that the plight of the destitute masses was attributable to their precarious economic situation, to their limited educational background, and to their cultural deficiency.

> For this reason, Maderismo, in an effort to improve the economic standard of the masses, strives to improve their moral and intellectual standards as well, through the school system. The school, according to Maderismo, must be found everywhere, whether in palaces or in slums; schools can be Christian, Mohammedan, Jewish, Buddhist —no matter—so long as they teach how to read and write, because this constitutes the beginning of the long process of learning to think and to understand, so that the masses

> might later be able to act conscientiously. The concrete tendency in thought and deed will be later determined by life itself. The State is not to impress its own seal in the public classrooms at the expense of freedom of instruction otherwise exercised by other institutions. This is why official instruction must be secular. The alphabet does not have a confessional origin, and teaching the alphabet, regardless of who teaches it, is a primary and vital necessity for all peoples. *Ultimately, however, it is the parents' right to instill in their children the motivation for learning.*[34]

It should be admitted at this point that, in their defense of private education, Panistas do depart from the Maderista thesis that education should be exclusively secular. PAN's position is clearly intended as a defense of the rights of the Mexican Church to participate in the educational process. Indeed, a defense of the private school system, whether in Mexico or in any other Latin American country, almost invariably entails a defense of the Catholic Church, since the majority of private institutions in the area are Church-operated. Like many other pro-Church movements in postrevolutionary Mexico, PAN often reflected, particularly in the earlier years, markedly anti-Protestant sentiments that betrayed a built-in religious prejudice in the party's defense of the legitimacy of private institutions. In the mid-1940s PAN literature dealt extensively with what it termed "Protestant infiltration in Mexico." José N. Chávez González, in an article written for PAN's *La Nación*, declared: "Every step forward won by Protestants in Mexico represents a step backwards for friendship with the United States."[35] While opposition to Protestantism has dwindled in recent years, it is evident that PAN still holds to its original position on religious unity in Mexico. Therefore, although PAN leaders reject the contention that their party is a Catholic party (but they do not dispute the fact that most of PAN's members are Catholics), they "recognize that religious unity [that is, Catholicism] forms the basis for national unity . . ."[36] Going one step further, Panistas often contend that truly humanistic politics can only develop in a Catholic atmosphere: "In order for nature to comply with its own law, it must rely on the supernatural. Christianity [Catholicism] shall be all the more effective in rectifying the bonds of nature, in helping politics to find its true path, if the law of nature recognizes its responsibility to supernatural law."[37]

PAN's perennial attacks on Article 3 of the Mexican Constitution, which incorporates the Maderista maxim of secular education in Mexico, however, are based on another point. The party does not reject the idea of secular education *per se.* What it rejects is the interpretation given to secularism by PRI, because PAN feels the government's interpretation implements anticlerical provisions in the Constitution which Madero, himself, in light of his recorded declarations on the subject, did not visualize. In other words, government leaders and Panistas, from opposite vantage points, invariably identify secularism with some sort of religious persecution. As suggested in the preceding chapter, Madero, the conciliator, clearly advocated a defense of Church rights in his own government, since, in his view, the Church and her allies represented a legitimate force in Mexican society. For this same reason Madero opposed the idea advanced by other contemporary revolutionaries that the National Catholic Party be abolished. In short, Madero sincerely felt that a distinction should be made between nineteenth-century Catholicism, and Catholicism within the revolutionary context. He also felt that the Church and her allies were entitled to play a meaningful role in the formation of modern Mexico. As Sánchez Azcona emphasized: "Madero considered religious creeds to fall within the exclusive domain of the individual's private and inner life, and denied the State any right to mingle in this domain."[38]

At the same time, of course, Madero opposed Church interference in politics. The point is that secularism for Madero meant some degree of individual choice in education, with only minimum controls exercised by the state, as the statement "ultimately . . . it is the parents' right to instill in their children the motivation for learning" suggests. This statement is often used by Panistas as a justification for their vigorous campaign in defense of the rights of Mexican parents to select for their children the type of education which they may deem appropriate. Admittedly, Madero's defense of secularism in education is close to PRI's position insofar as they, too, insist on secular education over all other forms. In contrast, PAN obviously has carried its own defense of Church participation in education to extremes. But it must be emphasized that, whereas Madero seemed to welcome the participation of outgroups in the state's efforts to improve the educational standards of the population, the PRI and post-Maderista governments have not encouraged—indeed, they have at times openly opposed—such participation. PRI, therefore, has also carried this issue of secularism to extremes, for the Maderista thesis had envisaged an educational program for Mexico that would genuinely reflect the joint efforts of both government-sponsored and private schools. The younger Panistas have come to accept the more moderate position of Maderismo, and if, at times, they still appear to be militant on the issue of Church rights, they suggest that excesses in their own doctrinal position merely reflect the excesses of the government, whose authoritarian attitudes Madero himself would not have approved.

In the last analysis, therefore, both PRI and PAN have interpreted Madero on this subject to suit the expectations of their respective constituencies. PAN's position is that education and the right of Catholics to secure avenues of representation within the pluralist arrangement was originally envisaged by the first leaders of the Mexican Revolution. This position is a clever manipulation of facts, but it is also not entirely incompatible with Madero's libertarian position. In fact, PAN makes the interesting suggestion that, in its early stages, the Revolution was principally motivated by religious and moral ideals. Party leaders contend that it was quite common in that period for revolutionaries to invoke moral values and religious principles. For example, they note that in the *Plan de Ayala*, Emiliano Zapata referred to Madero's Revolution as that "Revolution which he gloriously instigated with the assistance of God and of the people."[39] In short, PAN suggests that in those earlier days there existed "a far broader vision of man and of his dignity. The 1910 Revolution will attain its goals only and when it reassumes the profound Christian spirit which motivated the movement in the first place."[40]

Turning to another central problem inherited by the Revolution, the land problem, Madero's position again bore remarkable resemblance to PAN's own concepts. According to Madero, the solution was not large-scale, "irrational" reallocation of the land to the peasantry. The land question did not limit itself to a consideration of redistribution, but also encompassed improvement of production in terms of both quantity and quality. To be sure, Madero was an outspoken critic of all idle and unproductive land, and he opposed the existence of any *latifundios* (or large estates) that were uncultivated or designed for exploitation of the peasantry.[41] But at no time did he reject the idea of large landed properties, since he recognized that such estates might be required for the production of certain crops. Still, Madero was primarily concerned with government sponsorship of small farms, because he regarded this as the best means of securing an equitable distribution of the national wealth. It should be noted that Madero never regarded the joint sponsorship of both large and small landed estates as inconsistent with revolutionary ideals. On the contrary, both types of estates would complement each other in any effort to eradicate the land problem. Diversity in the type of farming was required because of Mexico's varied regional conditions. It is for this reason that Madero's 1910 Manifesto called for "state sponsorship of large estates and especially of small farms."[42] As for the *ejido* which has become the prevailing communal form of farming since the adoption of the 1917 Constitution, Madero agreed that communal lands that had been taken away from the Indians as a result of dictatorial abuses should be restored to them but he did not consider the establishment of an all-communal land regime as the sole solution to Mexico's land problem. Sánchez Azcona suggests that Madero knew that "communal property inevitably has the effect of engendering small, particularistic *cacicazgos,* somewhat akin to domestic tyrannies, which in time are placed above the law and social justice."[43] Madero was, therefore, positively convinced that as long as communal estates were subjected to the tutelage of government supervisors (whom Sánchez Azcona calls "official coyotes") there would always be a more astute co-owner who would, in turn, be in the position to impose his own will on others, thereby becoming a virtually omnipotent boss. The Maderista priority on small agriculture, then, is idealized in the farm, privately owned by each family and worked by each family, free from governmental interference.[44]

Madero's rationalized approach to land reform bears a remarkable resemblance to the position adopted by leading Panista ideologues. Summarizing Mexico's perennial agrarian problem, González Luna notes that it is the end product of three basic factors: man, his relation to the land, and land production. In discussing the first factor, González Luna poses two questions: Has the farmer been prepared technically by the regime? Is the farmer respected, does he enjoy political freedom and all other liberties essential to man? His answer to both questions is in the negative. "The farmer is in the eyes of the government simply a miserable object, a victim of *imposición* and of the perversion characteristic of Mexican politics. He has in a real sense lost everything: land, neighborhood, the chance to work, liberty."[45] Has the Revolution resolved the relationship of man to land? González Luna's answer: "No. The 1917 Constitution foresaw for the farmer, through the necessary and just efforts of the State, the acquisition of rural property, not its loss. But what do we see instead? The communal exploitation of the *ejido,* chaos in production, precisely because the regime is attempting to act deliberately in defiance of the Constitution; it seeks to prevent the farmer from acquiring property rights, because the moment when he acquires these rights, he will be free."[46]

Turning to the factor of land production, González Luna again places sole responsibility for the failure of agrarian reform laws on the government's refusal to consider the realities and limitations of the land situation in Mexico, and on the inequitable application of such laws. Manuel Gómez Morín clarified PAN's position regarding this problem in an interview:

> The problem has been poorly handled from the beginning: it has been approached, first, without taking into consideration that Mexico is a large country, with great regional diversity. The land problem in Chihuahua is not the same as the land problem in the Federal District, or in the State of Mexico, or in the *Bajío.* Yet the regime has pretended to resolve it through uniform measures; even

> the [constitutional] definition of small property has been applied indiscriminately for the entire country, irrespective of regional considerations. Thus, fifty hectares in Xochimilco are sufficient to turn a man into a millionaire, while fifty hectares in the desert of Chihuahua barely sustain a few goats. I believe that the fundamental error in the solutions which have been attempted thus far in the area of agriculture has been of a political, rather than a technical nature. Land was distributed without even attempting to define whether it was being distributed on an individual basis or collectively; we still lack a legal definition for the *ejido;* there does not exist, either juridically or practically, a clear delimitation of what is the *ejido,* of what constitutes *ejidal* property; no effort has been expended to organize labor within the *ejido,* nor to protect the worker, nor to give him guarantees of technical progress and social betterment.[47]

From these observations, it may be said that both Madero and Panista leaders opposed any form of demagoguery in Mexican land reform. The human dignity of the land laborer had to take priority above all other considerations. Blind imposition of a uniform agricultural regime for the entire nation, without due consideration of regional needs and limitations, serves limited short-range political purposes at best. Similarly, the insistence on *ejidal* farming, without exploring other complementary avenues, leads to a dead end. In referring to Eyler Newton Simpson's book, *The Ejido, Mexico's Way Out,*[48] Gómez Morín agrees that the *ejido* is not a viable solution. "It is the only road which leads nowhere."[49] Although basically opposed to the *ejido,* PAN ideologues do not oppose communal farming in principle. They recognize changing conditions in the country, and thereby depart from Madero's insistence on small farms for all farmers. As Gómez Morín notes, "this was considered back in 1910; today it is absurd."[50] According to PAN's founder, then, should the state continue to insist on preferential treatment of a collectivized arrangement, "we must give thought to examples and solutions which are perhaps better, such as the *kolkhoz* or the *kibbutz.* This is a task for all Mexicans, irrespective of whether they belong to PRI or not. The present *ejido* system, with its undefined legal status, applied uniformly in Chiapas or in Tamaulipas, in the coastal regions and in the northern desert regions, without organizations, without credit, without technical assistance, without market considerations, oblivious of demographic factors, makes no sense."[51]

The preceding comparative survey of Maderista and Panista tenets suggests that, within the context of the Mexican Revolution, PAN has a legitimate claim and a legitimate place. To be sure, if Madero were to reappear on the modern Mexican scene, it is not unlikely that he, too, might be labeled a conservative by his more revolutionary peers. If conservatism-á-la-Madero is used to identify PAN's ideology, then the label is defensible. But labels are deceiving, particularly if they reflect "official" propaganda, and must, therefore, be employed with extreme caution in the Mexican political context. Madero battled against political monopoly and on behalf of effective suffrage, and all the corresponding political liberties: protection of an effective, competitive multiparty system, with all parties organized on a permanent basis; defense of the federal system, with due respect for state and local autonomy; insistence on effective separation of powers, and on a genuinely independent legislature; respect for pluralist interests in Mexican society; free and open elections which do not violate the citizen's vote; syndical freedom, untampered by "official" union bosses; freedom of religion and of religious choice; liberty to select one's education; right to private property; social and economic development through rationalized, evolutionary policies in which legal and technical expertise take the place of demagoguery. This is the core of "conservative" Maderismo—a "conservatism" aimed at Porfirio Díaz, who ironically first ran for the presidency as a candidate of the Liberal Party. This, in essence, is also the core of conservative Panismo as expressed in PAN's original "Declaration of Principles" (see Appendix I), directed at the party which is called revolutionary but which monopolizes and insists on preserving the status quo.

Panistas readily recognize the striking similarities between their views and those advanced by Madero. Of all major Mexican revolutionary figures, only Madero has rated cover stories in PAN's official organ, *La Nación.* Indeed, Madero's picture hangs in the National Committee headquarters of PAN. If the administration of President Madero was marked by conservative policies, as some contemporary Mexican historians insist,[52] then it is likely that PAN would also accept the label for itself. But the "traditional conservatism" attributed to PAN by Brandenburg was referred to by party-founder Gómez Morín as a "gross distortion."[53] The evidence does suggest that PAN has progressively become a party representing moderate or middle-of-the road policies, and that its members are also members of the revolutionary family, which is, in the last analysis, the Mexican nation. That they are not members of *a* revolutionary family (PRI) does not automatically deny them their right to a front seat among the revolutionary audience. But scholars may ask: What about the Church? Does not PAN's defense of Church rights, adamantly advocated particularly in those early years of the party's existence, run contrary to the entire Mexican revolutionary tradition? Perhaps, it would be well to recall Madero's own views once more: "We do not consider it opportune to preoccupy ourselves with the Church's influence. The Church has already identified itself with national aspirations, and if it is to exercise moral influence on the voter in the future, such influence will be quite legitimate."[54]

4

The Influence of PAN on Public Policy

> I believe that your Party . . . represents the intelligence of the Nation and has the potential of becoming a guiding force in shaping its destinies, provided that you maintain the same clarity in political action which you now pursue in theory. In doctrine, you represent a just equilibrium of past and present, aimed at securing for Mexico a more just and civilized future.
> Jose Vasconcelos, letter to the 1939 Constituent Assembly of PAN

The noted sociologist, Lucio Mendieta y Núñez, once observed that whenever a political party fails to acquire power through the electoral process, it must search for other avenues in order to influence the orientation of public policy, if it is to remain a viable force in the political system.[1] Sigmund Neumann similarly attributes to all political parties the common characteristic of "participation in the decision-making process, or at least the attempt at, and a chance for such a mobilization for action." He notes, further, that "only in their fight for control and in their conscious influence on political forces do parties gain meaning and importance."[2] Manuel García Pelayo also emphasizes the natural drive of parties "to influence public policy *even if unable to win a meaningful share of public offices.*"[3] These three authors suggest that, in order to survive in a system in which the prospect of a major electoral victory is virtually nil, opposition parties must at least make a conscious effort to influence policy-making through means other than the ballot box, lest they lose their significance.

This chapter evaluates PAN's efforts to influence government policies in Mexico over the past thirty-four years. Admittedly, such an evaluation is not problem-free. As Ivan Vallier observes, even though the term *influence* "designates a general and extremely important category of social control . . . *and* is frequently employed as a synonym for power; [or as] a corollary of prestige . . . little cumulative progress toward a theoretical consensus is being made."[4] He adds that in his judgment,

> Influence should be equated with the capacity of a unit to generate commitments—loyalties, resources, behavioral support—in amounts sufficient to allow the agency of influence to impose a direction of its own choosing on the structure, and thereby to change a situation. An influential is thus a person or corporate unit that is able to place a distinct stamp on a valued sphere of interest or activity. The commitments gained may be of short duration or of a long-standing strength.[5]

Such a definition is obviously not fully applicable to the experience of PAN, since within a one-party dominant system like Mexico's, an out-group's capacity to generate the commitments identified by Vallier is always limited; this, in turn, reduces its own capacity to "impose" a direction of its own choosing, or its ability to place a "distinct stamp" on valued spheres of interest. However, considering the limitations imposed by the Mexican system on minority parties, it is important to note that PAN leaders and certain prominent members of the ruling coalition have occasionally agreed that certain systemic reforms were incorporated largely as the result of PAN influence, or, put in negative terms, provocation. In other words, this study contends that it is not enough to measure influence in terms of an ability to impose changes. It should be equally significant to determine to what extent individuals and groups *regard themselves* as influential (or even deceive themselves into believing that they are) and to what extent the ruling elite views them as such. Certainly in the case of PAN, the firm conviction expressed by many of its leaders that reforms have been introduced by the government because of PAN's own efforts serves, in part, to explain the party's perseverance as an opposition force for over three decades.

Without a significant share of political offices, and with a limited national electoral appeal even to this day (see chapter 5), PAN has had to search for other avenues to exert its pressure on the government. These have included (1) attempts at mobilizing public opinion against specific governmental policies that were particularly controversial, either through public conferences, campaign oratory, or the distribution of party literature; (2) direct cooperation with already existing alienated pressure groups; and (3) overt or indirect manipulation of individuals and groups within the Revolutionary Party that have been, under various circumstances, dissatisfied with the policies of their party, or that often have viewpoints parallel to PAN's.

Available data suggest that the degree of policy influence exerted by PAN was greatest during the years 1939-52 when the party was most adamant in its ideological commitment and orientation. As noted earlier, the founders of PAN realized that their party could not hope to cope with the powerful organizational structure of the Revolutionary Party, and they saw no prospects for an electoral victory in the immediate future. For this reason, the original founders consistently urged the delegates attending the party's earlier conventions to abstain from the electoral process and to spend their physical and financial resources elsewhere to propagate PAN's message. In a very real sense, therefore, the years 1939-52 marked a period of intense ideological confrontation under the guidance of PAN's most committed ideologues. Correspondingly, since 1952 PAN has steadily forfeited its impact upon policy-making by substituting greater mass appeal at the polls for clearly defined tenets. This shift in priorities came about with the advent of a new, younger, more vigorous breed of Panista, impatient with words, and demanding more political action.

In an interview, Adolfo Christlieb Ibarrola, a prominent exponent of this new breed of Panistas, suggested to me that, in reexamining his party's role in the first decade of its existence, he concluded that PAN's gravest fault had been that of sacrificing what had the potential of becoming a major national program in favor of a limited set of issues that were of particular concern to the party leadership.[6] While this exercise in reexamination is well-founded, evidence suggests that this concentration on a limited set of issues provides an additional explanation for PAN's greater effectiveness with key policy makers during those early years. I submit that the adamant, often repetitive quality of the demands exerted by such Panista luminaries as Manuel Gómez Morín, Efraín González Luna, Juan Gutiérrez Lascuráin, and others, facilitated a greater measure of positive response by government officials and by certain sympathetic sectors of society as well. By concentrating their efforts on a series of definable frontal attacks against certain aspects of the revolutionary legacy, in particular that legacy which had been formed under Lázaro Cárdenas and his leftist coalition, the PAN leadership succeeded in mobilizing certain sectors of Mexican public opinion to the point that the ruling party came to perceive the opposition in more sober and realistic terms. In contrast, more recent Panista leaders, such as Adolfo Christlieb and the current president of PAN, José Angel Conchello, have attempted to project an image of their party that is more akin to the over-all national aspirations of Mexican society and to the revolutionary tradition in general. They have, in effect, substituted their party's former adamant commitments for a policy of "out-doing-and-out-promising" the PRI. PAN's greater electoral appeal, particularly in state and local contests, has been accomplished at the cost of some of its immediate potential to influence policy. In all my interviews with prominent members of the PAN family, Manuel Gómez Morín, his son Juan Manuel, Adolfo Christlieb and Fernando Ayala Carrión, among others, I asked specifically if they could cite recent instances in which PAN might have directly or indirectly influenced PRI policies, and in every case the response was negative.

The ensuing examination of PAN's public policy influence has been divided into two major sections: the first includes certain issues which were clearly at variance ideologically with the developing revolutionary tradition. The second section incorporates the general question of political democracy (that is, effective separation of powers, decentralization of government, free and competitive elections) which did not in itself conflict with Mexican constitutional theory, but which nevertheless posed a challenge to the monopoly enjoyed by the ruling elites. Only a few of the more significant issues have been selected for discussion.

THE IDEOLOGICAL ISSUES: EDUCATION AND AGRARIAN POLICY

In preceding chapters, reference was made to the background of the educational controversy in Mexico and to PAN's position on the subject. To recapitulate briefly, Article 3 of the 1917 Constitution, while avowedly anticlerical in its exclusion of religious corporations from elementary and secondary instruction, did not originally commit itself much beyond the vague provision that education in Mexico would be secular [*laica.*] The religious civil war of the 1920s, however, had once again intensified anti-Church and anticlerical sentiments within the revolutionary family. In one of his last public statements, President Plutarco Elías Calles had stressed the necessity for greater governmental control of public education, and these views were subsequently echoed by Cárdenas and other key officials in his administration. In 1932, Public Education Secretary Narciso Bassols tried to implement a compulsory program of sex education and met with widespread resistance from parent associations throughout the country. By 1934, the Mexican Congress had amended Article 3, changing the original neutral secularism to "socialist education." PAN was later to characterize this amendment as "the greatest triumph of Mexican communism."[7] Leftist elements within the ruling party saw their efforts to extend the applicability of the new law to university communities defeated by the energetic Gómez Morín, but they made clear their intentions to do everything in their power to compel all other levels of instruction to submit to the letter of the new article. In 1939, for example, a law was approved to regulate the implementation, in practice, of socialist education.[8]

From the very beginning, PAN waged an active campaign against constitutional Article 3. Although PAN especially opposed the socialist provisions, its activities were directed against the entire spirit of the article, even in its 1917 form, as indicative of the government's ultimate objective to dictate every aspect of the educational process. PAN's *Declaration of Principles* accepted the notion that the state had an obligation to provide an equal opportunity for education to all members of the community, but opposed the propagandistic role which the state, through the ruling coalition, had assumed. It stated, moreover:

> Educational liberty must be guaranteed without any other limitations by the State than the determination of the technical requirements relative to method, the extension and enforcement of a minimum educational program, and those relative to the awarding of degrees which will enable the citizens to exercise a profession or a social function.[9]

In 1941, PAN submitted its first concrete program on education policy by calling for the following amendments to Article 3:

> The right to educate the children belongs exclusively to the parents. The tutorial role of the State may be expressed only in the following terms:
> 1) the formulation of a minimum program of compulsory education, but guaranteeing at the same time diversity in educational methods;
> 2) the obligation to provide free education, wherever private enterprise is insufficient, at the elementary level; and
> 3) the obligation to protect the morality of the children, and to protect the rights of private institutions.[10]

In its battle against Article 3, PAN was able to enlist the support of several citizen organizations, the most notable of which was the Unión Nacional de Padres de Familia (UNPF) (National Union of Parents), whose repeated declarations and protest demonstrations against Article 3 were noticed in official circles. By November 1941, the UNPF had staged large demonstrations in all the major cities; these upheld PAN's assertion that it was the right of parents to determine their children's education. Similar protests were raised in university circles which considered the article's objective of "creating in the youth a rational and exact notion of the universe and of social life" an intellectual affront.[11] The history of the Church hierarchy's opposition to the amended article has been amply documented elsewhere.[12] Of greatest significance to PAN's cause, however, was President Manuel Avila Camacho's own apparent disenchantment with much of the Cárdenas legacy, especially with the education measures adopted by his predecessor. Early in his campaign for the presidency, Avila Camacho had given evidence of this with an unprecedented affirmation of his Catholic faith. Relying, thus, on the president's sympathies, PAN wasted no time and effort to discredit leftist elements within the PRM, capitalizing on every official pronouncement which ran contrary to the objectives of the left.[13] Public Education Secretary Sánchez Pontón, an ardent supporter of socialist education and a leading member of the coalition's left wing, was "retired" early in 1941 and promptly replaced by the more moderate Octavio Véjar Vázquez. This rare action served to increase PAN's confidence and its leadership immediately attributed the ouster of Sánchez Pontón to its own pressures and to "the good intentions of Avila Camacho."[14] While Véjar Vázquez did little to implement the 1934 provisions, PAN, nevertheless, mounted its campaign for constitutional reform.

By December 1945, the administration already began to speak in terms of an impending amendment to Article 3. Although PAN realized that the proposed changes would not incorporate its own libertarian thesis which called for an almost total state disengagement from the educational process, they announced: "The very fact that a new project is being studied proves once more that public opinion can be a very powerful force in any system. The principal lesson to be derived from the public's struggle against Article 3 is an awareness of its own strength."[15]

While the project was being considered in Congress, the UNPF urged that the state recognize and guarantee liberty of education. The Mexican Archbishop, Dr. Luis María Martínez, declared in a press conference that the project represented "an important step toward liberty, because it clarifies concepts and removes those obstacles to spiritual tranquility which the 1934 provisions had introduced."[16]

The new text of Article 3 was approved by Congress and all

state legislatures, and went formally into effect a year later, on December 30, 1946. Although it fell short of the opposition's objectives, it represented a repudiation of socialist education. The article stated: "The education which the State shall impart is aimed at the harmonious development of all the faculties of the individual, and at instilling in him a sense of patriotism and an awareness of international solidarity, characterized by independence and justice." [17] It affirmed, further, that public education would maintain itself neutral on religious doctrine (Section I), but would, instead, be democratic (Section I, paragraph a) and nationalistic (Section I, paragraph b) in spirit. Restrictions on the operation of private institutions were maintained, but the approach was far more conciliatory. For example, Section III of the 1934 text had stated that "*no* private schools may operate *without* the previous and expressed authorization of the State." Section II of the 1946 version, on the other hand, maintained: "Private schools *shall be permitted* to operate at all levels, *provided that,* in the case of elementary and secondary education, they obtain previous authorization from the State."[18] Thus, while the conditions for the operation of private institutions were not really altered, there was a psychological difference between the negative "no private schools shall . . . operate without," and the positive "private schools shall be permitted . . . provided that." Similarly, the provision found in both versions to the effect that private schools were required to conform to the educational objectives set forth by the state acquired a new meaning after 1946, since it was easier for private institutions to justify collaboration with the state in the "harmonious development of all the faculties of the individual," than it had been with the 1934 socialist call for "a rational and exact notion of the universe and of social life."

Spokesmen for the left wing of the PRM publicly admitted that PAN had played a major role in the constitutional changes of 1946. Alberto Bremauntz, one of the chief engineers of the 1934 text, credited PAN with being the *one single group* which most directly influenced the government's change in educational policy. The vulnerability of the revolutionary party was attributed to its lack of unified doctrine. Bremauntz went on to declare:

> In contrast, the counterrevolutionary parties, groups and elements in our country have disciplined a large number of members, according to their own principles and doctrine. Therefore, there exists great ideological unity among them . . . It is in the ranks of Acción Nacional that we find the most prominent intellectuals and engineers of the counterrevolutionary movement. It is the most serious, strongest and best organized party of the reaction in Mexico. We affirm, therefore, that at the present time it is the anti-revolutionary movement which possesses the principal instrument of ideological formation, which is education.[19]

In addition to the government's departure from the socialist orientation of Article 3 in its 1934 form, Bremauntz noted that the conservatives also succeeded in convincing subsequent administrations to take a more permissive stand with private institutions. For example, during the Cárdenas years the government had gone so far as to conduct investigations into the ideology of individual teachers as a means of preventing counterrevolutionary instruction in schools, public or private. If the prospective teacher did not meet the "standards" set up by the Secretariat of Public Education, he would simply be dismissed. Such investigations were abruptly terminated under Avila Camacho and Miguel Alemán. Furthermore, private schools, most of which are Church affiliated, found it easier under those two administrations to conduct religious instruction, even though such instruction was illegal.[20] Both the allies of the Church and the government came to accept this tacit departure from constitutional standards, since the two sides realized that individual office-holders could not publicly compromise on the anticlerical tradition of the Revolution. As Brandenburg observes: "The Church measures the tolerance of a President by the degree to which he fails to enforce the legal restrictions on Church activities."[21]

The conservatives' campaign against socialist education, therefore, served to illustrate that, even though the Church hierarchy, by itself, did not represent a major force for government to contend with, "organized Catholic groups of citizens

. . . do represent a formidable challenge" to any administration.[22]

It is evident that the 1946 victory won by PAN and its sympathizers was, to a large extent, the result of indirect alliances on the issue of education. These alliances included, first and foremost, the president himself. Manuel Avila Camacho, often referred to as *El Presidente Caballero* (the gentleman-president) because of the conciliatory tone of his administration, was clearly not sympathetic to the dogmatism which had prevailed in the left wing of his party. His replacement of a leftist cabinet officer for a more moderate one was an early indication of his willingness to negotiate with the opposition. An additional source of indirect support for PAN was the moderate wing of the ruling party, which had taken over key governmental posts in the Avila Camacho Administration at the expense of leftist elements, whose influence had begun to dwindle following the presidential transition of 1940. The shift from adamancy to a resilient set of belief patterns on the part of the PRM under Avila Camacho gave PAN an excellent opportunity to stage its own ideological battle within official circles, at the expense of the equally adamant, but no longer so influential, left. PAN's success was, therefore, directly attributable to the accessibility of communication channels with the government—channels which had been characteristically closed during the previous administration. Had such a shift not occurred within the PRM—that is, had the left continued to prevail, the opposition forces would undoubtedly have been far less effective.

Also contributing indirectly to the cause of PAN was a group of prominent Mexican university intellectuals, whose prestige and influence extended to a number of former students who had since joined the ranks of the revolutionary family. This group of intellectuals, led by a man of the stature of Antonio Caso, had already manifested its opposition to the socialist clause in the amendment to Article 3, when it was first proposed in 1933. Although Caso and his followers had been particularly disturbed at the possible effects which that amendment might have upon the university community and upon academic freedom, the Mexican press had duly publicized the fact that Vicente Lombardo Toledano and other spokesmen for socialist education in Mexico had suffered a major setback at the hands of Caso, when the latter brilliantly challenged the entire spirit of the amendment in a debate with Lombardo Toledano.[23] The animosity between Caso and Lombardo Toledano persisted throughout the Cárdenas years, when the latter, together with Alberto Bremauntz and Narciso Bassols, fresh from their success in securing the approval of the socialist amendment, attempted to extend its effect upon the National University and other institutions of higher learning. As was documented in an earlier chapter, this invasion into the jealously guarded principles of university autonomy and academic freedom was successfully withstood by Manuel Gómez Morín, at that time Rector of the National University, with the support of the great majority of the faculty and students. From that point on, Lombardo and his associates met with the increased resistance of Mexican educators. In a very real sense, the leading proponents of socialist education became identified as militant foes of academic liberty and as political profiteers. Most of the respected members of the university community had little use for a position which seemed to threaten academic freedom. This atmosphere of discontent, of course, served to enhance the campaign which Gómez Morín, as PAN founder, was to stage at a later date against the 1934 revisions of Article 3.

Finally, mention should be made of the growing and organized popular resistance to the government's educational policies. This was especially evident within the ranks of the UNPF, a powerful pressure group, closely identified with Catholicism, which had refused to work within the ruling party as an organ under the command of the Secretariat of Public Education. The UNPF, founded on April 27, 1917, echoed PAN's demands that the education of Mexican children be left to the discretion of parents, and its active opposition by means of large protest demonstrations in most major cities dated back to 1933, when the then Secretary of Education, Narciso Bassols, tried to implement a program of sex education in primary and secondary public schools.[24] The *Ley Reglamentaria* of 1939, whereby officers of the Secretaría de Educación Pública were given authority to enforce the provisions of Article 3 to the fullest, resulted in a new round of public demonstrations staged by the

UNPF, which culminated in 1941 with organized marches in major urban centers. With the advent of a more moderate administration, the UNPF substituted its militant approach for one of persuasion by sending written petitions to key officials and urging a new reform of Article 3. The last such petition during this confrontation was presented to the Mexican Congress on December 18, 1945, when the legislature was already debating the modified reform project submitted by President Avila Camacho.[25]

Following the abolition of the socialist clause from the Constitution, PAN began to deemphasize its strong ideological commitment to educational freedom, even though Avila Camacho's concessions had fallen well short of the opposition's original demands. In so doing, PAN leaders were in effect following the example set by the Church hierarchy and other pro-Church organizations by tacitly acknowledging that a militant attitude towards the government would no longer be advisable, so long as administration officials showed restraint in the pursuit of any policies that might be adverse to parental rights in matters of education of children. Such discretion was evident in both the Alemán (1946–52) and Ruíz Cortines (1952–58) adminstrations, with the result that PAN's earlier militancy all but disappeared. Thus, in the ensuing national conventions of PAN, little mention was made of the education issue, an issue which had dominated the various platforms of the party before 1946.

It was not until 1962, midway through the administration of President Adolfo López Mateos, that the opponents of statism in education, once again led by PAN, openly challenged the government. On this occasion, the issue centered around free and compulsory texts for all public schools. Sponsored by the Secretary of Public Education, Dr. Jaime Torres Bodet, the new governmental policy stipulated that a standard textbook was to be distributed to all public school children free of charge. The text would presumably also be compulsory for private schools as well. This policy came almost immediately under vigorous attack from several sectors of Mexican society. In an official statement dated 29 July 1960, the Mexican Bar Association declared that such a policy of uniformism in education, as represented by the idea of a *texto único,* ran contrary to Articles 3, 7, and 28 of the Mexican Constitution, and argued further:

> Within a pluralist society as is Mexican society, one cannot pretend to implement cultural uniformity, without endangering democratic criteria . . . The integrity of the family constitutes another of the criteria which have inspired education policies, and this integrity is undermined whenever the educational rights and duties of the family are disregarded as is the case with the introduction of a standard, uniform, and compulsory textbook without the participation of the heads of family. Such a policy impedes the free access to truth, a specific attribute of the intellect, which constitutes the essential prerequisite for the respect of human dignity.[26]

Encouraged by the constitutional challenge posed by the Mexican Bar Association, both PAN and the UNPF stepped up their organized campaign against SEP Secretary, Torres Bodet.[27] Both groups argued that this new policy represented yet another effort on the part of the government to penetrate into the minds of the youth by propagandizing the "official truth," and they challenged the pedagogic merits of the text and challenged state intervention in the affairs of private schools in the sense that the government was claiming the right to determine which persons had the right to teach in such schools. They argued, further, that the new textbook policy had been directly inspired by pro-Soviet officials of the SEP, listing such names as Mario Aguilera Dorantes and Celerino Cano, and that the entire objective was to undermine family unity in Mexico. They cited as an example the guide text, *Unity of Work and Study* (1960), authored by Clara O. de Cardounel, a teacher at the Escuela Normal de Matanzas, Cuba. This text, they claimed, gave preeminence to material things and presented the State as the lord and master of all things.[29]

Rallying around the motto "In Defense of my Duties and Rights" *(Por mi deber y por mi derecho)*, the efforts of the UNPF culminated in Monterrey, on February 1, 1962, where it led a protest march of over 150,000 participants in front of the governor's office. For its part, PAN did little more than second the demands of the UNPF. It should be noted that both groups were not opposed in principle to the free distribution of texts. While this was understandable, since such opposition would have been political suicide, it nevertheless served to weaken their cause. Their vehement opposition to a uniform text had, after all, little meaning for those sectors that looked forward to the prospect of a free text, and *everyone did* agree that a free text was desirable.

Despite demands voiced by PAN and the UNPF, they did not alter the government's stand, and the free, uniform textbook was adopted. Why did opposition forces fail to repeat their earlier successes?

In contrast to the 1946 episode, several psychological factors, many of them insurmountable, worked against the cause of the education libertarians. First and foremost, was the uninterrupted period of acquiescence on the part of PAN and its associates to the state's legitimate role in imparting public education. Although Avila Camacho and subsequent administrations had shown a certain elasticity in pursuing a live-and-let-live policy with regard to private schools, it should be borne in mind that the 1946 revision of Article 3 still recognized the state as the principal agent of education. PAN, to be sure, had continued to question this arrangement, but because of the conciliatory tone of the Avila Camacho, Alemán, and Ruíz Cortines administrations, the party had, for all practical purposes, replaced its earlier intransigent position with a growing resiliency in ideological commitments. Former party leaders found it difficult, therefore, to instill or renew a spirit of militancy in the younger generation of Panistas, many of whom accepted the role of the state in this area. Indeed, much of the growing distantiation between the old and the new generations of PAN followers seems to lie in their conflicting views regarding the present and the future role that their party should assume. As was suggested earlier, the former group would still like to stress a limited set of issues in their confrontation with PRI forces, whereas the latter group is striving to emphasize PAN's viability as a progressive force of national proportions.

This conclusion is partially supported by a series of interviews I held with the late Manuel Gómez Morín and Adolfo Christlieb Ibarrola in 1968 and 1969. Gómez Morín, for example, had voiced his objection to younger Panistas eager to challenge the ruling PRI in all parts of the country and to run candidates for every conceivable office. He suggested, further, that the older generation, which was still bearing the bulk of party finance contributions, was weary of such expenditures, particularly in light of the poor electoral showing by PAN in areas outside of its traditional regional strength (see chapter 5 and Appendix III). Up to his death in 1972, Gómez Morín was convinced that PAN could never hope to win a national election, and he admitted to me that the party was not even prepared to cope with the implications of such a victory because of lack of personnel. Christlieb, on the other hand, took the opposite view, and was most critical of the particularistic orientation of PAN in the earlier stages of its existence.

A second psychological factor operating against PAN involved some of the leading personalities engaged in the 1962 confrontation. Unlike such controversial figures of the 1940s as Sánchez Pontón, Jaime Torres Bodet, as SEP Secretary under López Mateos, not only had a legitimate claim to the office as one of Mexico's most respected intellectuals,[29] but was himself above suspicion as far as pro-Communist or pro-Soviet leanings were concerned. Thus, neither PAN nor the UNPF could effectively shape general public opinion so that claims which, as noted, were largely based on the issue of communist influence in the Secretariat, failed to generate a significant response.

Finally, unlike the 1946 confrontation, neither President López Mateos nor the leadership of the PRI showed a willingness to discuss this issue with opposition forces and their representatives, particularly since the large majority of the Mexican people supported the government's free text program anyway.[30]

The question of land reform, governed by Article 27 of the 1917 Constitution, represented a second major area of ideological confrontation between PAN and the government. PAN was critical of the encouragement which the Cárdenas administration had given to class warfare, particularly that waged between *campesinos* and landowners and appealed to subsequent regimes for greater guarantees for small private farms.[31] While the party accepted the traditional Indian communes, or *ejido* system, it had strongly opposed Cárdenas' bias in favor of government-controlled cooperatives as well as mass expropriation of large estates without regard to their productive potential. At the same time, PAN charged that the government-sponsored peasant union, the Confederación Nacional Campesina (CNC), had created an even more subservient condition for the individual *campesino* than that which had plagued him under the traditional *latifundio* system. Furthermore, Panista leaders claimed, that, whereas in prerevolutionary conditions the peasant had suffered the abuses of individual landowners, he was now absorbed by the impersonal, often corrupt leadership of the unions, which placed priority on power and influence within the revolutionary family.[32]

Just as it had done in the education controversy, PAN again capitalized on the anti-Cárdenas sentiment which surfaced during the Avila Camacho and Alemán administrations. Partly as a result of PAN's pressures against stepped-up expropriation and collectivization of lands, some significant policy changes occurred in the 1940s.[32] Under Avila Camacho, the total redistribution of lands was drastically reduced. In contrast to the Cárdenas years, when a total of 17.8 million *hectáreas* had been distributed to the peasants, the number dropped to 6.6 million from 1940 to 1946. Later, during Miguel Alemán's term of office, the total fell further to 5 million *hectáreas.* Greater emphasis was placed, instead, on irrigation and colonization projects. Before 1944, for example, the total number of *hectáreas* under irrigation had been below the 200,000 mark. By 1950, it had risen to 1.7 million.[34]

When it became evident that Avila Camacho's successor would also be committed to policies of moderation, the revolutionary left began its own campaign of "redemption." Having lost to the conservative forces in the education issue, the left wished to make certain that no other setbacks would occur. With the consent of the union leadership, a series of disturbances erupted in the countryside, as peasants began to invade privately owned lands. These were followed by leftist-inspired workers' strikes in the cities against the government. In his *Manifiesto* of Guaymas, of October 25, 1946, ex-President Abelardo L. Rodríguez denounced these disturbances as communistic. At the inauguration of Zumpimito Dam, Lázaro Cárdenas announced that he was permanently retiring from political life (an announcement that was welcomed by the more moderate elements in the PRI), but he warned, at the same time, that small farms "must be fomented only in those regions where the peasants are not landless."[35] Shortly thereafter, many an eyebrow was raised at Cárdenas' failure to show up at the inauguration ceremonies for Miguel Alemán.

In the meantime, PAN was taking advantage of the agrarian disorders in the countryside by pointing to them as evidence of an imminent need for constitutional reform. On 17 October 1946, the PAN deputies presented a project in Congress, aimed at providing greater safeguards for private agricultural properties under Article 27. These included the restoration of the *juicio de amparo* to protect the individual constitutional rights of landowners. As expected, since the project was being presented by deputies of a minority party, it met immediately with strong opposition. Gabriel Leyva Velázquez, secretary-general of the CNC declared that the writ of *amparo* in this case would deal a mortal blow to the revolutionary principle of agrarian reform, adding that "this new attempt on the part of reactionary forces to destroy the Revolution's great accomplishments in the area of agriculture shall be energetically repressed by the progressive forces in the country."[36] Despite a favorable reception by the Mexico City press,[37] PAN's project was promptly shelved by Congress, which proceeded to consider other "more pressing" matters.

PAN, however, continued its campaign on behalf of small farming, and it did so by enlisting the support of other organizations. Prominent members of the Foro Nacional, all specialists in agrarian and constitutional law, came out in support of PAN's proposal.[38] A month later, the Instituto de Orientación Económica (Institute for Economic Guidance), whose membership was derived exclusively from the ranks of reputable economists, published an open letter in all Mexico City dailies, which recognized that "the revolutionary regime must offer legal guarantees to small property owners."[39] To those familiar with Mexican politics, this public recognition represented a clear sign that President Alemán himself had rejected the declarations made by the CNC leadership and indeed he had. On December 3, 1946, Alemán sent to Congress his proposals for the reform of constitutional Article 27. In essence, his was manifestly a conservative document aimed at restoring the legal personality of small property, or *minifundio.*[40] Coinciding further with PAN's position, the president called for the reinstitution of the *juicio de amparo* to the individual farmer. It is ironical to note that, although the president's own project followed PAN's earlier proposals almost to the letter, the Mexican Congress' reception was this time far more favorable; it was called a major revolutionary initiative.

PAN's assessment of the presidential initiative was favorable in general, although it stressed that its own project had been "more encompassing and congruent." It recognized, however, that the amendment "had the fundamental value of paving the way for the establishment of a juridico-social regime in the countryside, which would serve to stimulate genuine land reform and increase agricultural production."[41] The PAN deputies in Congress approved the amendment, and reasoned, "despite its defects, it creates a better situation than that which exists; we were unable to convince the other deputies that the reform should be more ample and clearer."[42]

Once again, the tables had been turned on the revolutionary left. As long as the president had remained silent, leftist elements had successfully pressured Congress to dismiss PAN's reform proposals as "reactionary." But it was the same Congress which unanimously approved the soundness of Alemán's project and repudiated those very same pressures which it had obeyed earlier, without demonstrating the slightest degree of perturbance at the fact that the president's and PAN's projects were substantially the same. Underscoring the victory of PAN and its allies in this confrontation of ideologies were the vigorous attacks waged against the administration (with little success) by the Partido Comunista Mexicano and other leftist spokesmen within the PRI, notably Narciso Bassols, and the leadership of the Confederación Nacional Compesina, (CNC) and the Confederación de Trabajadores Mexicanos. (CTM)[43]

The preceding case studies in ideological confrontation lead to several conclusions. First, they illustrate the fact that PAN's potential to influence policy was greatest in the decade which followed the presidency of Lázaro Cárdenas, when the ruling party under the leadership of Presidents Avila Camacho and Alemán veered toward more moderate policies. During that decade PAN never lost its own adamant ideological commitments (indeed one might argue that this was the secret of its relative success); and it was able to confront administrations which showed considerably less dogmatism than that prevailing from 1934 to 1940. With the appointment of key cabinet officers from among the ranks of revolutionary moderates, some of PAN's proposals were, in effect, absorbed into the revised revolutionary programs of Avila Camacho and Miguel Alemán. PAN's relative success, therefore, is attributable chiefly to the governmental shift to the center.

Second, and of equal significance, is the fact that, in concentrating on a limited set of vital issues, the PAN leadership was successful in projecting an image of consistency which it has progressively lost in the ensuing years. In earlier years the PAN had been unmistakably linked to a given set of ideological issues, a factor that lent the party a certain degree of credibility on the part of sympathetic circles and respect from its principal enemies, as attested by the declarations of Mr. Bremauntz.

Finally, it should be emphasized that PAN's influence rested largely if not solely, on its ability to capitalize on issues which were, in any case, representative of the public's discontent with some of the more controversial policies of the Cárdenas legacy. In other words, Mexican public opinion tended to be sympathetic to PAN's campaigns for constitutional reform. This is evident not only from the activities of such organizations as the UNPF and the Mexican Bar Association, but also from the largely favorable reaction of the Mexican press.

THE POLITICAL ISSUES

PAN's participation in the electoral process, limited though it was from 1940 to 1952 (see chapter 5), had represented a challenge to the dominant party's own interpretation of Mexican democracy. Since 1929, the Revolutionary Party, under its various names, had been the undisputed "umpire" of Mexican political life. The politics of the party became synonymous with the politics of the government. The resulting gap which developed between the ruling elite and the population, accentuated by the latter's noticeable lack of political sophistication, made it much simpler for the "ins" to assert themselves as the sole interpreters of the Revolution and of the needs of society. They reasoned that, since the aspirations of postrevolutionary Mexicans were commonly identifiable (that is, the masses were homogenous), a system of guided democracy, supervised by the direct heirs of the Revolution (the Revolutionary Party), would be most desirable to meet these needs. The accepted Western assumption of party competition according to an agreed-upon set of rules was, thus, replaced by an "emphasis on the right of the majority, not only to constitute the government, but also to take all power to itself without regard for the minority."[44] From this assumption that the ruling elite has the right to control and that "a minority is no more than a tolerated nuisance, it [was] a relatively small step to seeing it only as a niusance, no longer to be tolerated."[45] The success with which these justifications for guided democracy met in Mexico was undoubtedly attributable to the original popular support which the Revolutionary Party had been able to enlist. But once established in power, "the dynamics of the totalitarian procedures adopted in the name of happiness and plenty—which were never attained—won over democratic scruples, if they ever in fact existed."[46]

For its part, PAN opposed the very idea of "mass politics" and stated that pluralistic societal interests were very much in evidence in Mexico, and that a state, to be a just state, had the obligation to respect and to harmonize diversity in society.

> Democracy [the party stated] is that form of government in which, in order to guarantee the proper respect for the essential rights of man, in harmony with the requirements of the common good [Bien Común], the State recognizes both in theory and in practice the people's right to elect or determine the form of government, as well as the responsible holders of public office. It must also recognize that the source of all legitimate power rests in the people.[47]

Hence, in presenting what Emerson would term the Western view, PAN based its position on the assumption that,

> unless a variety of opinions, programs, and persons can be presented to the electorate for their approval or disapproval, the people are not in the position to make an informed choice between the alternatives which are open to them. Without full freedom for an opposition to canvass every possibility and speak its mind, the abuses and errors of the government cannot be brought to light, and, of even greater importance, nor can what may be wiser measures secure an adequate hearing. Only by establishing institutional safeguards for criticism and innovation . . . is it possible to ensure that all viewpoints have been heard, and that all means of achieving the public good have been explored.[48]

In the ensuing section, I will examine to what extent PAN has been successful in its campaign to preserve such institutional safeguards.

Case Study A: PAN in Defense of Its Congressional Candidates

During the first years of its existence, PAN limited itself to testing the most elementary safeguards for competitive democracy. Article 72, Section c of the Mexican Constitution provides for the establishment of electoral colleges at the federal and state levels, in order to determine the final outcome of executive and legislative contests. These tribunals are integrated by the out-going members of the lower house, or Chamber of Deputies. To ensure a fair hearing in case the outcome of an election is in doubt, all candidates concerned may, according to the rules of procedure of the electoral colleges, appear in person before the tribunal when it meets to decide upon the official results.[49] It was this built-in safeguard which PAN set out to test, particularly at the federal congressional level, because it was here that the party had directed its early electoral efforts.

One of the most colorful periods in Mexican legislative history was that after the 1943 congressional election, during which, for the first time, a permanently organized party of opposition (PAN) challenged the ruling party. Ever since the establishment of the PNR in 1929, the Mexican Congress had become a most exclusive "club". Senators and deputies thoroughly enjoyed the prestige and corresponding privileges and patronage pertaining to their status, although most of them, to be sure, hoped to occupy a more influential post in the future. All, however, were bound by one important, unmistakable, common denominator: membership in the Revolutionary Party.

It was against this background of exclusivity that PAN decided to confront Goliath. With twenty-one of its candidates claiming victory in various congressional districts, the party promptly declared that it would defend its case before the Federal Electoral College, which would begin its hearings one month following the election, on August 4, 1943. As the PAN delegation approached the premises of Congress, it noticed that the large iron front-gate was closed. This, in itself, was not particularly surprising. It had been a singular tradition that any Mexican, irrespective of class or party, was at perfect liberty to enter the halls of Congress, provided that the legislature was not in session. A member of PAN has vividly described the setting:

> The numerous interior doors open and close according to the climate. It is a coincidence, surely unintentional, but the truth of the matter is that, as one enters, all doors which are located on the right hand side remain permanently locked with a double turn of the key. Access to the basement is generously granted when not one soul is in sight. Yet, as soon as there is some interesting activity, this door is also promptly locked. And there, in the middle, behind locks, keys, and wooden frames, just like a safebox, stands the hall of sessions, where one speaks of everything, even of laws at times.[50]

The Panistas stood before the gate, and tried unsuccessfully to gain admission, while other individuals, displaying their

PRM credentials, were able to enter provided some evidence of "the right kind" of membership in "the right kind" of party was shown. By some unusual circumstance, one of the PAN candidates managed to pass unnoticed, and, once inside, he was cordially welcomed by everyone. Soon however, he discovered that he had been mistaken for someone else and he was quickly motioned out. Chaos erupted outside, with members of the PRM "elbowing" their way into Congress, while the PAN challengers were pushed aside from the gate. PAN called it *"la batalla de los empujones,"* the battle of the elbows. That same evening, Acción Nacional headquarters duly publicized the events:

> Pursuant to the provisions of article 3 of the Regulations of the Chamber of Deputies, which stipulates that all candidates in contested districts must appear, without the need of previous appointment, before the Electoral College to present their case, the candidates of PAN came to Congress. Although our candidates presented their respective credentials, they were denied access into the hall of sessions and even into the building itself.[51]

On the following day, the delegation went to the Secretariat of Gobernación, requesting a permit to attend the sessions of the electoral college. Officials there, however, held that it was not up to them to issue such a permit, and that the appropriate agent for these matters was the president of the electoral college. The appropriate agent, Deputy Fernando Moctezuma, suggested, in turn, after a lengthy meeting with the delegation, that he "might consider" allowing some of the "independent" candidates to be heard by the PRM bloc. The delegation spokesman, Miguel Estrada Iturbide, retorted that his party would never expose its case before the PRM bloc, because it constituted a strictly partisan, political organization, not born of law or any other rule.[52] He requested, instead, that the candidates be permitted to approach the Credentials Committee in Congress which was, in any case, an official organism.[53] Moctezuma, reluctant at first, finally acquiesced to this procedure.

While the credentials of the PAN delegates were being reviewed by the Committee, the Electoral College continued to decide on the outcome of contested elections, some of which included those very districts where PAN was claiming victory. Within three days, the College had awarded ninety deputyships, all to PRM candidates, without permitting a single opposition representative to defend his case. To accentuate the singularity of the proceedings, one of the PRM candidates, Jorge Meixueiro, of Oaxaca, upon hearing that the seat for which he had campaigned had been awarded to another more influential member of the party (Leopoldo Gatica Nerí,) mortally shot himself in full view of the session. Gatica, who had not even campaigned in that district, subsequently admitted: "I didn't win. Meixueiro was the real winner . . . but then, such is life, as you all know. . . ."[54]

The Meixueiro incident paralyzed all sessions for the rest of the week. It was not until the middle of the second week of proceedings that PAN won its symbolic victory: of the twenty-one contestants, two were allowed to defend their positions before the Electoral College. Amid catcalls and other types of unparliamentary vocabulary, Carlos Septién García and his Panista colleague, Filogonio Mora, announced:

> We are the first voices of Acción Nacional ever to address this assembly, and it is our duty to state that Acción Nacional has at least achieved one of its aims during this campaign: to bring out into the open the tactics of this fraudulent regime, to expose them, and to show that when it comes to democracy, we are vegetarians in foreign countries, and cannibals in our own.[55]

As expected, the decision of the Electoral College in these two cases was handed in favor of the PRM contenders, but PAN had made its own message clear: it would continue to fight for the effective implementation of existing institutional safeguards for election proceedings. This case study, which depicts an extreme situation, illustrates the extent to which the most fundamental safeguards for democracy had fallen into neglect as the result of the politics of exclusivism waged by the dominant party. Judging from subsequent confrontations, it can be asserted that the Revolutionary Party was compelled to react positively to PAN's challenge. For example, during the following two congressional elections (1946 and 1949), the regime agreed to permit the Electoral College to hear thirty-three PAN challengers, and, as a result of clear evidence, seven Panistas managed to win their cases and to be seated in Congress.[56] Over the past twenty-five years, in subsequent elections, the government has come to expect such challenges, and the very idea of allowing opposition candidates to argue their fate before electoral tribunals no longer results in headline coverage. At the time of this writing, the official results of the 1973 congressional elections had yet to be announced; almost three months after the election was held, PAN and other minority parties were still contesting the outcome in some 50 districts. To be sure, it had been a modest beginning back in the 1940s, but a beginning that contributed to the recognition of pluralist interests in Congress.

Case Study B: PAN and the Issue of Electoral Reform

Among PAN's major political concerns has been the establishment of an electoral system which would enable several permanent political parties to participate, and one which would ensure impartial electoral procedures. Neither the 1911 nor the 1918 electoral laws had proved to be adequate safeguards for these conditions. They had set forth very permissive conditions for the establishment of new parties, so that Mexico's two earlier experimental periods in multiparty politics (1910–13 and 1917–29) had proved chaotic and unfruitful for a genuinely competitive democratic system.[57] Similarly, when the Revolutionary Party was created, these laws were promptly converted into tools for self-enhancement since all electoral agencies were soon entirely dominated by the ruling coalition.

PAN lost no time in urging reform of these outdated laws. The party approached some of the more sympathetic officials in the administration in the hope of obtaining additional support for this cause. In October 1942, PAN leaders delivered to President Manuel Avila Camacho a project for electoral reform which called for the establishment of impartial institutions and for stricter qualification for the creation of new parties.[58] No significant response came from the administration at that time. Following the 1943 federal elections, however, PAN stepped up its campaign, backing its demands for change with examples of widespread irregularities in state and local elections. By 1945, opponents of electoral reform began to concern themselves with PAN's adamancy. In September of that year, PAN submitted another project to the secretary of Gobernación, which was similar in content to that which it had urged the president to adopt three years earlier. Amid speculation that the administration was indeed giving serious consideration to an overhaul of the existing electoral system, several voices of protest within the revolutionary coalition began to be heard, charging that such a concession to the demands of a minority group would seriously undermine the unity of the Revolutionary Party. The President of the PRM, Antonio "Roque" Rodríguez warned:

> Once again the reactionary faction, enemy of the people, which calls itself a political party, insists in pursuing its unjustified attacks against our united country. The members of PAN sustain unpatriotic positions, disorienting and agitating the masses, with the pretext that the present electoral system does not guarantee the efficacy of the people's political rights.[59]

Leaders of the powerful labor sector (CTM) echoed the PRM president:

> The present electoral law must be maintained, since it effectively guarantees the existence of revolutionary regimes which, themselves, encourage through an evolutionary process the exercise of civic rights.[60]

The leadership of the agrarian and popular sectors also affirmed that the existing law "essentially satisfies the needs of the national electorate, and does not, therefore, call for any major modifications."[61]

In addition to PAN, however, several members within the coalition challenged the views expressed by Rodríguez and the sector *jefes.* The president of the Chamber of Deputies, Medrano Valdívia, who evidently had already been informed by the administration of an impending electoral reform, affirmed that a new law would ultimately be submitted to the Congress, and that "the views of Acción Nacional are as respectable as those of any other group."[62] The transient Mexican Democratic Party (PDM), which was to nominate Foreign Secretary Ezequiel Padilla as its 1946 candidate for the presidency, stated that "the declarations made by the PRM leadership against a reform of the electoral law have been interpreted by public opinion as an acknowledgement that the present law is the ideal instrument for fraud and the violation of the citizen's vote."[63] Two leading aspirants to the PRM presidential nomination, Ezequiel Padilla and General Henríquez Guzmán, voiced similar views. Padilla declared: "No one can deny the atmosphere of intimidation, of insecurity and abuse in our electoral system. This is the somber picture which we in Mexico call *imposición.*"[64] General Henríquez, Commander of the Mexican Armed Forces, stressed that "the Revolution, which was essentially a democratic movement, has improved in part the economic plight of the people; but it has not progressed in the electoral area. There is no question but that the present law suffers from grave defects. I also feel that the PRM, our party, no longer corresponds to our present political situation."[65]

On December 6, 1945, the Secretariat of Gobernación sent the administration's project for a new federal electoral law to the Congress. This move represented a repudiation of the leadership of the president's own party, the PRM, which, as noted, had committed itself to the status quo. A further source of embarrassment to the opponents of electoral reform was the fact that the government's project incorporated the basic proposals which had been made by PAN, including stricter membership requirements for political parties, the creation of a Federal Electoral Commission (Comisión Federal de Vigilancia Electoral), and of a National Registry of Voters (Consejo del Padrón Electoral).[66] However, while PAN's ideas had found textual acceptance, the party felt that the provisions of the new law regarding the composition of these newly instituted organisms would greatly disfigure their intended impartiality, since the PRM would still be overrepresented, and thereby have the final say. For example, PAN had stipulated that, to be truly effective and impartial, the Electoral Commission would have to be composed largely of members from outside the PRM bloc. The new law, however, established the membership as follows: two from the cabinet (with the Secretary of Gobernación acting as chairman), two from Congress (a senator and a deputy chosen by the majority of their respective colleagues), two representatives from the Supreme Court, and two from existing political parties. Under this plan, a minimum of five of the eight commissioners would invariably come from the ranks of the ruling party.

Despite the lack of technical safeguards which might have made the law truly effective, PAN commented:

> The mere fact that this project is being submitted is of great interest, because it recognizes the public's right to demand a reform of our present system of fraud and because it admits in principle the need for institutional safeguards which public opinion has demanded, such as an autonomous electoral commission, an authentic census, and permanent and responsible political parties. But most significantly, because it proves the power which public opinion can and must exert.[61]

While the revolutionary coalition's monopoly over the electoral process was largely unaffected by the law of 1945, PAN had rallied sufficient public and official support to force its foes into the defensive. Following the highly publicized mass killings in the León, Guanajuato, municipal elections (see next chapter), and during President Alemán's administration, PAN continued to demand a seat in the Federal Electoral Commission, which it had been denied in 1946, when the Commission first met. Indeed, it was ironic, although not unintentional, that the very party that had initiated the demands for electoral reform should have been denied a seat in the Electoral Commission when it was first established. In an effort to put an end to the division in the ranks of the Revolutionary Party, prompted by Ezequiel Padilla's defection during the 1946 presidential election, the Commission had awarded the second party seat to Padilla's "permanent" party. It goes without saying that the other seat went to PRI.[68]

Despite this "oversight," PAN continued to urge additional reforms, including the abolition of the partisan electoral college system by substituting for it a tribunal which would be independent of the three branches of the federal government. Arguing against this proposal, government representatives noted that such a tribunal would bring about the development of a fourth branch in the political system.[69] Also pressuring for additional changes was the newly formed Partido Popular (PP), a leftist offshoot of the PRI, which was founded by Vicente Lombardo Toledano in June 1948. The PP's proposals included: (1) a change to a system of proportional representation; (2) a provision that would enable all parties to participate indiscriminately in the preparation, organization, and vigilance of electoral activities; and (3) a system of public computation of all election results.[70] This project was also turned down by Congress.

Early in 1949, President Alemán met these renewed demands for reform with a project for a new electoral law, which he sent to Congress in February.[71] While this law proposed no significant institutional changes from those already introduced in 1945, there were already extralegal indications that the regime was willing to concede PAN a role in the supervision of elections. On March 3, 1949, the Federal Electoral Commission (FEC) voted to award the seat occupied until that date by the representative of the PDM to PAN.[72] From that year on, the government has recognized PAN's right to a seat in the Electoral Commission. Brandenburg observed that in 1949, "the Commission worked fairly well and its representative from PAN concurred in most decisions rendered."[73] It would be unfair, however, to suggest that the PAN representative's role in the Commission was exclusively one of passive acquiescence. Indeed, the party's first commissioner, Roberto Cossío y Cosío, contributed significantly to the formulation of procedural questions taken up by the Commission. For example, in 1949, the Commission agreed to PAN's demand that the lists of election officials for every polling place be distributed to all political parties participating in the election, and it also accepted the less discriminatory ballot form proposed by Cossío. The Commission then took up the question of personnel of the various state electoral boards. At that time, each state electoral board was composed of three members whose appointment first had to be submitted for approval to the FEC. To this day, these boards have been responsible to the FEC for the preparation, organization, and proper operation of elections in their respective entities.[74]

Through its commissioner, PAN was able to exert considerable supervisory powers over all the candidates proposed by the individual states. In certain instances, particularly those involving states where PAN has traditionally enjoyed some popular appeal, Cossío was able to veto some of the nominees. One such instance involved the three canditates proposed by the state of Jalisco, where PAN entertained some electoral hopes. Cossío objected to all three, basing his case on their previous professional connections with the government. The Commission finally agreed to accept his thesis that employees of decentralized agencies had to be regarded as public employees, and consequently were not qualified to apply for membership in electoral boards. The Commission also agreed at this time to allow PAN representatives to supervise the upcoming elections in as many as 23 of the 29 federal entities.[75]

Questions relating to electoral reform have continued to play a major role in PAN campaign literature. As has been noted elsewhere, the issue of electoral reform is PAN's major thrust.[76] The principal reform proposals submitted by PAN ever since the party came into existence may be summarized as follows:

1. The establishment of an impartial tribunal. Although PAN had in mind the creation of an organism wholly independent of the other branches of the federal government,[77] a demand which to this day has never been met by any administration, it regarded the introduction of the Federal Electoral Commission as a major concession, imperfect though it was, to pressures exerted by the Panista leadership. Since 1949, PAN has successfully legitimized its claims to a seat in the Commission. Indeed, on several occasions the government has bypassed other minority parties which might have played a more servile, or less controversial role in the Commission. In 1954, for example, the Federal Electoral Commission agreed to give party seats to PRI, PP, and PAN, and ignored the demands for representation raised by the nascent conservative Partido Nacional Mexicano. In so doing, the ruling coalition has, in effect, conferred upon PAN the status of the official right. This, in

turn, has brought charges against PAN that it accepts payoffs from PRI, but no documentation exists to substantiate them. For its part, PAN has generally admitted that most of the proposals submitted by its commissioners before the FEC "have been given due consideration."[78] In the Commission, therefore, PAN has been able on repeated occasions to press for the elimination of deficiencies inherent in recent electoral law reforms.

2. The adoption of a National Registry of Voters. On this point, PAN has been especially adamant. Although a registry had already been introduced in the 1945 electoral law, it was based on such questionable sources as lists provided by the various syndicates and agricultural communities, or on census data. In all cases, the individual citizen was not required to be present to apply for his voter's card. Upon the insistence of PAN's representative in the Federal Election Commission, Rafael Preciado Hernández, that body finally agreed in 1954 to perfect the registry by requiring that each identification card be accompanied by a photograph of the voter.[79]

3. Finally, PAN has consistently urged that the personnel at each polling station be impartial and representative of all the principal parties vying for public office. As noted earlier, PAN's membership in the FEC has enabled it to exert considerable influence in the selection of personnel at the polls, although, to be sure, fraud is still a major problem in Mexican elections, especially in more remote areas of the country where local *cacicazgos* still prevail.

Except for some minor modifications in the 1945 Electoral Law, it was not until 1962 that a sweeping reform was enacted by the ruling coalition. Someone once observed that "PAN's incessant campaign for reform may have had some influence in increasing public opinion for an extension of democracy," but that "PRI's concern with a democratic image, which it had been trying to project, was more important and determined the degree of reform."[80] This view finds support in my own interviews with members of PAN, who felt that the electoral regime established by the 1962 reform actually reinforced PRI's grip over minority parties.

This reform directly affected the composition of the Federal Chamber of Deputies. In addition to the prescribed seats for

Mexico's 178 congressional districts, minority parties were assigned a maximum of twenty seats each, dependent on the percentage of the national vote which they received. Hence, a minority party that was able to secure at least 2.5 percent of the national vote would in turn be entitled to a minimum of five seats, and to an additional seat for each .5 percent, until the maximum of twenty seats was obtained. All 178 deputies who actually won the election in their respective districts were to be designated as majority deputies (*diputados de mayoría*). Those representing minority parties on a vote-percentage basis would be referred to as party deputies (*diputados de partido*). While minority parties could thus obtain a deputy delegation which reflected more accurately their overall national strength, the practical result of this reform tended to boomerang against PAN more than against any other of the minority parties.

PAN had initially hailed the 1962 law because in previous years, despite an average national vote total of 8 percent, it had only been able to secure three to five congressional seats through an outright victory at the polls. Had the 1962 reform been in effect earlier, PAN reasoned, the party would have been entitled to sixteen additional party seats. PAN, therefore, thought that the reform would serve to improve PAN's own position in Congress and that it would at the same time undermine government-financed "splinter" parties by exposing their actual lack of national popular support and driving them out of Congress. This latter point is significant because, in emphasizing the need for permanent national opposition parties, PAN had actually been attacking all along certain groups which it felt were neither entitled to registry as national parties nor to seats in policy-making bodies. Among these, PAN has always included the Partido Auténtico de la Revolución Mexicana (PARM), which in effect has never averaged more than 3 percent of the total vote, and its archrival, the PPS, whose vote averages have not been much higher. In contrast, the PAN leadership is quick to point out that the party's own vote totals have risen steadily since 1964, to an all-time high of 16.5 percent in 1973.

In short, it is probable that, in their original support of the 1962 reform, PAN had hoped that in the not so distant future it would be able to win a greater share of congressional districts through electoral majorities, and that, in the meantime, the proportional scheme would serve to prepare the Mexican electorate to accept the legitimacy of a meaningful opposition in Congress. In other words, these reforms were to render a service that was considered instrumental to PAN's needs. Actually, the immediate discernible effect of the reform did not validate this assumption. For example, during the 46th Congress (1964–67) only two PAN candidates, Luis Manuel Aranda Torres, of the Federal District, and Florentián Villalobos, of Parral, Chihuahua, won their seats by means of electoral majorities. The remaining eighteen Panista deputies were all *diputados de partido.* During the 47th Congress (1967–70), only one of the nineteen deputies representing PAN, Javier Blanco Sánchez (D. F.) was a *diputado de mayoría.* In fact, during the 48th Congress (1970–73), PAN did not seat a majority deputy, and the PRI claimed all 178 districts. This was a strange turn of events, indeed, particularly when one considers that from 1964 to 1970, PAN's national percentages had been rising, not declining! Fortunately for PAN, this downward trend has been reversed temporarily, and the upcoming Congress (1973–76) will include at least four PAN majority deputies.

Understandably disappointed by the 1962 Electoral Reform, not only because it had failed to produce a larger number of majority deputies for PAN, but also because national vote percentages were not accurately reflected in the number of *diputados de partido* assigned to minority parties by PRI (too many for the PPS and PARM and not enough for PAN), Panistas renewed their efforts for electoral reform following the 1970 presidential election. These efforts culminated in the enactment of the most recent statute, the Federal Electoral Law of 1973.[81]

The 1973 law, however, has not substantially altered the electoral regime already established in 1962. The only departure from the previous scheme is that it has increased the number of party deputyships from twenty to twenty-five, presumably to accommodate the gradual increase of PAN's national vote totals. (In 1970, with a respectable 14.18 percent of the vote, PAN had been granted twenty party seats, even though, from a strict percentage basis, it could have been entitled to as many as twenty-nine, assuming, of course, that no ceiling had been set for the maximum number of such seats.) But even with this "accommodation", PAN is still compelled to accept a situation which fails to genuinely reflect the party's national strength. PAN continues to be underrepresented in Congress, and PRI will probably continue to agree to the demands made by the PPS and PARM for a larger number of party deputyships than that to which they are actually entitled, as it did in 1970.

It seems that the psychological tactic envisaged by PAN in terms of preparing Mexicans to accept greater representation for opposition views has veered in a different direction. Public pressure on the PRI has not increased but decreased, since, in the eyes of the electorate, the government has already consented to allocate a fair share of additional seats to minority parties. At the same time these parties, with which PAN is invariably associated because of its own status as a minority party, cannot escape the image, encouraged in the mind of the Mexican voter by PRI, of political servilism—of beggars content with a compromise *mordida.* In the words of a disenchanted former Panista, Jesús Guisa y Azevedo, who was also one of the founders of PAN: "They (PRI) have delivered to a so-called opposition party the 'gift' of twenty deputy salaries. These deputies are not elected by the people, but by PRI, because they cater to the designs of PRI. They thus deceive themselves into believing that they share in the task of governing, when they actually serve only to entertain, amuse, and provoke."[82]

From a more positive standpoint, however, it must be conceded that PAN's adamant crusade for electoral reform has caught the public's attention, as the 2 million-plus votes which the party recently obtained attest. The crusade has also introduced some remedies in an electoral regime that has traditionally been subservient to one-party praetorianism: minority representation in the legislature is now a right prescribed by law, and the atmosphere in the Mexican Congress today is a far cry from those earlier chaotic days when PAN first decided to challenge its political homogeneity.

Case Study C: PAN and the Democratization of PRI—the Issue of Nominating Procedures

In February 1965, the late Carlos A. Madrazo was selected as PRI party president. Deeply concerned by his party's deteriorating popular image, he elaborated proposals which were to win for him many plaudits in the press and the more enlightened sectors of Mexican society, but an equal number of political foes who precipitated the fall of the reform-conscious Madrazo later that year. Madrazo placed special emphasis upon the democratization of the selection of PRI's municipal committes and candidates for local government posts.[83] He was particularly critical of the party's preassembly decisions, and of the manner in which these decisions, arrived at by the party elite in Mexico City, were railroaded through the remotest of municipal assemblies. When it came to the selection of PRI candidates for mayor, state legislature, and governor, the respective assemblies met only to voice their "unanimity" with the selections made by PRI's powerful National Committee. As one writer suggests, "Madrazo pointed out that the growing image of the party as the instrument of a few must be changed through actual expansion of popular participation, [and] said publicly that the party was in danger of losing the university students and that more must be done to recruit the able, politically articulate student."[84]

Such an uncommon exercise in self-criticism and reevaluation was promptly met with vigorous opposition on the part of the revolutionary elite, with the result that Madrazo was compelled to resign from his post scarcely eight months after he had taken office. It took a vigorous challenge at the polls by an opposition party to bring Madrazo's reform proposals out of the archives.

The setting was Uruapan, the second largest city in the state of Michoacán, long dominated by the powerful former president and native son, Lázaro Cárdenas. Early in 1943, the Paricutín volcano had erupted near Uruapan. On 1 December 1968, an election for city mayor was held, which was to have the effects of a major political eruption. In Uruapan, the PAN had been run by a highly respected small businessman, Salvador Segovia, who operates a very modest specialty button shop. A journalist described him as follows: "He has a passion for politics and spends much of his time propagandizing the virtues of PAN to his clients and anyone who will listen in the narrow streets of Uruapan as he walks (he does not own a car) from his shop to his house."[85]

With the upcoming race for mayor at stake, Segovia and other local Panistas urged Dr. Francisco Solís, a philanthropic surgeon and native of Uruapan, to postulate himself as PAN candidate for the post. Solís' popularity with fellow Michoacanos was firmly based upon his longtime activities as a civic leader who had headed the Red Cross, taught at the local prep school, and was the former director of the city hospital. With these activities, he had built a solid reputation for honesty and humanitarianism.

In contrast, the PRI, in its usual style, refused to measure public opinion in its selection of a candidate, since it considered Uruapan to be a "safe" city. The Mexico City PRI machine hand-picked a "carpet-bagger," Rafael Genel, who was virtually unknown in Uruapan, having lived there only three years. On election day (December 1), after a heated campaign, many PRI voters stayed away from the polls. It became clear that the PAN candidate was running ahead, and Solís and his supporters held a victory parade on the following day. On December 3, the PRI candidate proclaimed that it was he who had won the election. Sixty buses loaded with PRI supporters, allegedly paid by PRI, rolled into town for their victory parade. In the short span of two days, Uruapan had become a tense city. "I told you so," people told each other cynically. The more militant voters, however, talked about the possibility of taking up arms in defense of Solís. Finally, on December 4, the government anounced the official returns and declared Solís the winner with 8,728 votes to the PRI's 5,858. Asked why his victory was recognized in spite of Genel's declarations to the contrary, Solís suggested that the government was probably still worried over the student disturbances that occurred during the controversial elections held earlier in Baja California (see chapter 5), in which PAN was denied the victory to which many citizens believed it was entitled, and that the government "didn't want to chance any more trouble."[86]

The major significance of this election was not that the PRI was forced to admit a humiliating defeat; rather, the significance lies in the statement released later at the national headquarters of PRI in Mexico City, in which the party admitted that it had "made a mistake, in general terms, in the selection of those who aspired to the offices of mayor and councilman." The statement went on to say that the PRI recognized that more attention must be given to selecting candidates who are "sensitive to public opinion."[87]

In my conversations with Manuel Gómez Morín and Adolfo Christlieb Ibarrola in August 1968, this statement by PRI came up as a subject. Neither man considered it to be anything more than a propaganda effort, aimed at temporarily quelling public criticism of PRI tactics in elections. They did grant, however, that it was significant that these words were expressed by those very elements which had vituperated Carlos Madrazo, even though the words would not be accompanied by deed in the foreseeable future.

The isolated election in Uruapan, like recent student disturbances, has apparently served to shake the long-entrenched PRI establishment. In the words of the late Rubén Salazar, "The PRI may, at long last, recognize that candidates imposed by Mexico City on municipal elections are highly resented by local people, and that Mexicans are becoming more militant when it comes to having their votes respected. Uruapan was a classic example of this."[88] As an educated guess, it seems safe to conclude that, without the vigorous opposition of PAN in elections at the local and municipal levels, PRI headquarters would hardly have deemed it necessary to admit deficiencies in the party's nominating procedures. As a result, many political observers in Mexico believe that PAN is playing a major role in forcing democratization within the PRI.

5

Three Phases in PAN's Electoral Participation

> Decorate the polling booth with PRI propaganda; place the ballot box on the table, and hide another underneath; add a touch of registered voters to taste and bring in the brigades; mark the ballots at your discretion, blend all the ingredients, simmer with a few bullets, and the cake will be ready.
>
> PAN's Version of PRI's Electoral Recipe.

In this chapter I will discuss PAN's electoral efforts from 1939 to 1973. During this period, the party's participation in the electoral process has undergone three distinct phases that corresponded to the type of office for which PAN most actively campaigned. In the first phase, extending roughly from 1939 to 1952, party leaders placed heaviest emphasis on the office of federal deputy, and, as such, it might be properly labeled the Legislative Phase. The second phase (1952 to approximately 1964) saw the party's major efforts directed to the presidency, and will be referred to as the Presidential Phase. Finally, since 1964, PAN has shifted its electoral priorities away from national offices and toward state, local, and municipal contests. For this reason, the label Municipal Phase is appropriate for this latter stage. This threefold categorization does not imply that PAN ceased to participate in contests at the other levels when emphasizing a given phase. It suggests, rather, conscious efforts on the part of party leaders to establish electoral prioritites according to their assessment of PAN's potential to win certain offices. Furthermore, an evaluation of PAN's electoral capabilities is best developed by considering the types of electoral contests that were emphasized by the party leadership. Since a marked shift of emphasis on political offices did take place, the division of this period into three separate phases is justifiable, as long as one bears in mind that they are not mutually exclusive.

THE LEGISLATIVE PHASE

In the preceding chapter it was noted that, in this initial phase (1939–52), PAN was identified mainly as an ideological exponent of postrevolutionary conservative interests in Mexico. As such, PAN was a reflective, meditative party by its own admission: "Acción Nacional at first was a reflective party. It mediated for a long time over national problems, and this joint meditation was the end-product of numerous individual views."[1] In the opinion of party-founder, Manuel Gómez Morín, the organization was not established to seek immediate success at the polls, since it was not even prepared to accept the responsibilities of such a success. In those early years, therefore, the party represented a small group of professional men who, while recognizing the significance of political action, preferred not to make such action an occupation. Panistas of this period did not regard themselves as politicians, but merely as citizens interested in politics, dedicated to the formation of public opinion and of a "national conscience."[2] Such a self-evaluation was bound in time to lead to a dichotomy, which PAN, if it were to become a viable, permanent opposition party, had to resolve. On the one hand, the party was more concerned with projecting the image of a spiritual movement than of a political party. On the other, however, PAN had been founded with the avowed purpose of being intimately connected with politics.[3]

It has been suggested elsewhere that had PAN been anything other than an organization of reflective intellectuals during this formative phase, the preponderantly powerful government party would have crushed it in its infancy.[4] While this may be a plausible thesis, two additional considerations should be taken into account: first, the party leadership, much of it derived, as indicated in chapter 2, from Catholic youth organizations such as the ACJM, had to some degree inherited the failure of those organizations to distinguish in practice between civic and political action. Because of their close association with the Church, the youth movements had often tended to place full responsibility for Catholic political action on the Church hierarchy itself. This attitude of dependency had originated in the excessive respect which these organizations held for ecclesiastical authority.[5] Second, it should be remembered that the party was founded in a period when ideological issues dominated the Mexican political scene. In the opinion of many leading Panistas, the foundations of the country's cultural values had been threatened by the leftist orientation of the Cárdenas years, so much so that the party seemed "predestined" to emphasize ideology over all other considerations as the most effective means to counteract the Cárdenas legacy. As Calderón Vega explains: "Cárdenas was responsible for the intensification of our fierce and ashen political system. To the already primitive and barbaric militarist fury, he added the primitive demagoguery of socialism. This socialism to which the nation was subjected from 1936 to 1940 was not 'scientific.' Rather, it represented an anarchic, senseless, and irresponsible waste of the people's material and cultural resources, and bankruptcy for Mexican institutions."[6] Such statements serve to underscore the fact that PAN in those days tended to place minor emphasis on electoral activism.

Despite the leadership's preference for an ideological "crusade," many delegates present at PAN's First National Convention in Mexico City (September 24–27, 1939) felt that to remain viable, the party would have to seek public office. During this convention, Manuel Gómez Morín presented his first address as the newly-instituted president of the party. This address was to have divisive effects on the membership of PAN for almost two decades, as they are, incidentally, still manifest today. In it he offered to the delegates a lengthy exposition of the implications of either electoral participation or abstention. Participation he construed as an adequate means to awaken public opinion in a country of such insufficient political preparation as Mexico at the time. Similarly, it would simplify and concentrate the objectives of political action and would serve to unite the greatest number of wills opposed to the existing political arrangement. Abstention, on the other hand, would serve to stress the party's nonconformity with the political process and with the government's undue influence over the ballot and elections. It would also encourage PAN's efforts in forming politically conscious groups, which in any case were a necessary prerequisite for an effective opposition at the polls. In conclusion, Gómez Morín warned the delegates:

> Electoral participation at this time could very well become an open escape-valve to put an end to public pressures, a means to exhaust the impulse of the citizenry, a path to dissolve—possibly through superficial concessions that would conceal the real issues—the collective impulse and to produce once more, in a very short time, conformism and the lethargy of a new deception.[7]

Among the more prominent delegates who openly supported the decree of the National Organizing Committee (Comité Nacional Organizador) as summarized in Gómez Morín's address was party cofounder, Efraín González Luna. He best summarized the abstentionist position in an emotional appeal to the delegates. "The technique for salvation," he declared, "is no other than subordinating the passing episode to destiny, and if we speak of the problem of saving Mexico, we cannot achieve this by submitting ourselves to the peripheral demands of our present woes."[8]

The more militant elements in the party, however, refused to abstain from an active role in the electoral process. Led by Gustavo Molina Font, Aquiles Elorduy, and Manuel Herrera y Lasso, they insisted that PAN present its case to the people, even if the prospects for a victory at the polls were remote. The abstentionists were successful in imposing their view that PAN would be unprepared to cope with a contest of the magnitude of a presidential campaign (it was not until 1952 that the party selected a candidate from within its own ranks to run for that office). PAN limited its participation to a rather subdued statement of support of General Juan Andrew Almazán, who had earlier postulated his candidacy for the presidency as a result of the PRM's decision to bypass him in favor of the Cárdenas hand-picked Avila Camacho. But by a vote of 89 to

40, the activitists won a victory in the sense that the PAN would participate at other levels in the upcoming elections.[9]

In this first phase, the party clearly showed its preference for contests to the national legislature. In an interview with Gómez Morín, I questioned him about the reasons behind this preference. He replied that the Congress at that time, despite its servility to the executive,[10] still represented the only national forum where PAN's views might be heard. He noted, further, that in those earlier years of the party's existence, national press coverage of its major pronouncements and activities was most meager, so that the only place where the government would be unable to shelve PAN's views would be during congressional debates, which are in any case always recorded.[11] The quest for a forum within which PAN might obtain a certain degree of national exposure seemed, therefore, to constitute the principal motivation for the party's choice. Undoubtedly it was also motivated by expediency. As already noted, most delegates, activists and abstentionists alike, concurred that participation in a presidential campaign was out of the question, so long as PAN did not have party committees operating throughout most of the Republic. As for state, local and municipal contests, the party would have had to face the perennial problem of *caciquismo,* whereby local political bosses almost assuredly violated the citizen's vote.

PAN directed its efforts from 1939 to 1952 to the restoration of the Maderista ideal of a legislature which would authentically represent all sectors in Mexican society. Although the electoral capabilities of the party in the congressional elections of 1943, 1946, and 1949 were low in terms of actual vote-getting power—of the 154 candidates for the office of federal deputy which PAN postulated, only seven were seated—these contests are not entirely devoid of significance. In the first place, the congressional campaigns contributed greatly to the structural development of PAN as a permanent party of opposition. They also provided a more reliable indicator of the party's regional strength and growth potential.[12] Conforming to the wishes of party leaders, PAN consistently stressed ideology over practical politics, so that the campaigns conducted by individual candidates often took on the semblance of an academic exercise. But as the campaigns progressed, and when the Panista candidates saw their loyalty to Mexico questioned by their opponents, the party's efforts were often distracted from doctrinal propagation, to an actual defense of the "virtues" of its own candidates.[13] The congressional campaigns conducted by PAN served, therefore, to convince the party leadership of the necessity of incorporating practical politics into the higher realm of ideological dialogue. Indeed, one of the earliest indicators of the leaders' growing willingness to accept the legitimacy of practical politics was the substantial drop in abstentionist sentiment within the PAN. Even González Luna, the most outspoken critic of electoral participation at the First National Convention in 1939, admitted as early as 1946: "Enough organization . . . now on to a political victory!," and he agreed to run for office.[14] Table 1 indicates the decline of abstentionist sentiment among delegates at the three conventions which preceded the 1943, 1946, and 1949 congressional campaigns.

TABLE 1

National Convention	*Percentage of Delegates for*	
	Participation	*Abstention*
7–9 May, 1943	61.2	38.8
2–5 February, 1946	89.8	10.2
25–27 February 1949	92.3	7.7

Source: *La Nación* (Mexico City). See corresponding issues.

Of equal significance was the growth of PAN's campaign involvement from 1943 to 1949. The number of candidate slates gradually increased and, consequently, so did the number of entities in which the party offered organized opposition to the dominant party. In the 1943 contest, PAN had run candidates in only 21 out of 147 districts, or 14.3 percent of the total, and in only 12 of the 29 federal entities. In 1946 the number of contested districts rose to 64, or 43.5 percent, in 20 entities, and in 1949, to 69 (47.5 percent) in 23 states.[15]

The 1943 campaign is noteworthy only in terms of the experience which both PAN and the PRM gained as a result of renewed opposition in congressional politics. Most of the opposition movements in postrevolutionary Mexico had concentrated their efforts on politics at the presidential level. The year 1943, on the other hand, marked the first time in almost two decades that a permanent opposition party had challenged the ruling party for seats in the legislature. The long range effects of PAN's challenge on the government party have been analyzed in the preceding chapter. For this campaign, PAN selected some of its most prominent personalities as candidates. The list tended to include the younger, more militant members of the party, who were willing and eager to assume the personal risk of waging an active battle against local *caudillos,* and the firmly entrenched PRM machine.[16] The atmosphere of the campaign is vividly depicted by Luis Calderón Vega, himself a candidate for a district in Michoacán:

> The secret of victory was reconquering the public *plaza* . . . but to achieve this objective, we faced two traditional enemies: the first consisted of the bands of municipal gunmen who often established a fence of rifles around our propagandists and candidates, or raided the hotels and boarding houses where we were lodged; the second was the fear of the citizenry. Whenever we managed to stand upon some platform, we would soon discover the groups of gunmen, or the armed police ready to commit any conceivable form of aggesssion . . . and, standing against the facades, close to the doors of their homes, were our sympathizers, ready to flee or take cover.[17]

In spite of PAN's claims of victory and charges of widespread fraud, the Federal Electoral College refused to grant seats to a Panista candidate, so that the new Congress was once again, as on past occasions, composed exclusively of PRM sympathizers. Following the July 4, 1943 elections, the National Committee of PAN made the following declarations:

> This election proved once more that the obstacles to the normal and effective operation of a constitutional regime of authentic political representation are artificial, and that they are derived exclusively from the incapacity or from the corruption which sustains the official party and its machinery for political monopoly.[18]

At the same time, the PAN leadership vowed to step up their

efforts to organize public opinion in order to put an end to this monopoly.

In contrast to 1943, the vast majority of the delegates present at PAN's Fourth National Convention in 1946 enthusiastically agreed that the party should run as many candidates for Congress as possible. That year not only were the federal deputyships at stake, but the 58 senatorial seats as well. Despite the frustrations of the 1943 contest, there was among the delegates a sense of expectancy of imminent victories. PAN increased its number of candidates for the office of federal deputy, as previously observed, and supported twenty-three candidates for senator. More significantly, the party leaders this time agreed to run for office alongside the younger, more militant Panistas. Efraín González Luna was selected by the PAN Regional Convention in Jalisco as candidate for the state's first district. For the first time, party president and founder, Manuel Gómez Morín, agreed to run for the second district seat in his home state, Chihuahua.[19]

As in 1943, PAN once again focused its campaign propaganda on the decisive preeminence of legislative powers, on its dignity and importance to democratic theory and to the Mexican constitutional system, and on the need for restoring the concept of genuine popular representation.[20] In contrast to 1943, however, the party attempted this time to impress the electorate with the fact that it was ready to assume the obligations of a possible victory at the polls. Its campaign, although subject to financial limitations, was the most vigorous which PAN had waged to date. By June 30, 1946 a week before the general election, the party had conducted 850 major rallies in sixty-four districts in twenty states, all within sixty days.[21] Although PAN tried to make some inroads in states with large Indian populations such as Campeche, Oaxaca, and Yucatán, its greatest efforts were still being directed in the Bajío region, especially in the states of Guanajuato, Jalisco, and Michoacán, where it conducted a combined total of 182 rallies, and to the large industrial centers of Monterrey (Nuevo León) and Mexico City (D.F.), with over 381 rallies. Traditionally it has been in these areas that independent political movements have found greater popular support.

To the surprise of governmental circles and the press, PAN

admitted publicly that the election of July 7, 1946 had been the first peaceful election ever held in Mexico. The party also praised the role played by the federal troops as guardian of the ballot box, but it pointed out that in the more remote areas, the tradition of fraud and violence had not been eradicated. Unlike 1943, PAN spokesmen expressed great faith in the response of the citizenry. *La Nación*'s election issue ran a cover with Gómez Morín's celebrated phrase: "The spirits [of the people] were moved!" (*Se movieron las almas!*)[22]

Fearing, however, that the Electoral College would again dismiss its claims to victory, PAN reverted to the tactics of political alienation by voicing repeated charges of electoral fraud. The party openly claimed victories in twenty-seven districts and in two senatorial contests.[23] It was not until mid-August, after a vigorous battle in Congress, that the Electoral College awarded three deputy seats to PAN.[24] Although this concession fell well below PAN's expectations, it nonetheless represented a major psychological victory for the party. For the first time since it had been established, PAN had secured some kind of representation, small as it was, in the national legislature.

The 1949 congressional elections came at the height of PAN's involvement in the electoral process during this first phase. By this date, the party structure had reached national proportions, with regional committees formally organized in twenty-six federal entities.[25] Although in actual numbers the party ran only a few more candidates for deputy than it had in 1946, it is noteworthy that, whereas in the preceding election seventeen of the sixty-four candidates had not been card-carrying members of PAN, but sympathizers who had been urged to run under the party's banner by prominent figures within PAN, in 1949 *all* sixty-nine candidates were pledged members of the Panista family. Otherwise, PAN's intensive 1949 campaign closely resembled its efforts in the preceding campaign, despite the fact that this was an off-year, or non-presidential election.

As it had in 1946, PAN campaigned primarily in the large cities and in the *Bajío.* Its largest slate of candidates (twenty-four) ran in the Federal District, followed by fourteen in Michoacán and twelve in Jalisco. The importance given by the party to these areas was also reflected in its campaign activities there. In the Federal District alone, PAN held over 325 rallies in all twelve districts, and an average of thirty rallies per week in the states of Jalisco and Michoacán.[26] More so than on any previous occasion, PAN was able to combine forces with the still powerful Sinarquistas, whose regional appeal coincided with PAN's major victory ambitions. With the support of the Unión Nacional Sinarquista, PAN was able to make some additional inroads with the *campesino* masses of the *Bajío.* This added support came as the direct result of the punitive action taken by the government against the UNS, whereby the organization's own Fuerza Popular Party was permanently outlawed.[27] Even though in previous years the Sinarquistas had come out in support of certain PAN candidates, they had primarily backed candidates of their own party. In 1946, for example, Fuerza Popular had postulated forty candidates for deputy and six for senator.[28] Deprived of a formal party organization by 1949, however, the UNS joined and actively supported PAN in the latter's campaign efforts. The PAN leadership evidently welcomed this association. Gómez Morín, for example, affirmed that "the doctrinal and programmatic proximity of the UNS and PAN was evident. I do not see any reason that would prevent a close collaboration."[29]

In terms of actual electoral capability, the results of the 1949 elections were again disappointing for PAN. At first, the government refused to recognize but one victory by PAN, however three other candidates later won their cases before the Electoral College.[30] As on previous occasions, PAN again voiced charges of electoral fraud and demanded that the Mexican Supreme Court investigate election irregularities, a demand which the Court rejected.[31] Still, the mere fact that PAN was awarded four seats in the Chamber of Deputies that year was significant enough, since "it was the first time that an opposition party had been awarded deputyships in an off-year or nonpresidential election."[32]

The frustrations of these earlier electoral efforts, coupled with growing demands of Panista activists to participate in elections that might give the party greater national exposure, resulted in a gradual shift of priorities from congressional politics toward presidential contests. It should be noted, however, that PAN continued to present candidate slates for deputy in the congressional elections (1952, 1955, 1958, 1961, 1964,

1967, 1970, and, most recently, in 1973), thereby remaining true to its commitment as a permanent party of the opposition. Indeed, the number of slates grew steadily as the organizational maturity of the party developed. In contrast to the 1949 election, when the party contested what had been in this early phase an unprecedented sixty-nine congressional districts out of a total of 147, PAN had by 1964 committed itself to contests in 174 out of the 178 districts, and, in 1967, to an all-time high of 176 out of 178.[33] Yet the enthusiasm that marked the earlier years of the Legislative Phase declined noticeably after 1952, because it was redirected to other types of contests. The lack of enthusiasm in congressional politics has become even more evident in recent years, largely because of the adverse effects of the 1962 and 1973 reforms in legislative representation discussed earlier (see chapter 4). As matters stand now, minority parties can hope to be assigned a maximum of twenty-five party seats based on their proportion of the national vote, a number which corresponds to 12.5 percent of that vote. Therefore, it makes no difference if minority parties were to win a larger percentage, as PAN did in 1973 with 16.5 percent of the national vote, since they will still be entitled to only the maximum number of *diputados de partido* prescribed by law. The reforms presume, of course, that if a party is able to secure over 12.5 percent of the vote, it will also be in the position to win several congressional districts by majority vote. This supposition, however, was negated in 1970, when PAN secured 14 percent of the national vote but was not awarded any district by majority.

In conclusion, it may be argued that, had the 12.5 percent "freeze" not been set by the government, PAN might have reverted to its earlier priorities on congressional contests. One should emphasize, however, that while PAN's own negative assessment of its legislative fortunes from 1943 to 1952 had the effect of shifting electoral priorities away from congressional politics in most states, party leaders still continue to give much attention to congressional races in the major urban centers, but most notably in the Federal District. Indeed, as electoral trends in the D.F. since 1964 suggest, PAN has good cause to regard itself as a worthy competitor of PRI. In 1964, for example, PRI outpolled PAN in the Federal District by a margin of

66.1 percent to 29.4 percent. In 1973, however, PRI's majority dwindled to an all-time low 52 percent (a 14 percent net loss), whereas PAN's vote total rose to an unprecedented 38.4 percent, which represents nearly a 10 percent net increase.[34] (See Appendix II.)

THE PRESIDENTIAL PHASE

By acclamation, Efraín González Luna was nominated as PAN's candidate for president of the Republic at the party's 1951 National Convention. The selection of González Luna as PAN's national standard-bearer was significant for two reasons: first, it marked the first time that the party agreed to participate actively in the arena of presidential politics with a political figure from within its own ranks; second, González Luna was ideology-oriented and his acceptance of the nomination for the nation's highest office substantially reduced those proabstentionist sentiments voiced from time to time during the first phase of PAN's electoral history.

As suggested earlier, PAN's position toward presidential politics before the 1952 national elections had been that of an "interested" observer. Before PAN was established, many personalities who were subsequently to play a decisive role within PAN, such as Gómez Mórin, had actively participated in the ill-fated campaign for the presidency waged by José Vasconcelos. Vasconcelos' "defeat" resulted in the realization that the presidential office was indeed beyond the reach of any challenger to the revolutionary coalition. It is no small wonder, therefore, that an attitude of pessimism prevailed among the founders of PAN, who in 1939 saw little hope to challenge the PRM. At that time, it will be remembered, the party leadership, headed by Gómez Morín and González Luna, had to confront a dissident group of young, activist Panistas who, exhilarated by the 1940 presidential campaign, had wished to involve their party in the contest. Most of those delegates who favored active involvement were avowed supporters of General Juan Andrew Almazán, who, like Vasconcelos a decade earlier, had split away from the revolutionary family, and was already in the process of waging a personalistic battle for the presidency against PRM candidate, Manuel Avila Camacho. In Almazán they saw a man who, while not openly sympathetic to PAN's overall ideological position, was nonetheless conducting a campaign against political monopoly and corruption. They believed, further, that, because of his great personal magnetism, Almazán could launch PAN to a position of national prominence. Thus, they urged other delegates not only to opt in favor of electoral participation in general, but also to pursue the politics of "national unity," which in their view could be attained only by supporting a figure of national prestige and appeal. This implied, in effect, not selecting a candidate from within their own ranks who would, in any case, be a candidate of lesser national exposure. Gómez Morín and the party leadership were understandably upset at this suggestion, since the party's doctrine aimed to dissociate itself from the perennial plague of *personalismo* in Mexican politics. It was their conviction that parties should exist to serve doctrine, and not individual personalities or *caudillos,* and that movements such as Vasconcelismo and Alamazanismo were doomed to oblivion, because their future depended solely on the immediate electoral fortunes of their standard-bearers. If PAN was to operate as a permanent party of opposition, party leaders felt that its activities should not become subordinate to the selfish interests of such figures.

Although, as observed earlier, the activist group won its battle to participate in the elections, Gómez Morín made a final appeal against supporting Almazán. He described Almazán's opposition as superficial, a mere shadow of existing policies, "an opposition without head, without heart, and without a man." He added that if the party membership still felt that Mexico could only be saved by one man, then it might as well be one who was a "living example of the nobility and generosity of our tenets." Such a man, he felt, was Efraín González Luna, whose nomination he proposed. Because of his open opposition to any form of participation in the elections, González Luna declined the candidacy, leaving the National Convention with no other alternative than to adopt the activist position on behalf of General Almazán.[35]

The victory of the activists in terms of getting PAN to support Almazán's candidacy in 1940 was a relative one, however.

Even though their position had found favor among a majority of the delegates, it lacked the support of the party's founding fathers. On December 22, 1939, three months after the Convention, the leadership established a National Executive Council which successfully managed to play down PAN's involvement in Almazán's campaign, and instead channeled the party's major efforts in the direction of doctrinal propagation. This became particularly evident during a series of party meetings held at the height of the presidential campaign. The first of these was an interregional convention held in the city of Tampico, January 7–8, 1940, which, under the auspices of the abstentionist González Luna, dealt exclusively with ideological matters. Similarly, on March 30, 1940, the party held another convention in Guadalajara which served to outline PAN's position on municipal freedom. The predominance of ideological issues was also evident at the party's Second National Convention in Mexico City, April 20–21, 1940. Although this convention was held less than three months before election day, the normal practice of voicing support for a presidential candidate was conspicuously missing. Neither Gómez Morín nor González Luna, the Convention's principal speakers, made mention of Almazán, but spoke rather against the Cárdenas administration and other leftist elements in government circles.[36]

In each of these meetings, PAN, while endorsing a candidate from outside its ranks, showed a marked reluctance to translate this endorsement into an active role in the Almazanista movement. As Padgett suggests, the party resigned itself to the fact that, to be effective at election time, it had to support at the presidential level a figure that appealed to the masses. In the case of General Almazán, it had meant endorsing an individual whose only affinity to Panista ideology was his challenge to PRM's monopoly. Yet the leaders of PAN were also bent on preserving the party's "definite elitist orientation, thinking only in terms of a small number, and refusing to compete for mass support."[37]

Election day was marked by widespread violence characteristic of most presidential elections, up to then. The area most affected was Mexico City, where an hour after the polls had closed, over 30 persons were shot, and more than 300 wounded.[38] The authenticity of the returns was equally questionable. The government's PRM began to broadcast during the early hours of the voting that its candidate, Avila Camacho, had won large majorities in all states, but it is noteworthy that the victory bulletins were distributed to the various radio stations hours before the polls were even opened![39]

In 1946, PAN was again faced with the decision whether to participate or abstain in the presidential contest, and whether to nominate a candidate from within the party or from the outside. Certain significant contrasts to the 1940 experience were in evidence. First, PAN had successfully established itself as a permanent opposition party, officially registered with the Secretariat of Gobernación under the stricter terms of the Federal Electoral Law of 1945.[40] Second, PAN had gained by 1946 considerable electoral experience. In addition to its half-hearted involvement in the 1940 presidential elections, it had vigorously participated in the congressional elections of 1943 and in a few state and local contests. Thus, the question of participation had by 1946 become somewhat perfunctory, as indicated by the delegate vote (115 in favor to 13 against), so that the discussion centered primarily on the choice of candidate.[41]

The list of possible presidential nominees included Panistas as well as other prominent individuals whose critical views of the Revolutionary Party were well-known. Among the former, the names of Efraín González Luna, Aquiles Elorduy, Rafael Preciado Hernández, and Miguel Estrada Iturbide were mentioned. The non-Panista possibilities included Teófilo Olea y Leyva, Mexican Supreme Court justice, and a leading critic of Mexico's "guided democracy"; Ezequiel Padilla, Foreign Secretary in the cabinet of Avila Camacho, who, like Almazán, had temporarily abandoned the PRM to challenge the government candidate, Miguel Alemán; and Luis Cabrera, who, in Gómez Morín's view, represented the last of the revolutionaries in the Madero tradition.

On the basis of this list, the delegates had three possible avenues to follow. They could either support a leading Panista, or a dissident revolutionary who already enjoyed some organized popular support (that is, Padilla, who had already accepted that year the nomination of the Mexican Democratic Party (PDM)), or, finally, they could nominate an outsider who, while retired from the political scene, might agree to represent the party in the presidential contest because of his affinity with PAN's ideology (that is, either Olea y Leyva or Luis Cabrera).

At this convention, the views of the delegates coincided with those of the party leadership. They unanimously agreed that postulating a candidate from their own ranks would still be premature. They also dismissed the candidacy of Padilla, whose rivalry with Alemán was viewed as a mere intraparty squabble.[42] With the approval of Gómez Morín and González Luna, the delegates opted for the third possibility by casting 153 out of 166 votes for Luis Cabrera for the 1946 candidate of "national unity."[43] It is interesting to note here that PAN made its selection without even being assured of Cabrera's acquiescence. Salvador Novo, the prominent Mexican journalist, observed at that time that "this irregular procedure might have a significant psychological explanation, because it reflects the only freedom in the electoral process that the members of Acción Nacional are permitted to exercise."[44] The freedom of which Novo spoke was, of course, that of nominating whomever they pleased, whether a party member or not.

Cabrera made a brief appearance on the closing day of the Convention, declaring that the nomination "is the greatest honor ever conferred on me."[45] However, he declined the nomination, citing age and ailing health as pretexts. In perspective, it is clear now that his publicly expressed reasons for not accepting the "honor" did not in fact coincide with the reasons which he advanced in his private correspondence with Panista leaders. Although Gómez Morín had asserted at the Convention that Cabrera was a true candidate of "national unity," a term which directly suggested a general base of popular support, Cabrera himself had no such illusions.

Following the National Convention, the various PAN state delegations met in their respective regional conventions to ratify the resolution adopted in Mexico City to support Cabrera.[46] This news was promptly conveyed to Cabrera by Gómez Morín in the hope that he would accept these renewed affirmations of Panista regional support as evidence of the voice of the people. On April 12, 1946, Cabrera sent an open letter to the Mexican press, stating that he was still not convinced that there was a general will backing his candidacy, although he did admit that various other groups besides PAN had urged him to campaign actively. He concluded in a note of hope for PAN: "If I soon become convinced that the postulation initiated by PAN is going to assume wide-scale proportions, I shall be willing to meet my obligations as citizen and revolutionary."[47]

To most political observers, it was clear that this message was nothing more than a national opinion poll in disguise, especially since he proceeded to outline a five-point campaign program. This program was unmistakably consonant with PAN's own ideological commitments, and Cabrera offered a boost to the party's cause by asserting that the program of PAN "was acceptable to any sane revolutionary."[48]

At last, in a letter dated April 27, 1946, Cabrera made a final decision not to seek the presidency. He emphasized therein that no movement of national unity had come about from his presence in the political scene, but that, on the contrary, most independent groups had split into separate factions, rather than united behind him. He concluded, therefore, that he could not in conscience run as the candidate of PAN alone, since he was not even a member of the party.

Cabrera's decision left PAN with no other choice but to remove itself from the presidential contest and to concentrate its efforts on the congressional campaign. Judging from the past electoral experience, however, Cabrera's chances for occupying the presidency would have been remote indeed. This was reflected in the outcome of the election that year, in which even Ezequiel Padilla's recognized popularity with the Mexican electorate was given only token expression in the election returns. The official returns posted by the PRI were: Alemán 1,786,901; Padilla, 443,357; others 64,470.

Following the ill-fated attempts of 1940 and 1946 to lift PAN to the status of a party representative of national unity by recruiting national candidates of wide popular appeal from outside its ranks, Panistas realized that in future presidential contests, they would have to rely on their members for candidates. But in order to conduct a meaningful campaign for national office, the party faced the task of organizing regional and state committees throughout the country which would be assigned the duty of mobilizing popular support in their respective areas for the candidate during the campaign. Thus, the single most significant outcome of PAN's decision to run party members for the office of president was the motivation which it instilled in the leadership of PAN to structure the party along national lines. In other words, had PAN opted to count itself out of the presidential contest, it would have undoubtedly continued to direct its electoral efforts along regional lines, and thereby permanently consolidate its image as a party of mere regional appeal. With the growing conviction that PAN could indeed hope to participate directly in a presidential election, party members accepted the task of "nationalizing" PAN's structures. According to Gómez Morín, this task was accomplished in time for the 1952 elections.[49]

As one surveys the four presidential contests in which PAN participated up to 1970, it is evident that the type of campaign waged in each case reflected closely the changes which were taking place within the party itself.

After ten years of service as party president, Manuel Gómez Morín handed over the reins of leadership to Juan Gutiérrez Lascuráin, one of PAN's first three victorious candidates for federal deputy in the 1946 elections. Gutiérrez, who was to serve as party president from 1949 to 1956, was instrumental in mapping out PAN's first presidential campaign, and, according to Panistas, his major qualities consisted of "firmness and loyalty to the party."[50] As successor to a person of the stature of Gómez Morín, loyalty for Gutiérrez naturally meant loyalty to the views of the party's founding fathers, which, in turn, meant loyalty to ideology over all other considerations. It came, therefore, as no surprise when in the course of PAN's 1951 National Convention, the name of the party's principal ideologue, Efraín González Luna, was once more submitted to the delegates for consideration. As Lux suggests, the choice of González Luna was an example of the influence retained by the "old guard."[51] But no less significant is the fact that González Luna's acceptance of the nomination clearly pointed to the "old guard's" realization that ideology had to be carried out of the seminar, or conference room, and into the political arena.

For a man who had had very little exposure to the world of practical politics, González Luna conducted a remarkably aggressive campaign in a total of 161 districts (or nearly all), giving at times three speeches per day. But throughout the campaign, it became evident that González Luna had an innate distaste for "politicking," and a content analysis of his 160 campaign pronouncements reveals that they were primarily ideological in content. As one of his close collaborators has written, González Luna's main campaign themes consisted in acquainting the electorate with the doctrinal principles which motivated the creation of PAN. Thus, his oratory was basically academic and serene, except when he occasionally displayed militancy and adamancy while lashing out against previous administrations.[52] As the prominent Mexican journalist Pedro Vásquez Cisneros suggested in an article written shortly after González Luna's death in 1964, the entire campaign represented for González an extreme sacrifice for a man of his profession and of his intellectual tastes and habits.[53] González Luna himself confirmed this distaste for practical politics when he wrote in his diary:

> There presently exists a frightening possibility that I might be selected as my party's presidential candidate, should those who are more qualified reject the nomination. This would represent for me a crushing effort, the very contradiction of my habits, inclinations, plans, temperament, and personal constitution.[54]

It is clear, therefore, that PAN's first direct participation in a presidential campaign reflected largely the primacy given to ideological matters, and, correspondingly, the uneasiness with which the party's candidate approached the active political arena. It is also clear that González Luna was never able to create for himself an image of national appeal, and that his vote total of 285,555 (or 7.9 percent) to PRI's Adolfo Ruíz Cortines' 2,713,419 was, in spite of the usual "irregularities" in the computation of election returns, fairly accurate.[55]

By the time of the 1958 presidential election, the leadership of the party had changed hands once again. During PAN's 1956 National Convention, the delegates elected Alfonso Ituarte Servín as party president. Ituarte, like Gutiérrez Lascuráin, had been elected to the Chamber of Deputies a year prior to his selection as titular leader of PAN.[56] But unlike Gutiérrez, he was no longer as directly bound to "live up" to the standards of party founder, Manuel Gómez Morín. Instead, he interpreted his election to the presidency of the party as the direct by-product of the support which he had received from the activist camp. During his brief tenure of office (lasting only until March 21, 1959), Ituarte took an active role in the institutional growth of the party. He was instrumental in reorganizing two major groups previously indirectly associated with the party, the Youth Sector and the Feminine Sector, in such a way as to officially incorporate them into PAN. This move was aimed at increasing the control of the new generation. "The youth, educated by Acción Nacional's intellectuals, were now the party leaders while the old guard intellectuals acted at best as a restraining force."[57] Ituarte was also instrumental in encouraging party members from the lower echelons to seek the presidential nomination of PAN. One such party member was Luis H. Alvarez of Chihuahua, who was to emerge as PAN's presidential standard-bearer at the party's 1957 National Convention.

By October 1957, three Panistas were already actively seeking their party's nomination. These were: Rafael Preciado Hernández, selected by the regional convention of Michoacán; José González Torres, selected by the Federal District convention; and Luis H. Alvarez, by the Chihuahua convention.[58] Later that month, additional names were suggested by other regional conventions, including that of the mayor of Mexico City, PRI's Ernesto Uruchurtu. The highly competitive nature of PAN's preconvention activities, as reflected in the numerous candidates vying for the party's nomination, signaled the introduction into the Mexican political system of a practice previously unheard of: the prospect of an open convention, in direct contrast to the government party's perennial practice of *tapadismo.*[59] Indeed, this contrast became readily observable. Following PRI's national convention (Mexico City, November 15–17, 1957), during which the preordained selection of Adolfo López Mateos was unanimously acclaimed, PAN inaugurated its Thirteenth National Convention on November 23, 1957. As presiding officer, Ituarte Servín took into account the nominations made by the various regional conventions and added the names of other candidacies which arose from the floor of the national convention itself.[60] After some candidates withdrew their names for different reasons, the final list included the following: Luis Castañeda Guzmán, José González Torres, Luis H. Alvarez, Alfonso Ituarte Servín, and Juan Gutiérrez Lascuráin. One of the addresses supporting Luis H. Alvarez pointed to the changing mood within PAN. "Let us not engage in demagoguery," declared one delegate, "Luis H. Alvarez has by far *the greatest political experience.*"[61] According to the party's convention rules, 80 percent of the total delegate vote was required for a first-ballot victory. In the first ballot, the results were 178 votes for Alvarez, 100 for González Torres, 22 for Castañeda Guzmán, 15 for Gutiérrez Lascuráin, and 10 for Preciado Hernández. The second ballot produced a run-off match between Alvarez and González Torres, with the former winning 215 to his opponent's 112 votes. After the second ballot, González Torres readily conceded defeat and released his delegates to make the vote unanimous.[62]

The most significant fact is that Alvarez' strong convention support derived entirely from his own political *experience* and not from his ideological identification. Thus, unlike Gómez Morín's speech in support of González Luna's candidacy six years earlier, which had stressed González' personification and embodiment of Panista principles, the delegates present in the 1957 meeting were eager to give PRI a fight on the latter's own terms. This shift in mood was reaffirmed by González Luna himself in one of the keynote speeches at the 1957 convention:

> . . . the hour of polemics has passed. We are now turning to the hour of construction, with this magnificent laborer named Luis Alvarez, capable of understanding the meaning of political duty, and to build for us a new house.[63]

It is also noteworthy that Ituarte's presidential report to the party dealt exclusively with political problems of an electoral nature. No mention of ideological issues appeared in the entire report.

Alvarez' campaign was perhaps the most aggressive ever conducted by PAN. Certain students of Mexican politics in the United States have labeled Alvarez' manifold declarations throughout his campaign as demagogic and irresponsible.[64] Such conclusions, it would seem, are derived primarily from the fact that the Alvarez campaign did not follow the usual pattern of campaigns waged by PAN. As a former candidate for governor of his home state, Chihuahua, Alvarez represented essentially the embodiment of the young, activist, aggressive brand of new-generation Panista, and these attributes became readily observable in the course of his extensive campaign for the presidency. The general tone of his campaign oratory was in direct contrast to the sedate, academic atmosphere that had prevailed during the González Luna campaign. Alvarez' major theme was the reaffirmation of political and social democracy. He also emphasized war on poverty, liberty and peace for the farmer, social justice for the laborer, municipal autonomy, and a genuine federal system with effective separation of governmental powers.[65] Thus, the conclusion reached elsewhere that "Alvarez was openly the spokesman for clerical interests and for some members of the financial aristocracy," is unfounded.[66] If Alvarez' "irresponsibility" is attributed to the fact that during his campaign he consistently "blamed all the ills of Mexico and of the world on the PRI," then it must be admitted that Alvarez' critics were willing to concede to PAN only a marginal role in Mexico's one-party "democracy."[67] The candidate and his campaign staff, however, interpreted the role of their party differently. Alvarez saw in PAN the beginnings of a genuinely national political movement, capable of enlisting sufficient popular support to dethrone the PRI. For Alvarez, his campaign marked an end of his party's role as a secondary organization, operating, as it had in the past, as an ideological interest group. This changing mood within PAN under the leadership of Alvarez and Ituarte Servín is reflected in the intensive battle waged by PAN for all offices during the 1958 campaign; this was in direct contrast to the meager opposition staged by other minority parties that year.

Table 2 shows that PAN's involvement in the campaign, measured in terms of the number of offices sought, was considerably more intense than that of its nearest competitor, Lombardo Toledano's Partido Popular. PAN had postulated senatorial candidates in twenty-six of the thirty federal entities, while PP had done so in only twelve states, followed by PARM in ten, and by the PNM in five. For the office of federal deputy, PAN had candidates in thirty entities, the PP in seventeen, PARM in twenty-one, and PNM in fifteen. Finally, PAN registered complete slates of candidates in eighteen states, while the PP did so in only five, the PNM in one, and PARM in none. Of all minority parties, only PAN had a candidate running for the presidency.

TABLE 2

PAN's 1958 Campaign Involvement Contrasted with that of Other Minority Parties

Party	*Candidates for Senator*	*Candidates for Deputy*
PAN	52 (out of 60)	139 (out of 162)
PP	21	70
PNM	9	49
PARM	13	47

Source: "Observatorio," *Excélsior,* (Mexico City), May 5, 1958.

This suggests that in almost two decades of existence, PAN had begun to seriously consider the possibility of nationwide victories, and if a major charge can be levied against Luis Alvarez' style, it would not be one of irresponsibility; perhaps unrealistic is more appropriate.

A detailed analysis of the Alvarez campaign leads to the conclusion that the candidate attempted to pattern his activities very much along the lines of presidential campaigns in the United States. He initiated his tour of the nation in his native town (Camargo, Chihuahua) on December 8, 1957. From then on, in the company of his wife, he visited every state in the Republic and a total of 510 towns.[68] A pictorial survey of his major rallies, contained in *La Nación,* shows no indication that the crowds were small, as some observers have suggested.[69] On the contrary, they were unusually large, particularly in the major cities. The great majority of the Mexico City press praised Alvarez and the PAN for their courage in attempting to strengthen democracy in Mexico.[70] Horacio Cortina, special envoy of *El Universal* assigned to the Alvarez campaign, made the following statement regarding the candidate's campaign before the Mexican Association of Reporters on July 2, 1958:

> Alvarez' political journey represented without doubt a marvelous civic lesson, as he urged the inhabitants of the entire Republic to fulfill their duty as citizens by participating actively in the electoral process. I consider it an obligation to stress Luis H. Alvarez' courageous handling of such topics as *caciquismo* . . . It is also noteworthy that in none of his speeches did he seek out votes for himself and other candidates of Acción Nacional; rather, he stressed that every citizen should analyze and reflect upon the situation seriously before casting his vote . . . Finally, I want to make special mention of the dignified and highly civic attitude adopted by Mrs. Blanca Magrassi de Alvarez, wife of the candidate, who remained at her husband's side throughout the campaign, providing with her presence an extraordinary example to all citizens, an example which is until this day unique in the political history of Mexico.[71]

It is, therefore, understandable that, after such an intense campaign, Alvarez should have displayed an uncompromising attitude toward the system, as he learned of the "official" election results. Out of 7.5 million votes, PRI's López Mateos was accorded a record 6.7 million to 705,303 for Luis Alvarez.[72] Shortly after midnight, on July 7, 1958, Alvarez made the following announcement: "The returns received until now from several regional committees and from the Federal District give evidence to a gigantic effort on the part of the regime to cynically dismiss the will of the Mexican voter. That is all I have to say!"[73]

On July 13, 1958, PAN declared the elections invalid, charging government authorities with partiality and tactics of *imposición.* During an extraordinary session of PAN's National Council, held on that same day, the majority agreed to remove the party's representative in the Federal Electoral Commission, as a protest against the entire electoral process, and it recommended that the five Panistas who had been granted seats in Congress refuse to accept the government's "cheap gift." In subsequent meetings, Ituarte Servín admitted that four of the newly elected PAN deputies refused to accept the recommendation of the National Council, and were thereby expelled from the party.[74]

Howard Cline observes that these postelection developments "underline not only PAN's weakness at the polls, but also its basic irresponsibility, divided and poor leadership, and lack of any constructive contribution to a real multi-party political system."[75] Does Cline really believe, though, that PRI's token concession of five congressional seats was aimed at establishing in Mexico a "real multi-party political system?" Even Christlieb admitted to me that the PAN candidates had not really won those seats, and that they represented mere gifts.[76] And, one might ask further, had PAN accepted the PRI's gifts, would PAN have been in the position to make any "constructive contribution" to ending that practice? On the contrary, evidence seems to suggest that PAN's intransigent mood following the 1958 elections compelled PRI to adopt a more conciliatory spirit. Indeed, the PRI became then, and still is, far more sensitive to charges which might undermine Mexico's "democratic facade" for foreign consumption. Hence, even though the government initially echoed Cline's views, it later found it expedient to request that PAN reconsider its position, and to admit that "certain irregularities" had indeed occurred during the computation of the votes. This admission prompted PAN to reappoint its commissioner to the Federal Electoral Commission (Adolfo Christlieb Ibarrola) in 1960.

The aftermath of the 1970 election left another bitter imprint, and PAN's president, González Hinojosa, decided to withdraw the party's representative on the Federal Electoral Commission.[78] Thus, PAN's frequent attacks on the electoral process, also reflected in the recent abstentionist mood on the part of the Mexican voter, are indicators that it is perhaps PRI, and not PAN, as Cline suggests, that has failed to provide the proper climate for a "real multi-party political system."

Following the 1958 elections, there were growing fears among the young, militant Panistas that the abstentionist mood which had characterized the party in the earlier stages would again come to dominate PAN policy as a result of Alvarez' wounded ego. The four elected PAN deputies who had defected from the party in 1958 prompted a series of subsequent defections that have plagued PAN to this date. In 1959, the delegates present at the party's National Convention elected, from among nine candidates, José González Torres as new PAN president. The desire on the part of delegates to replace Ituarte was undoubtedly motivated by the feeling that Ituarte had, with Alvarez' blessing, in effect "sold out" to the intransigent position that had characterized the party for so many years. Denied by the actions of the party leadership any form of representation in Congress for the first time since 1946, the delegates saw in González Torres a man who was committed both to activism and to bringing PAN's image closer to that of a "loyal opposition." Because of his background, they also felt that he could eventually shape the party into a Christian democratic movement, whose progressive ideals were, in any case, more in line with those held by the younger generation of Panistas.[79] In 1962, González Torres reaffirmed the delegates' vote of confidence in him by extending an invitation to Rafael Caldera, leader of Venezuela's Christian Democratic party (COPEI), to address PAN's National Convention that year. On this occasion, Caldera urged PAN to establish ties with the international Christian Democratic movement, an invitation which was welcomed by the younger generation, but adamantly opposed by the party's old guard. I questioned Gómez Morín about large-scale defections as a result of his stand against Caldera's proposed union:

> Yes. For the past four years a significant group of very young Panistas have stepped out of the party to form a Christian Democratic movement of their own. This group first became active in the state of Chihuahua, and has been advised, among others, by Professor Alejandro Aviles, ex-Director of *La Nación.* In my opinion, this group has posed a serious confessional problem with which we in PAN cannot go along. Christian Democracy is clearly an international confessional movement which does not suit the Mexican experience of deep-seated anticlericalism. It has met with success in countries such as Chile and Venezuela, but it must be kept in mind that these two countries never did experience the bitter religious wars that have taken place in our country. I am a personal friend of many Christian Democrats, including

> Rafael Caldera, but this has nothing to do with our accepting their theses.[80]

Gómez Morín's personal interpretation of Christian democracy was, of course, open to question, since the Christian Democrats themselves emphatically refute such an interpretation. Mexican electoral decrees which ban parties that cater to religion (the word Christian after all does suggest a religious preference) have undoubtedly contributed to the fears expressed by Gómez Morín. On this same subject, my conversation with Gómez Morín proceeded as follows:

> Q. There is the added legal impediment in Mexico in the sense that no party or movement which caters to religion, race, or to foreign influence may be officially registered as a national political party. How then has the Christian Democratic movement of which you speak been permitted to participate in our political system?
> A. Because PRI knows well that the movement poses no significant threat to the present system. The government also knows that the only party that will eventually suffer and be weakened by this group is PAN. This is really why it has allowed the movement to exist, even though everyone knows that the movement is supported by certain German bishops.[81]

In any case, Caldera's controversial appearance brought about a sudden change in PAN's leadership, since the office of party president was vested in the more moderate Adolfo Christlieb, who, like the party's old guard, had also opposed any type of association with the Christian Democrats. Christlieb thus faced the major task of consolidating the various factions which had developed within PAN.[82]

In their preparations for the 1964 presidential elections, Christlieb and PAN were confronted by the potentially divisive effects of the newly-formed Christian Democratic movement, the Movimiento Social Demócrata Cristiano, largely composed of young Panista defectors. The electoral threat posed by this group was further aggravated when, together with the Unión Nacional Sinarquista, which had in previous years often come out in support of PAN candidates, they agreed to back the Partido Nacionalista de México (PNM). In March 1964, however, at the height of the presidential contest, the registration of the PNM was suddenly canceled by the Secretariat of Gobernación on the grounds that the party no longer complied with the legally established membership of 75,000, required for official registration. Although this information is nowhere documented, it has been suggested that the original demand for cancellation of the PNM came from the National Committee of PAN, since PAN feared the loss of its own status as Mexico's principal opposition party. "In acceding to the PAN demand, PRI not only acknowledged the political relevance of the satellite right, but also co-opted PAN as an 'official opposition' of the Right."[83]

González Torres was criticized for his role in the Caldera controversy, but the 1963 National Convention agreed that he was still the most qualified candidate to run for the presidency. Under the general framework of increased concessions to PAN by the government, reflected in such actions as the reaffirmation of PAN's legitimate role as an opposition party (confirmed by the cancellation of the PNM registry), and in the formulation of new electoral laws that would guarantee minority parties a minimum representation in the Congress, Christlieb and González Torres conducted their party's 1964 campaign, stressing moderate, constructive, and "loyal" opposition. In the words of Christlieb:

> In a democracy, the opposition is not simply a negative force, a dead weight stifling government action . . . We wish to participate legitimately in governmental decisions, in order to discuss long-range reforms. We wish to integrate ourselves into the responsibilities of power, but not to govern in favor of any particular group.[84]

Thus, in contrast to Alvarez, González Torres' campaign was considerably more restrained. His major speeches had every characteristic of "loyal" opposition. Contrary to the views expressed by Kenneth Johnson, who suggested that González' campaign pronouncements paralleled those of Barry Goldwater in the United States,[85] the PAN candidate actively campaigned for social democratic goals which were attuned to Mexico's revolutionary commitments, such as land for the peasants and increased social benefits for the workers. His speeches did not include specific criticisms of the PRI and its candidate, Gustavo Díaz Ordaz. The officially announced election of Díaz Ordaz, as Johnson suggests, marked an important "first" in recent Mexican political history. "It was the only time in PAN's history that one of its candidates publicly acknowledged defeat without charging fraud or disparaging the outcome. On July 11, 1964, President-elect Díaz Ordaz openly thanked PAN for its attitude and lauded the concession of defeat as an example of Mexico's maturing democracy."[86]

The restrained attitude adopted throughout the campaign by candidate González Torres reaped certain fruits for PAN. Although the election returns solidly confirmed Díaz Ordaz' victory (8.4 million votes or an impressive 89 percent of the total), it was the first time that a PAN presidential candidate was able to poll over 1 million votes, with the highest total national percentage ever accorded to PAN (10.5 percent).[87] Although the average national vote total was only slightly above previous PAN efforts (see Table 3), it should be noted that in the more urbanized centers, González Torres' vote was considerably more impressive. In the Federal District, for example, the PAN candidate polled 383,399 votes to PRI's 861,302, or 30.81 percent of the total.[88] In contrast, the vote received in the Federal District by other minority parties did not even approach the total amassed by PAN, with the PPS and the PARM polling only a combined vote of 37,000. As Robert Scott has suggested:

> The emerging pattern seems to show that opposition parties capture a larger share of votes, though not necessarily of elective offices, in the more urbanized areas. This suggests that a correlation exists between independent political action and social-economic awareness, a factor that may have important consequences in the future, as Westernization proceeds.[89]

Paralleling the 1958 effort, PAN also conducted in 1964 an intensive campaign for political offices at all levels. It ran a total of 174 candidates for federal deputy, and senatorial candidates in all states except Tabasco. In all, the 1964 election saw a total of 457 PAN candidates running for public office. It should also be noted that the national percentage polled by PAN in the

1964 congressional elections was 11.52 percent, or 1 percent higher than the vote received by the party's presidential candidate.

TABLE 3
Percentage of Presidential Vote Polled by PAN

1952	Efraín González Luna	285,555	7.9%
1958	Luis Héctor Alvarez	705,303	9.5%
1964	José González Torres	1,034,337	10.5%
1970	Efraín González Morfín	1,945,204	13.9%

Sources: *Diario de los Debates,* 12sp., 1952; 10sp., 1958; *Declaratoria por la Cámara de Diputados,* 8sp., 1964; and *Excélsior,* (Mexico City), July 1970.

The 1970 presidential campaign was in many ways reminiscent in style of PAN's efforts in 1964. From my conversations with members of the party in 1969, there seemed to be widespread hope that Adolfo Christlieb would accept PAN's presidential nomination for the 1970 contest. Indeed, by all measures, Christlieb would have been an aggressive and effective candidate, for even members of the Mexican left, such as Jorge Cruickshank García of the PPS and the noted muralist David Alfaro Siqueiros greatly respected his intellect and dedication.[90] Christlieb's untimely death (at 50 years of age) left PAN temporarily without leadership and compelled the party to look for other alternatives.

The choice of the 1969 National Convention eventually fell on Efraín González Morfín, son of PAN's first presidential hopeful. Unlike his father, González Morfín patterned his campaign along the same conciliatory lines adopted by José González Torres in 1964. This apparent continuity in tactics has led some observers to refer to PAN as the loyal opposition, but to this writer such a designation seems premature for two basic reasons: first, PAN's official statements in the years following the 1964 election reverted to a spirit of intransigency and alienation, and second, it is presumptuous to apply terms fashionable in competitive Western democracies to a situation which still can hardly be said to pose an even contest.

In any event, González Morfín proved to be by far the most attractive candidate that PAN has ever postulated for the presidency. Since he was the only leader of a minority party willing to challenge the PRI for the nation's highest office (both the PPS and PARM decided to back Luis Echeverría), he was able to draw considerable public attention and press coverage, particularly in the major cities. His gallantly conducted campaign, however, could not match the PRI organization, nor could it cope with the apparent rising popular dissatisfaction with the political regime, especially following the aftermath of violence and bloodshed which had preceded the 1968 Olympic Games. Neither could he mitigate the strong campaign for abstentionism waged in several circles, not the least of which was to be found within the ranks of his own party. As noted earlier, of approximately 25 million registered voters, 10,607,603 million, or 43 percent, failed to show up at the polls in 1970, a trend which was again apparent in 1973, with 46 percent abstaining.[91]

González Morfín's efforts did not go entirely unrewarded, however, since the country delivered to PAN its highest presidential vote total to date, nearly 2 million ballots, or 13.9 percent.

THE MUNICIPAL PHASE

In addition to congressional and presidential elections, PAN has participated since 1939 in a number of local contests, presenting candidates for governor, state legislatures, and counties (*municipios*). However, it was not until the mid-1960s that the party was finally able to challenge with some effectiveness PRI's absolute monopoly over state and local politics. The increased prospects for success caused PAN's leaders to shift their emphasis to contests at this level.

As noted in chapter 3, from the outset PAN ideology had placed great stress on the municipal autonomy necessary if Mexico were to enjoy an effective and genuinely democratic political system. In the Mexican political arrangement, the basic politico-territorial unit of government is the *municipio*, a counterpart of the county in the United States. Under the Mexican system, the public administration is in the hands of an *ayuntamiento*, or city council. This council is composed of a mayor, or municipal president; several councilmen (*corregidores*), whose number is set according to the population of the county-seat, and a county attorney (*síndico-procurador*).

The council is assisted by a judge, a chief of police, a treasurer, several secretaries, and a citizen's committee for moral, civic, and national betterment. Because of the one-party dominance characteristic of the system, the executive power is found exclusively in the person of the mayor, who is solely answerable for his administration to the governor of the state, who, in turn, answers personally to the president. In practice, also, the mayor has been the titular local leader of the Revolutionary Party, thus becoming the determining force in local elections, and enjoying great power in endorsing the other candidates on the ticket.[92]

In emphasizing the need for municipal autonomy, PAN aspired, in effect, to break this chain of command that had placed the revolutionary coalition in such a firmly-entrenched position; but the pursuit of this goal meant that the party had to confront *caciquismo* at its worst, for the local brand of *caciquismo* was not only the most primitive, but also it had no use for or understanding of constitutional norms, nor of democratic processes and guarantees.[93] In those earlier years following the establishment of PAN, the party placed clear priority on doctrine in its state and local campaigns, since PAN felt that it had no imminent prospects for victory. This self-evaluation proved to be correct. For example, from 1940 to 1959, only two minor victories at the municipal level were accorded to PAN.[94]

One of the more characteristic and publicized municipal contests in which PAN participated during those earlier years was held in León, Guanajuato, in December 1945. The party had conducted a very vigorous pre-election campaign and was convinced that it had won at least some of the minor offices. The local machinery, however, thought differently and declared all the revolutionary candidates victorious. Following a massive popular demonstration at the main plaza, thousands of citizens gathered in front of the municipal palace to protest the outcome of the elections. These demonstrations were promptly and brutally dissolved by federal troops, who opened fire at the fleeing crowd. At day's end, over 300 persons were wounded and more than 40 killed.

PAN reacted immediately, addressing a note to the Mexican Supreme Court, requesting its intervention in the case. Similar requests were received by the Court from the national press, the Mexican Bar Association, and numerous prominent citizens residing in Guanajuato. For the first time in the history of postrevolutionary Mexico, the Court agreed by a vote of 20 to 1 to investigate the events. This represented a major triumph for PAN. President Avila Camacho soon thereafter dissolved the powers of the state. It should be noted, however, that despite clear evidence of fraud, no PAN victories were recognized by the government.[95]

In subsequent municipal elections, PAN made several attempts to involve the Supreme Court further, but with little success. In 1946, for example, the party had hoped to duplicate its earlier victory in getting the Court to intervene. In this case, the municipal elections in Monterrey were at stake, and PAN once again called for an investigation of the results. The Court refused to conduct such an investigation, reasoning that it was not prescribed in the Constitution that the Court should decide on the final results of an election, to the detriment of one political party or another. It reasoned further that its intervention in the León case was conducted for entirely different reasons, since in that instance it had not been called upon to deliver an opinion on the election returns themselves, but rather to investigate the alleged violations of citizen liberties and the right to peaceful assembly.

In spite of the electoral setbacks at the municipal level, the party did not desist in its ideological attack against local *caciquismo.* PAN's Fifth Extraordinary National Convention in 1947, for example, dealt exclusively with municipal problems. Seven commissions were established to study such questions as constitutional provisions, structure, and the internal legal regime of the *municipio,* as well as the problems of municipal finance and public services.[96] Indeed, from 1947 to 1948, the overriding issues in PAN's ideological message included municipal autonomy and reform. In 1948 alone, PAN reported active campaigns for municipal offices in 150 counties, in 9 states, but none of these renewed efforts met with success.[97] Similarly, PAN ran many candidates for governor, state legislatures, and counties from 1948 to 1959, but won no victories.[98]

In every instance, PAN placed the blame for its defeats upon widespread *caciquismo* and electoral fraud. Party leaders noted that in state contests in which the PRI was virutally assured of a resounding victory, local election officials would make certain that such victories were the product of full citizen participation, that is, of near-100 percent voter turnout. But whenever a contest was regarded as close, the percentage of citizens voting would inexplicably decrease. This phenomenon was seen during the gubernatorial election held in Chihuahua in 1956. In this race, Luis H. Alvarez challenged the PRI candidate, Teófilo Borunda, and all pre-election reports suggested that the PAN candidate had an outside chance of carrying the election. Yet, despite the intensive campaign waged by the two candidates throughout the state, only 143,739 voters, or less than 30 percent of the state's 400,000 registered voters were said to have voted. In Ciudad Juárez, out of 75,000 potential voters, only 41,181 voted, and in Chihuahua City (100,000 registered voters), the actual vote was slightly over 20,000. And it was in these very cities that the PAN vote was expected to be very high. This low voting turnout in a country where the government normally boasts of almost total citizen participation suggested to PAN that, because of the closeness of the race, there was a widespread theft of votes. This suspicion was further reaffirmed by the voting totals accorded to the candidates in certain key cities, which were extremely close. In Ciudad Juárez, for example, the official results gave Borunda 24,576 votes to 20,551 for Alvarez.

After two decades of fruitless electoral efforts at the state and local levels, PAN began to shift its emphasis more and more to non-national offices. This shift occurred especially following the 1964 presidential election, when regional committees of PAN in areas of the party's traditional strength (Jalisco, Nuevo León, and Michoacán), as well as in new areas where there was widespread citizen dissatisfaction with the graft and corruption of PRI local officials (Baja California, Sonora, and Yucatán) began to work toward the consolidation of forces opposed to the government. This wave of citizen dissatisfaction, which persists to this day, was first evidenced in the state of Baja California. Elections for city councils (*ayuntamientos*) and state deputies were scheduled for June 2, 1968. The PAN committee in Baja California had been actively preparing for these elections several years in advance, and had by 1968 enlisted the support and sympathies of a great number of *bajacalifornianos.*[99] When the election returns began to be tallied it seemed that PAN had scored impressive majorities in the municipal elections of the state's two most important cities, Mexicali and Tijuana. In Mexicali, the initial results showed a total of 61,957 votes for PAN candidates to 49,724 for those of PRI. Similarly, in Tijuana, the vote favored PAN over PRI by a vote of 30,269 to 24,272.[100] PAN also won clear majorities in the contests for deputy to the state legislature in six out of the eight districts, but in all cases the official "recounts" altered the initially established vote figures in such a way that PRI was able to claim victories in every district but one. (See Table 4.) Unable to tamper with PAN's victory margins in Mexicali and Tijuana, the Baja California Legislature subsequently declared those elections null and void.

TABLE 4

The 1968 Election Results for State Deputy in Baja California

District	*Original Vote*		*Official Recount*	
	PAN	*PRI*	*PAN*	*PRI*
1	10,715	6,883	4,970	5,279
2	11,818	7,601	6,418	6,021
3	17,046	10,216	4,607	4,862
4	7,727	11,101	6,709	10,695
5	6,362	10,008	5,012	8,572
6	8,208	7,956	Comp. Discont.	
7	8,951	6,703	6,703	8,951
8	9,030	6,365	5,401	9,962

Source: Adolfo Christlieb, Memorandum to the Mexican Supreme Court, 27 August, 1968.

Table 4 exposes PAN's accusations of fraud. In Districts 1 and 3, both originally claimed by PAN, the PRI machinery seems to have discounted over 15,000 votes on grounds of incorrect marking of the ballots, while the PRI suffered a corresponding loss for the same reason of only 7,000 votes. This recount enabled PRI candidates in those districts to manage a slight victory. In contrast, in Districts 4 and 5 where PRI apparently established majorities from the very outset, vote tampering was practically not discernible. But in Districts 6, 7 and 8, where the early returns indicated a very close race, PAN claims that PRI "borrowed" votes from PAN's own column in such a way as to post the original opposition margins of victory on its own side. In District 2, the only one awarded to PAN, PAN's margin was reduced from 4,000 to a mere 400 votes.

Official circles today reluctantly admit that PAN did win the 1968 Baja California elections, but as one civil servant noted, it would have encouraged a run in the stocking which would have eventually destroyed the stocking itself. The "run in the stocking," however, was not averted by PRI's handling of the Baja California elections. By 1969, PAN had elected mayors in three major cities (Hermosillo, Mérida, and Uruapan), and in fifteen other smaller communities in nine different states. (See Table 5.)

TABLE 5
Elected PAN Municipal Presidents (1968–69)

Name	*State*	*City*
J. Santos Esparza	Chihuahua	Santa Barbara
D. Miguel González	Chihuahua	Villa Aldama
Rafael Pérez Aguirre	Jalisco	Teocaltiche
Dr. Francisco Solís	Michoacán	Uruapan
Norma V. de Zambrano	Nuevo León	Pedro Garza G.
Apolonio G. Elizondo	Nuevo León	Abasolo
Juan Benavides	Oaxaca	Sn. Andres
Bernardino García	Oaxaca	Sn. Mateo Nejapa
Florentino Cisneros	Oaxaca	Tlachichilco
Maximino Clemente	Oaxaca	Suchitepec
Eliseo Córdoba Loyola	Puebla	Xiutetelco
Jorge Valdés Muñoz	Sonora	Hermosillo
Mariano Ruiz Rivera	Sonora	Santa Ana
Hermán de la Vega	Sonora	Ordepe
Gerardo Tapia Limón	Sonora	Sn. Miguel
Fermín Contreras B.	Sonora	Bacoachi
Fco. Sixto Agapito F.	Sonora	Cumpas
Victor M. Correa Rachó	Yucatán	Mérida

Source: PAN National Committee Headquarters.

The increasing number of victories by PAN in municipal elections over the past few years tends to refute the contention made by some students of Mexican politics that no headway has been made toward the creation of a free *municipio.* Such a contention is gounded on the following questionable conclusion: "It has seemed that the intransigent attitude of the party on some national problems lessens the party's appeal to the mass of Mexican voters. Where modification of attitude by PAN has occurred, difficulty is encountered in transmitting this modification to the public and making it believable."[101]

While PAN's appeal has been slight in contests for national offices, it can hardly be proposed that at the municipal level, where the party has been able to secure 18 mayoralities, PAN has lost its appeal with the Mexican voter. To be sure, this marks a modest beginning for PAN, but election trends show no relation between the popularity of individual local PAN candidates and the national party line adopted by PAN in Mexico City. Thus, in this most recent phase in PAN's participation in the electoral process, the party and its candidates seem to have succeeded in moving closer to the people, as they have, indeed, scored victories in areas where PAN was previously an unknown political force, such as Baja California, Sonora, and the predominantly Indian states of Oaxaca and Yucatán.

SUMMARY OF PAN'S PARTICIPATION

The preceding survey of PAN's participation in the electoral process suggests that each of the three phases in the party's electoral involvement closely corresponds to the interpretation of PAN's objectives and role as an opposition party given by its leaders. Thus, during the Legislative Phase, which saw PAN actively seeking seats in the Federal Congress, it is clear that party leaders were concerned primarily with obtaining a national forum for themselves in order to propagate PAN ideology. The first phase, therefore, parallels those earlier efforts by party leaders to shape PAN into an effective ideological movement to challenge the socialist forces which had acquired a dominant role in the decade immediately preceding the creation of PAN. During this phase, PAN had to rely primarily on those regions that had been sympathetic to conservative causes for its electoral support, such as the *Bajío* and the larger urban centers. As such, the party remained during these early years, both by choice and necessity, one of limited regional appeal.

In the second, or Presidential Phase, party leaders agreed to run candidates for the nation's highest office in an effort to secure a genuinely national audience. As was shown, the four contests in which PAN participated with a candidate from its own ranks again paralleled the leadership's changing interpretation of PAN's role and objectives. Efraín González Luna, the first Panista presidential candidate, saw his candidacy primarily in terms of an extension of the earlier phase. The objectives consisted in the propagation of ideology, but, because of PAN's very limited success in congressional politics, González Luna agreed that a national forum and a national audience could be more effectively secured by means of the rostrum of a presidential campaign. In direct contrast, the campaign of Luis Alvarez reflected those years of reevaluation in which the party leadership regarded PAN no longer as an association committed to academic pursuits, but as a party dedicated to an active participation in practical politics. "Enough doctrine—now, on to action!" became the dominant slogan of Panistas, who now saw themselves as militant crusaders against the political status quo. An analysis of Alvarez' statements, during and after the campaign, however, suggests that in his unrealistic expectations of PAN's electoral potential, he actually threatened to lead the party out of the Mexican political framework. Thus, the major lesson derived by PAN from Alvarez' campaign was that practical politics can be effectively waged only if parties are willing to abide by, or "suffer", the system's prescribed rules. That this lesson was learned is attested by the general tone of the campaign of its third candidate, José González Torres. Unlike Alvarez, who had shown no willingness to compromise with PRI, González Torres clearly ran as a candidate of moderation. His campaign oratory supported Mexico's revolutionary tradition, and was devoid of any personal attacks against the PRI candidate. When the election results were announced, he readily conceded defeat and offered his party's support to the victorious candidate. In short, González Torres' campaign reflected a growing resilient outlook evident in younger members of the Panista family, an outlook that was carried over into the 1970 campaign of Efraín González Morfín.

The Muncipal Phase which has largely characterized PAN's electoral efforts in recent years was a direct by-product of the second phase. As was noted, an effective presidential campaign could not be waged without the existence of permanent regional, state, and local party committees, dedicated to enlisting and organizing the support of their respective constituencies for the traveling candidate. Whereas PAN could not hope to effectively challenge PRI in presidential contests, the establishment of these committees throughout the country has brought the party closer to the people, as is attested by the growing number of victorious PAN candidates in state and local elections. In a very real sense, then, PAN has finally found its place. It has found the place where, ultimately, every opposition party will have to begin its challenge to the system's characteristic one-party dominance.

6

Prospects for the Future: A Conclusion

Seguimos continuando . . .

Efraín González Luna

In September 1969, PAN celebrated its thirtieth anniversary as a permanent opposition party. And now, five years later, there is no reason to believe that PAN is giving up on the task which it initially set out to accomplish: to offer the Mexican electorate a competitive political dialogue, and alternative candidates and programs.

This study noted at the beginning that all the literature on Mexican politics readily admits that the country continues to be governed by one-party rule. This is not disputed. What has been contested in this study, however, is that one-party rule can provide a genuine sense of participation for the Mexican electorate. Almond and Verba, for example, are undoubtedly correct in their conclusion that "Mexicans have been exposed to a revolutionary ideology that places a high value on political participation," and that "exposure to these norms may create a tendency to confuse aspiration with performance."[1] On the other hand it is inconceivable that, after admitting that "Mexicans have had direct experience with bureaucratic authority, and they reject that authority as corrupt and arbitrary," they should conclude that "these civic aspirational tendencies in Mexican political culture are important evidence that the democratic aspiration of the Mexican Revolution and the political elite is meaningful to the population."[2] How is it *meaning-*

ful? Is the embodiment of democratic aspiration in the political elite the by-product of exposure to official fountains of information? Is the role supposedly performed by the political elite in advancing the democratic aspiration of the Mexican Revolution meaningful to the population when the population at the same time perceives the elite as *corrupt* and *arbitrary?* How does one explain that 16.5 percent of Mexicans chose to censure PRI by voting for PAN in 1973? What about the 38.4 percent of the electorate which showed preference for PAN over PRI in the Federal District? Or, more significantly, what about those 10,840,814 alienated voters that chose to remain home rather than vote without a voice?

These questions arise from time to time, and they now dominate Mexican press coverage. Yet some scholars refuse to deal with them. Indeed, the pervasive manifestations of alienation in postrevolutionary Mexico contradict the assertion that the Mexican political system is increasingly offering significant "opportunities for political experience."[3] These questions should certainly stimulate a desire to investigate just why it is that, contrary to official declarations, uniform popular acceptance of the democratic goals of the Mexican Revolution does not necessarily imply uniform popular support for PRI. It is hoped that this study illustrates such a desire.

La Palombara and Weiner suggest that "a one-party pattern is by definition hegemonic and not turnover."[4] As such, it represents a departure from Western norms that call for political competition. How, then, did this one-party situation develop in a Western country? La Palombara and Weiner suggest that such a development can usually be attributed to: (1) a previously existing competitive party situation; (2) serious conflict among existing parties; (3) a catalytic crisis such as war, revolution, depression, or policy paralysis; and (4) the emergence of a strong externally created party with an explicit mission to "discipline," that is, to repress all other political parties.[5]

All these conditions have manifested themselves in the Mexican political environment. From 1911 to 1929, with only a minor interruption, Mexico experimented unsuccessfully with multi-party politics. The Revolution of 1910 later served to manufacture a gigantic government agency referred to as the

Revolutionary Party. Presently, this Revolutionary Party "suffers" the presence of a limited number of minority parties which are nonetheless duly disciplined to conform to prescribed standards. Critics of PRI have called this democratic simulation. As they see it, the PRI is now surrounded by a number of opposition parties whose maximum representation in the government has been "institutionalized" by decree. PRI "awards" electoral contests if they are localized and do not suggest statewide or nationwide discontent with its iron rule. The victory of a Panista mayor or a PPS deputy makes a newsworthy item abroad. Internally, however, the admission of defeat in a senatorial or gubernatorial contest would be disastrous to PRI. PRI holds elections, but the tribunals that ultimately review the results of those elections all reflect the all-encompassing one-party dominance. PRI readily recognizes the rights of workers and peasants to organize politically into unions but insists these unions be committed to sustaining PRI in power, and union bosses are duly screened to ensure they comply. Union bosses, therefore, are seldom security risks for the Mexican government. PRI subscribes to basic educational freedoms, but it persecutes groups which are not subservient to the truth, government-defined, by using a compulsory, uniform text for all Mexican children. PRI advocates freedom of the press, but it is the State that controls all newspaper production. Paper is provided gratuitously in "credit" form to the media that bows to official policies, but in the case of a deviant newspaper, the quotations may be deleted from the word credit. The list of PRI political manipulations could be much longer.

Yet, Mexico has not moved away from ideologically inspired politics. This is the first conclusion of this study. Analysis of the prevalent political styles in Mexican party politics reveals the absence of interparty communication and of a live-let-live attitude. Although at times the intensity of ideologies has decreased, one must again recall Sartori's admonition that "a lessening of this intensity should not be confused with a withering away of ideology itself."[6] Both PRI and the "satellite" parties may have pragmatized their respective social doctrines, but both retain those firm commitments that represent their reason for existing. PRI will invariably continue to subscribe to the one-party authoritarian pattern, which calls for the domination by a single, monolithic, ideologically-oriented, but nontotalitarian party.[7] Within PRI, ideological orientation has been toward instrumental preservation of the status quo, which is an ideologism of sorts. On the other hand, minority parties such as PAN will persist in their claim of being sole legitimate representatives of alienated sectors of society. Pragmatism, therefore, as defined in an earlier chapter, is not an immediate prospect for the political life of Mexico.

One-party authoritarianism and political alienation, the two current general manifestations of earlier readily definable class ideologies, have retained old clichés and slogans. The Mexican political system and its students still fabricate the kinds of deep-seated animosities that prevailed among the various sectors of prerevolutionary Mexican society. Labels dominate political dialogue; PAN becomes a Church party, or a bourgeois party, or a banker's party, or a traditional conservative party. The PPS, in turn, is characterized as inflammatory, radical-leftist, Soviet-dominated, and so forth. And PRI, taking advantage of this political labeling, proceeds to characterize itself as the only legitimate heir of Mexico's revolutionary tradition, places the name of its candidates on every major mountaintop, and reserves for itself the national colors of red, white, and green for its campaign propaganda and ballot forms and denies any other party the right to use such colors. This leads to this study's second conclusion. Slogans notwithstanding, every political party in the Mexican political scene today is committed to the tradition of the 1910 Revolution, which, contrary to often-voiced assumptions, is not readily definable. Specifically, PAN, perhaps more than any other party, has been charged with betraying the revolutionary tradition. PAN has not really opposed this tradition, especially if one subscribes to the Almond and Verba thesis that the majority of Mexicans today can identify only the goals of political democracy expressed by Madero as the core of revolutionary tradition. PAN has, however, opposed the ruling party's interpretation of that tradition, and has challenged the contention by PRI of being the sole guardian of Mexican revolutionary values. By these actions and on the basis of evidence presented in the earlier chapters of this study, Panistas may appear to be ideological

1. Lic. Manuel Gómez Morín, founder and first national president of PAN, 1939–49.

2. Lic. Efraín González Luna, first PAN presidential candidate, 1952.

11. Arquitecto Ignacio Limón Maurer, national president of PAN, 1968.

12. Lic. Manuel González Hinojosa, national president of PAN, 1969–71, and federal deputy, 1967–70.

13. Efraín González Morfín, presidential candidate in 1970 and federal deputy from 1967 to 1970.

14. Lic. José Angel Conchello, presently serving as PAN president and federal deputy.

15. Rally in Ciudad Delicias, Chih. during 1958 presidential campaign of Luis H. Alvarez.

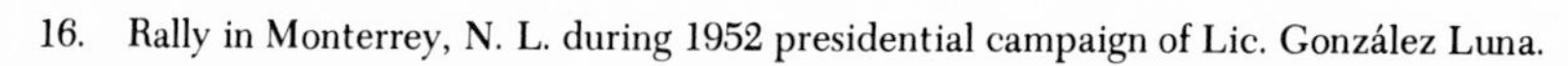

16. Rally in Monterrey, N. L. during 1952 presidential campaign of Lic. González Luna.

exponents of the political and social aspirations of the Maderista tradition, the flame which originally enkindled the revolutionary movement. This assertion may cause some skepticism, but it is hoped that the comparison of Maderista and Panista statements reproduced in this study result in careful examination of labels. Scott perceived that the electorate in the more urbanized centers in Mexico was displaying evidence of independence in political action and dissatisfaction with facile labels. Today, more than ever, PRI's margins in the large cities are not impressive. In Mexico City, 38 percent of the voters indicated belief that PAN was not an association of "traditional conservatives," unless, of course, one should subscribe to the notion that traditional conservatives are somehow multiplying themselves in Mexico City. This would necessitate, however, explaining Tijuana, Mexicali, Hermosillo, Uruapan, Mérida and many other smaller cities where Mexican voters have accepted PAN as legitimate opposition. PAN's role as a political movement, operating in post-revolutionary Mexico, should become clearer when the political and intellectual origins of the party are recounted (see chap. 2). Chapter 2 concludes that these origins form an integral part of Mexico's revolutionary tradition; that, along with most other groups representing alienated sectors in society, PAN has consistently rejected violence as a means of securing stated objectives; and that such objectives can best be attained through the established constitutional framework. The marked tendency of Mexican scholars is to equate postrevolutionary conservative thought with the reactionary policies of the old Conservative Party of the nineteenth century; they overlook the fact that PAN's own brand of conservatism, as its political and intellecutal origins attest, acquires meaning only in the context of modern Mexican society.

The initial aim of this study was, therefore, to clarify certain misconceptions about Mexican politics in general today and about the exact nature of the forces that led to the founding of Acción Nacional. The study then investigated the impact which PAN has exerted over the last thirty-five years in policy formulation against the background of one-party authoritarian rule. The conclusion is that from 1939 to 1952 PAN played an important role in influencing government policies in Mexico.

The birth of PAN coincided with the closing year of the Cárdenas administration, a period marked by intense "ideological heating" on the part of the ruling coalition. Constitutional issues that had become dormant were suddenly revived under the dynamic leadership of President Cárdenas. As an essentially counter-ideological movement, PAN from 1939 to 1952 was almost exclusively in the hands of the party's ideologues. These men, led by Manuel Gómez Morín and Efraín González Luna, concentrated all their party's efforts on specific constitutional issues. This study also concluded that PAN's earlier successes in influencing policy makers coincided precisely with that pervasiveness with which the leadership propagandized a limited set of issues that stood high on its priority list. This provided the policy makers with a clear perspective of the opposition's viewpoint on such issues as constitutional reform of articles dealing with education and land reform. As was shown, PAN's efforts during this earlier period were enhanced by its ability to enlist the indirect support for many of its proposals from such key figures as the more moderate Presidents Manuel Avila Camacho and Miguel Alemán. It was admitted that PAN's successes were limited, in the sense that the government showed a willingness to incorporate only minimal demands formulated by PAN. In no instance, as might be expected in a one-party dominant pattern, was the minority party able to *impose* its own views upon the ruling coalition. Furthermove, PAN's limited success could never have been accomplished, if its position had not found a sympathetic audience and a certain degree of support within the ranks of PRI. In other words, PAN *complemented,* rather than *implemented,* certain demands for the rationalization of earlier radical policies that were already breathing their way into some moderate groups within the revolutionary coalition. In those early years, therefore, PAN's principal victories were in the battle of ideologies that had begun *within* the Revolutionary Party.

Since 1952, PAN's capability to influence public policy seems to have decreased sharply. The new generation of Panista leaders has largely opted to keep out of any clear-cut battle of ideologies characteristic of the efforts of their predecessors, because they feel that the continuation of such tactics would permanently "institutionalize" the party's appeal to a restricted number of groups in the Mexican electorate. Thus, the old issues of educational and agrarian reform are given token expression in order to temporarily bridge what appears to be a growing gap between the old guard and today's *político* -conscious Panistas, but they have been largely replaced by such general procedural issues as electoral reform, free elections, and a more autonomous local and municipal regime. It may be asserted, therefore, that PAN's influence in policy-making can no longer be measured in the terms of specific rules incorporated in the 1917 Constitution. The modern Panista family has ceased to question many of the objectives of the post-Maderista tradition. The younger Panistas are, after all, a product of the contemporary Mexican system, and as such they may be less prepared to argue against public education or against state prescriptions for private schools, since they have been more exposed to state-sponsored education than were their predecessors, whose early educational experience seldom transcended the Church-run private school. Thus, the new party leadership has become ardently committed to goals of continued social change, although it still emphasizes rationalized evolution instead of demagogic change. Any assessment of the influence exerted by PAN in the decision-making process during this second period must, therefore, be made in terms of the role which the party now plays in the democratization of the prevailing authoritarian patterns within the political system. As evidenced in the three case studies discussed in chapter 4, PAN's success has been very limited, and depends more than ever on governmental and public support. It is important to keep in mind, however, that PAN's desire to provide a meaningful permanent opposition, in spite of seemingly insurmountable obstacles, has produced the kind of incentive that is required if the democratization of the Mexican political system is to take place.

Chapter 5 suggested that a close correlation exists between PAN's shift away from "ideological heating" and the party's increases in electoral potential since 1952. As long as the party's strategy had been one of adamantly propagating certain clear-cut social issues, as it was under the leadership of the old guard before 1952, it was evident that PAN's efforts in electoral contests would automatically be restricted to winning over the ideologically sympathetic voter. At the same time, the very perseverance on the part of the leadership at that time in their campaign for a limited but important set of reforms, tended to increase PAN's potential to influence certain decision-makers. This case study of PAN, therefore, advances two central hypotheses regarding the relationship of policy influence and electoral potential:

1. Adamancy in ideological expression tends to increase a minority party's potential to influence governmental policy formulation under a basically one-party authoritarian pattern, provided that the ruling party has settled for a more resilient set of belief patterns, which in turn allows for a degree of infiltration by the more adamant outgroups. Before 1952, PAN exploited such a situation. Its own adamant position on certain social issues did not meet with an equally adamant challenge of that position by the ruling coalition, so that, in spite of the government's continued emphasis on the preservation of the political status quo, PAN's ideas were able to infiltrate the decision-making process. Correspondingly, an adamant expression of ideology on the part of a minority party in a one-party authoritarian pattern decreases its potential in the electoral arena, since such an expression consciously sacrifices programs that might engender a broader base of popular appeal to a list of priorities that are visualized and understood by a more limited sampling of the Mexican electorate.
2. In contrast, the emergence of a more resilient set of belief patterns in the ideology of a minority party tends to reduce that party's ability to influence decision-makers, as is attested by PAN's own experience since 1952. At the same time, this resiliency increases a party's prospects for scattered victories in certain types of elections. Chapter 5 concluded that these prospects are best in municipal and urban areas.

Chapter 5 showed that PAN's limited electoral potential from 1939 to 1952 might be attributed as much to PAN's own political strategy as to factors inherent in the Mexican political system. In an absolute monopoly exercised by a single party, the ruling elite controls the entire electoral process from the polling place to the deciding Federal Electoral College, a political patronage system distributes rewards among those individuals or groups directly identified with the policies of the dominant party, and a politically-conscious electorate that is prepared to choose from alternative policies is absent. But it was PAN's strategy to push for constitutional revision by resorting to pressure tactics other than electoral opposition that resulted in PAN's poor showing in earlier elections. PAN was well aware that its own internal organization was too much in its infancy to hope to compete against the machine of the ruling party. Contrary to claims made by some Panistas, the party membership during this early stage was not representative of most sectors of Mexican society. Neither did the party wish to give semblance of a mass organization, since, as noted earlier, it denied the very notion of "mass politics." Furthermore, the party's earlier ideological orientation was not compatible with a national policy of moderation and adjustment that is characteristic of party systems in modern democracies. Rather, its demands were directed toward "a fundamental restructuring of the general pattern of policy and the general institutional framework."[8] Cognizant of PAN's limited ability to achieve this end through elections, party leaders consistently urged voter abstention from the electoral process. They felt that PAN's list of priorities could best be attained by infiltrating the rank and file of the ruling party or, to put it differently, to set one group in the ruling party against the other. In sum, PAN did at no time during this first phase place major emphasis on immediate electoral success, because it knew that such success was impossible. Its electoral goal was avowedly long-range: that of creating a politically-conscious and responsible citizenry. Therefore, an electoral contest in the years preceding 1952 was hardly a contest at all. Confrontation was exclusively in terms of the out-group versus the in-group, or, to borrow another classification, it was a contest between a party of principles and the party of patronage. The static nature of this arrangement allowed no significant prospects for modification through the electoral process. Instead, the two parties gravitated toward the danger points of such a division: corruption of the "ins" by power and irresponsible dogmatism of the "outs."

In contrast, PAN's present leadership, which began to take control in the mid-1950s, has stressed a radical departure from tactics that characterized the party during the first phase. Satisfied that the initial set of priorities in constitutional revision had been partially met, contemporary Panistas have gradually phased out the politics of infiltration; they have prescribed programs and platforms of wider national appeal; and, encouraged by trends that suggest greater electoral potential, they have decided to give the PRI a run for it at election time. The younger Panista no longer philosophizes, as did his tutors. He is an activist. The younger Panista talks no more of depersonalized politics. Instead, he searches for candidates with personalities more appealing than those of their PRI counterparts. The classroom politician has been replaced by the populist politician. In making this shift, PAN has had to pay a price. PAN has been criticized severely by some of the more reactionary sectors of the population from which it previously received some support and has also lost considerable monetary contributions.[10] More important, however, has been the loss in potential to directly influence national policies, a loss which the old guard decries but which new leaders have tended to settle for in exchange for brighter horizons that might lie ahead in the electoral sphere.

What, then, are PAN's prospects for the future? After the 1970 and 1973 elections, Mexicans are once more referring to the indispensable opposition. Of all the minority parties, PAN has made the greatest inroads in vote-getting potential and is the only party that has left an indelible mark on Mexico's attempt to experiment with competitive democracy. One has to admit, though, that this vote-getting potential has yet to develop into truly national proportions. PAN was and has remained a party of limited regional appeal. (See Appendix III.) Even in the 1973 elections, when PAN received a record 2,211,852 votes, almost half of those ballots (917,875) came from the Federal District alone (see Appendix II.) The urban appeal enjoyed by PAN has led the PRI leadership to refer sarcastically to its opposition as "a party of the sidewalks, whose popularity ends where the unpaved roads begin."[11] Panistas naturally are not perturbed by these charges: "Let the PRI pave some more roads," is their obvious retort. The PAN leadership, however, must not completely disregard such accusations, for it could be true that the party's future would be seriously compromised if PAN abandons its efforts to secure a more representative sample of the Mexican electorate in favor of electoral escapades limited to the Federal District. For example, I was particularly disturbed at PAN's decision in 1973 not to participate in the Baja California contest, a state which, at least up to 1970, had been a bastion of recent Panista support. The rationalization I was given was that internal party divisions had dictated such a move, and that, in any event, the rise in abstentionism should "teach PRI a lesson" that the government no longer enjoys the support of a substantial number of Mexicans.[12] Maybe this is so, but Panistas should wonder why some of this substantial number have not defected to PAN. It is evident that not all alienated voters believe that PAN provides the answers.

The 10 million-plus "Pedros" who remained home because they did not agree with PRI do not agree with PAN either. To them, neither PRI nor PAN are "lovers." They are both "potbellied" aristocrats. Therefore, increased alienation in the contemporary Mexican ideological setting has failed to generate a truly coordinated effort that will result in meaningful alternatives to pressing national problems. On certain occasions, diverse alienated groups may have been on the verge of producing a consolidated front against PRI, but, at election time, communication channels among these groups seem to disappear, and the political dialogue reverts to empty slogans and old clichés. For its part, PAN may have contributed to the internal democratization of PRI or to the introduction of a sense of purpose in the electorate. But its future threatens to become sterile unless the party sorts out its electoral priorities, very much in the same way that the old guard established ideological priorities when it confronted PRI. It is praiseworthy, to be sure, that PAN continues to present candidates for nearly all offices, and it is also praiseworthy that PAN's own presidential candidate can now poll 2 million votes.

Ultimately, however, the transformation of the Mexican political system depends on the system's ability to adhere in practice to a Constitution that calls for a federal arrangement. The power monopoly presently exercised by PRI in Mexico is the end-product of the hierarchical party structure which negates independence at the local level, and which requires the subservience of public officials at all levels to the dictates of the revolutionary elite in Mexico City. The need for PAN to establish electoral priorities becomes clearer when viewed in the context of the three phases in the party's electoral participation discussed in Chapter 5. That PAN received 9, or 14, or 16 percent of the national vote is not a significant factor. In any case, PAN's presidential candidates cannot hope, in the foreseeable future, to bring their party to national office. The servility of the Mexican Congress, despite token concessions now made to minority parties, should convince party leaders that they must turn elsewhere. Perhaps the adage that age brings wisdom may have some elements of truth. Gómez Morín once indicated to me that he disapproved of the perennial waste of party funds to finance "impossible" campaigns. Recent developments indicate that the least impossible campaigns are those that correspond to the so-called Municipal Phase. If PAN has increased its national vote totals, it is because of the party's efforts in local and state contests. These campaigns have made the average Mexican voter more aware of the existence of PAN. As the party founders consistently suggested in the past, the secret of an opposition party's success in Mexico eventually rests in reconquering the town plaza. PAN's more productive challenge of local *caciquismo,* graft, and corruption in recent years indicates that the plaza will not be reconquered by unsuccessful presidential or congressional candidates. It will first have to be won by bright, honest, popularly identifiable state and local candidates. Today the free, competitive *municipio* offers Mexico the most immediate prospects for an effective multiparty system. If parties are unable to legitimately compete for state and municipal offices, competitive presidential politics, and a multiparty legislature will remain, as in the past, myths that will serve to consolidate PRI's democratic image abroad and encourage the proliferation of research projects on Mexico's fancied one-party democracy. Whether genuine multipartyism will include PAN as a major participant remains to be seen. It is hoped, however, that despite so many frustrations, Panistas will remain true to the commitment expressed by its founders: "*Seguimos continuando. . . .*"—we shall continue.

Notes

Introduction

1. See, for example, L. Vincent Padgett, *The Mexican Political System,* (Boston: Houghton Mifflin, 1966); Frank R. Brandenburg, "Mexico: An Experiment in One Party Democracy," (Ph.D diss., University of Pennsylvania, 1955); Howard F. Cline, Mexico, *Revolution to Evolution, 1940–1960* (London: Oxford University Press, 1962); and Robert E. Scott, *Mexican Government in Transition* (Urbana: University of Illinois Press, 1959).
2. Joseph La Palombara and Myron Weiner, eds., *Political Parties and Political Development* (Princeton: Princeton University Press, 1969), pp. 177–200.
3. Giovanni Sartori, "Politics, Ideology, and Belief Systems," *American Political Science Review* 63, no. 2 (June 1969): 398–411.
4. *Ibid.* See also: Daniel Bell, *The End of Ideology* (New York: Collier Books, 1962); Milton Rokeach, *The Open and Closed Mind* (New York: Basic Books, 1960); and Hannah Arendt, "Ideology and Terror: A Novel Form of Government," *The Review of Politics* (July 1953).
5. James W. Wilkie and Edna Monzón de Wilkie, *México visto en el siglo XX: Entrevistas de historia oral* (México: Instituto Mexicano de Investigaciones Económicas, 1969).
6. Andrew J. Milnor, ed., *Comparative Political Parties* (New York: Thomas Y. Crowell Co., 1969), pp. 104–105.
7. *Excélsior* (Mexico City), July 11, 1970.
8. The Popular Socialist Party (PPS) and the Authentic Party of the Mexican Revolution (PARM) received 6.8 percent and 2.6 percent of the vote, respectively. *La Nación* (Mexico City), July 30, 1973, p. 13.
9. *Excélsior* (Mexico City), July 12, 1970. See also: *La Nación* (Mexico City), July 30, 1973. At the time of this writing, the official results of the 1973 elections had not been posted; however, the figures cited here are expected to be an accurate reflection of the final outcome.
10. William Robert Lux, "PAN: The Conservative Political Party of Mexico" (Ph.D. diss., University of Southern California, 1967).
11. Interview with Adolfo Christlieb Ibarrola, Mexico City, August 13, 1969.
12. Frank Brandenburg, *The Making of Modern Mexico* (Englewood Cliffs, N.J.: Prentice-Hall, Inc., 1964), p. 127.

13. Efraín González Luna, *Humanismo político* (México: Editorial Jus, 1955).

Chapter One

1. "Democracia en pantuflas: el partido que necesitamos," *Excélsior* (Mexico City), July 15, 1970.
2. Once a journalist was attending one of PAN's national conventions, and, as he read the PAN slogan "por una patria ordenada" (for an orderly fatherland) spread out over the speaker's platform, he approached one of the party leaders: "My friend," he observed, "I fail to see the distinction between your slogan and that of the opposition. You say 'por una patria ordenada' while PRI echoes 'por una patria ordeñada' (for a milked fatherland)."
3. Sartori, "Politics, Ideology and Belief Systems," p. 399.
4. Ibid., p. 400.
5. Ibid., p. 401. See also Rokeach, *The Open and Closed Mind,* p. 44.
6. Ibid.
7. Ibid.
8. Ibid., pp. 402–403.
9. Ibid.
10. Ibid., pp. 404–405.
11. Ibid.
12. "Frentes Políticos," *Excélsior* (Mexico City), July 12, 1970.
13. La Palombara and Weiner, *Political Parties,* pp. 27–28. (Emphasis added.)
14. Ibid.
15. *Continuismo* refers to the perpetuation in power of one group or party. *Imposición* is the authoritarian method of imposing elite policies on all levels of government.
16. *Excélsior* (Mexico City), August 6, 1969.
17. Ibid., August 18, 1969.
18. See especially Frank Brandenburg, "Mexico: An Experiment in One Party Democracy," (Ph.D. diss., University of Pennsylvania, 1955); and L. Vincent Padgett, "Popular Participation in the Mexican 'One-Party' System," (Ph.D. diss., Northwestern University, 1955). I make special reference to these, because in their dissertations both authors were considerably more complimentary in their respective evaluations of Mexican "democracy" than in their subsequent published works.
19. Sartori, "Politics, Ideology and Belief Systems," pp. 405–406.
20. *The News* (Mexico City), August 4, 1969.
21. Ibid.
22. *Excélsior* (Mexico City), August 7, 1969.
23. Scott, *Mexican Government in Transition,* pp. 194–95. "Even in a presidential year, if conditions are right, in certain types of districts the opposition may pile up a larger aggregate vote than the official party, leaving it to win by a simple plurality." See also Appendix II.

Chapter Two

1. Padgett, *The Mexican Political System*, pp. 9–10.
2. Ibid.
3. See especially Gastón García Cantú, *El pensamiento de la reacción mexicana: historia documental 1810–1962* (México: Empresas Editoriales, S.A., 1965). The author sees the origins of Mexican conservatism in the two edicts issued against Hidalgo (dated September 24 and 30, 1810), and proclaimed by Manuel Abad y Queipo, Bishop of Michoacán (pp. 33–36).
4. Ibid., p. 27.
5. In a fine essay, Ivan Vallier notes that the term "Church elites" for Latin America cannot be limited to the higher clergy, but must also include laymen and members of the lower clergy who "possess a capacity for exercising influence or power." In Seymour M. Lipset and Aldo Solari, eds., *Elites in Latin America* (New York: Oxford University Press, 1967), pp. 190–232.
6. Ivan Vallier, *Catholicism, Social Control, and Modernization in Latin America* (Englewood Cliffs, N.J.: Prentice-Hall, 1970), p. 7.
7. *La Nación* (Mexico City), October 31, 1954, p. 16.
8. Daniel Cosío Villegas, *American Extremes* (Austin: University of Texas Press, 1964), pp. 3–4. Incidentally, the survey conducted by Almond and Verba in *Civic Culture* supports Cosío Villegas' views when it notes that even today a substantial number of Mexicans are unable to identify the objectives of their revolution. Of the respondents, a sizable 35 percent could not name any of the goals, and the 65 percent that could do so tended to give priority to the Maderista principles of democracy, political liberty, and equality.
9. Antonio Roa Hernández, "La doctrina de los partidos políticos y el Partido Revolucionario Institucional" (Thesis, Facultad de Derecho, Universidad Nacional Autónoma de México, 1961), p. 79.
10. Cosío Villegas, *American Extremes*, p. 5.
11. Charges have been made, for example, that many Catholics later betrayed the Madero revolution by siding with the conspirator, Victoriano Huerta. It should be noted, however, that the leadership of the then officially recognized conservative National Catholic Party refused to have any dealings with Huerta when the latter offered 100 seats in Congress in exchange for the party's support. Indeed, during the November 1913 elections, the PCN backed the Federico Gamboa-Eugenio Rascón ticket against Huerta. See Luis Calderón Vega in *La Nación* (Mexico City), February 27, 1950, p. 15.
12. Ibid., p. 14.
13. Ibid.
14. This party was a direct outgrowth of the National Catholic Circle, founded on August 18, 1909, by Gabriel Fernández Somellera.
15. The PCN went on to declare: "Mr. Madero, who has understood that the Catholic Party is willing to work within the framework of existing political institutions, has agreed to permit our Party to compete democratically with all other parties; but neither has he entered into any deals with us, nor

would we accept them. Such conduct would only reveal that Mr. Madero had the intention of governing with the same dictatorial tactics employed by General Díaz, and, further, that he did not actually intend to guarantee independent suffrage to all Mexicans." Francisco Barrera Lavalle, *En defensa del Partido Católico Nacional* (México: Juan Aguilar Vera, 1912), pp. 42, 84.

16. Francisco I. Madero, *La sucesión presidencial en 1910.* "The best-governed countries, wherein liberty and progress are most evident, are those which have strong political parties that effectively oppose governmental policy when it runs contrary to their ideals."

17. Barrera Lavalle, *En defensa,* p. 56. (Emphasis added.)

18. Ibid., p. 81. The Laws of the Reform (La Reforma), known also by the name of Ley Juárez and Ley Lerdo, incorporated those anticlerical provisions enacted by President Benito Juárez in an effort to combat the temporal powers of the Catholic Church, and were later added to the Liberal Constitution of 1857.

19. Ibid. (Emphasis added.)

20. Ibid., pp. 87–88.

21. Vicente Fernández Bravo, *Política y administración* (México: Costa-Amic, 1965), p. 71.

22. It is interesting, and perhaps not entirely accidental, that *La Nación* is also the name given to PAN's own publication years later. Gómez Morín assured me, however, that this was a mere coincidence. The PCN-oriented press at that time also included: *El Tiempo* and *El País* (Mexico City), *El Amigo de la Verdad* (Puebla), *El Regional* (Guadalajara), and *El Correo* (Chihuahua).

23. The intransigent position was represented in the daily *La Voz de México* (Mexico City).

24. "The Catholic Party's *raison d'être* is evident: the Church is a state agency that has duties to fulfill and rights to demand; through its various associations it is intimately tied to matters of public education and welfare. But since the State is called upon to grant freedoms of association, assembly, and education, it is necessary to form a political party that will in turn protect the sacred rights of Christians in the various municipalities, local legislatures, and in the National Congress." Barrera Lavalle, *En defensa,* p. vi.

25. Brandenburg, "Mexico: An Experiment," p. 20.

26. *La Nación* (Mexico City), February 27, 1950, p. 14.

27. Brandenburg, "Mexico: An Experiment," p. 20.

28. *La Nación* (Mexico City), February 27, 1950.

29. Ibid.

30. This organization fell into disrepute when it allowed itself to become a party to Huerta's suppression of Emiliano Zapata, rather than rally to the defense of Veracruz. *La Nación* (Mexico City), February 27, 1950, pp. 14–15.

31. Juan Gutiérrez Lascuráin, national president of PAN from 1950 to 1956, had been a member of ACJM since 1935; Alfonso Ituarte Servín, party president (1956–9), since 1936; his successor and PAN's 1964 presidential

candidate, José González Torres, was elected national president of the ACJM in 1944. This list is not exhaustive but should be indicative.

32. These included pastoral letters dated November 17 to 20, 1917, from the Prelates of Panama, Santo Domingo, La Plata, Paraná, Santa Fe (Argentina), Loja, Santiago de Cuba, San Salvador, and Guatemala; the Pastoral of the French Bishopry (March 19, 1919); the collective pastoral letter from the Bishops of the United States (December 12, 1926); and statements issued by Popes Benedict XV and Pius XI. *La Nación* (Mexico City), March 13, 1950, pp. 12–13.

33. Luis Calderón Vega, *El 96.47 porciento de los mexicanos: ensayo de sociología religiosa* (Morelia, Michoacán: 1964), pp. 89–90.

34. The interview referred to appeared in *El Universal* (Mexico City), on February 4, 1926. Reporter Ignacio Monroy quoted the Archbishop as follows: "Church doctrine is unchangeable because it derives from divine revelation. We are firm in our protest which we, the Mexican prelates, raise against the 1917 Constitution, particularly against those articles which oppose religious beliefs and liberties. The story published by *El Universal* on January 27, stating that we were prepared to wage a campaign against unjust laws that run contrary to natural law, is perfectly true. The Bishopry, clergy, and Catholics do not recognize these laws, and we shall combat articles 3, 5, 27, and 130 of the present Constitution." The official response to these declarations came from Secretary of *Gobernación,* Alberto Tejada: "The State allows the Catholic Church full exercise of its functions up to the point that these do not pose an obstacle for progress and the development of our people; but it cannot and must not tolerate those elements who propose to 'combat and ignore' constitutional laws, as the Archbishop asserts." *Excélsior* (Mexico City), February 5, 1926.

35. Antonio Ríus Facius, *Méjico cristero* (México: Editorial Patria, S.A., 1960), p. 11. See also Carlos Pereyra, *México falsificado* (México: Editorial Polis, 1948).

36. "We protest in the name of the most elementary justice and good sense, which affirm that a law contrary to natural law is no law at all. Any law which provokes the indignation of an entire nation must be reconsidered. It is absolutely impossible that an antireligious law should emanate from the will of a people that is fundamentally religious. As Mexicans we demand constitutional reform and we vow before the entire nation that *we shall employ all legal means to secure these reforms.*" Ríus Facius, *Méjico cristero,* p. 29. (Emphasis added.)

37. New ACJM groups were formed in Cuáutla, Morelos; Tamazunchale, San Luis Potosí; Arroyo, Nuevo León; and throughout the State of Oaxaca.

38. For example, in Colima the state legislature fixed the maximum number of priests at 26 for a total population of over 60,000; in Nayarit, 40 priests for a population of 167,000; Tamaulipas, with a population of 350,000, was assigned 13 priests; and Aguascalientes, 1 priest for every 50,000 inhabitants. Ríus Facius, *Méjico cristero,* pp. 30–43.

39. The respective official designations for these laws were: *Reglamento para la inspección y vigilancia de las escuelas primarias particulares del*

Distrito y Territorios Federales; and *Ley que reforma el Código Penal para el Distrito y Territorios Federales sobre delitos del fuero común y para toda la República sobre delitos contra la Federación.*

40. Carlos Velasco Gil, *Sinarquismo* (México: Edición del Autor, 1944), p. 321.

41. For the complete text of this important message, see Estados Unidos Mexicanos. Congreso. XLVI Legislatura de la Cámara de Diputados. *Los Presidentes de México ante la Nación: informes, manifiestos, y documentos de 1821 a 1966.* President Calles admitted that, due to "violations of Article 27," 42 churches had been shut down, nuns had been evicted from all charity institutions, and 73 convents had been compelled to close down. The government had, furthermore, deported 185 foreign-born priests from Mexico, including the Apostolic Delegate, Monsignor Jorge José Caruana, a United States citizen.

42. For the complete statement of the League, see "Memorial presentado a la Cámara de Diputados por el episcopado," in García Cantú, *El pensamiento de la reacción,* pp. 922–28. Congressional debate on this petition is found in *Diario de los Debates,* September 23, 1926.

43. In an article headlined "The Real Cause for the Actual Disturbances in Mexico," *L'Osservatore Romano* (August 11, 1926) actually approved of the armed revolt on the basis that *Ley Calles* prevented Mexican Catholics the use of legitimate avenues of protest. Similarly, in terms openly sympathetic to the Cristero revolt, the Papal Encyclical, *Inquis Afflictisque,* (November 18, 1926) dealt with the situation in Mexico.

44. Two fine day-by-day accounts of the revolt can be found in Ríus Facius, *Méjico cristero,* and in García Cantú, *El pensamiento de la reacción.* Consult also Alicia Olivero Sedano, *Aspectos del conflicto religioso de 1926 a 1929: sus antecedentes y consecuencias* (México: INAH, 1966).

45. García Cantú, *El pensamiento de la reacción.* "In the truest sense of the word, González Flores was the real protagonist of the reactionary movement." p. 909.

46. Carlos Pereyra, *México falsificado,* pp. 341–42.

47. See Anacleto González Flores, *El plebiscito de los mártires* (México: Comité Central de la Asociación Católica de la Juventud Mexicana, 1961).

48. "Our nation is a vast prison ever since the 1917 Constitution was promulgated." (*En la carcel.*) "Revolutions are fearful because they all must ultimately face the judgment of history, and because all the war machines, while they might destroy the living, cannot destroy the bones of the dead." (*El miedo de la revolución.*) For excerpts of these and other works by González Flores, see García Cantú, *El pensamiento de la reacción,* pp. 910–28.

49. Carlos Pereyra, *México falsificado,* p. 383.

50. As L. Vincent Padgett suggests, there are numerous interpretations as to the reasons for Calles' decision to establish a revolutionary party. It seems, however, safe to assert, as he does, that the party "was organized to unite the divergent revolutionary groups and reconcile personality differences among leaders. It centered groups of the revolutionary tradition with a symbol of common interest." *The Mexican Political System,* pp. 47–49.

51. Ríus Facius, *Méjico cristero,* pp. 315–16.

52. Ibid., p. 373. Calles is said to have personally questioned León Toral in prison. The latter vowed that he had acted on his own. Asked why he had done it, León Toral responded: "So that Christ might reign in Mexico." Calles: "What kind of kingdom is that?" Leon: "It is a kingdom over souls, absolute." (Biblical parallelism here is almost carried to extremes.)

53. The organizational development of the Revolutionary Party, over its various stages, has been subject of detailed analysis elsewhere. See especially Antonio Delhumeau, *México, realidad política de sus partidos* (México: Instituto Mexicano de Estudios Políticos, A.C., 1970).

54. *La Nación* (Mexico City), April 3, 1950, p. 13.

55. Wilkie and de Wilkie, *México visto en el siglo XX.*

56. José Vasconcelos, for one, had publicly justified the Cristero rebellion by characterizing it as a movement inspired by civic conscience. Pereyra, *México falsificado,* p. 344.

57. Luis Calderón Vega summarizes the Vasconcelista opposition to Calles: "From Madero to Calles, internal politics rotated around military men. But Calles imposed a General Plan of his own creation: a real 'tabulation' of duties and compensations. He introduced democratic verbalism in order to settle the squabbles of second-rate militarists who knew nothing about political parties. He established the PNR, and thereby obtained not only everyone's submission to the federal government's crushing machine, but also the compulsory obedience of bureaucracy to the state party." *La Nación,* April 3, 1950, p. 12.

58. Alfonso Taracena, *La revolución desvirtuada* (México: Costa-Amic, 1966), pp. 111 and 243.

59. Padgett identifies Vasconcelismo as a "transient" political movement which, like others of its kind, is characterized by a "pattern of personalism," its objective being "the division of the Revolutionary Coalition," with "no intention of becoming a permanent, loyal opposition." *The Mexican Political System,* p. 63.

60. Ibid., p. 49.

61. The 1917 text of Article 3 read: "Instruction will be free, but in the official establishment as well as private establishments where primary, elementary and advanced education is administered, instruction shall be secular. No religious corporation or minister of any sect shall enjoy the right to establish or direct primary schools. Private elementary schools will only be allowed to operate, subject to official supervision. In all public schools education will be imparted gratuitously. *Constitución Política de los Estados Unidos Mexicanos.*

62. The controversial aspects of the Six-Year Plan are discussed in Salvador Novo, *La vida en México en el período presidencial de Lázaro Cárdenas* (México: Empresas Editoriales, 1964). Novo comments: "The Six-Year Plan which was approved by the PNR sounds like the Five-Year Plan which was approved by the Communist Party of the Soviet Union, but it also bears resemblance to the Four-Year Plan adopted by Hitler and his Nazi Party," (p. 64). For an excellent account of this period, see also Sebastián Mayo, *La*

educación socialista en México (Rosario, Argentina: Editorial BEAR, 1964), pp. 170–183.

63. Mayo, *La educación socialista en México,* pp. 226–27.

64. *Diario Oficial,* December 13, 1934.

65. Novo, *La vida en México,* p. 73.

66. The "Grito de Guadalajara" was a major speech in the "revolutionary tradition" pronounced by Calles on July 20, 1934. (In Mexico, most of the pronouncements made by leading figures in the movements of independence and revolution are often labelled either "gritos" or "planes").

67. Others in this select fraternity included Narciso Bassols, Daniel Cosío Villegas, Alfonso Caso, Miguel Palacios Macedo and Octavio Medellín Ostos.

68. During his lifetime, Antonio Caso was probably the scholar with greatest authority in Mexico. Not only was he the most distinguished professor of philosophy in his day, but he enjoyed an unparalleled moral authority over members of the revolutionary family, many of whom had been his students.

69. Mayo, *La educación socialista,* pp. 82–96.

70. The first convention of this group was held in Cárdenas' home state, Michoacán, from July 16 to 21, 1933. Ibid., pp. 56–58.

71. Manuel Gómez Morín was born in Batolipas, Chihuahua, in 1897. During his early childhood, his family moved to Mexico City. His brilliant studies in law at the National University won for him the admiration of his classmates of the famous 1915 student generation. He became professor of public law at the university at the age of 21, and in 1924 he was appointed Director of the Law School. His role as a leading economic consultant to President Calles and as the chief engineer of the Banco de México, as well as his earlier liberal leanings, have brought charges that he was a Callista and a Marxist. (Robert Scott and Frank Brandenburg have made these charges, respectively.) In my conversations with him before his death, Gómez Morín dismissed these accusations with his characteristic smile, and he pointed out that his services had been of a purely technical nature, for which he had received no financial compensation. He also indicated that, at the height of the religious conflict, he had been living in Europe (1926–28), returning only in time to actively contribute to the Vasconcelos presidential campaign. It should be noted, however, that Mexicans fitting the Scott-Brandenburg theses did include such prominent personalities as Herminio Ahumada, son-in-law of Vasconcelos, and Alfonso Caso. Gómez Morín died in Mexico City in the spring of 1972.

72. Novo, *La vida en México,* p. 426.

73. Ibid., p. 427. Novo notes that even the Rector's car was raffled in an effort to obtain additional funds for the University. The winner would in turn donate the car back to the University, and the car would be raffled again.

74. This messianic attitude was evident in the numerous meetings of the Confederación Nacional de Estudiantes. Of particular importance were the 11th and 12th congresses, held in San Luis Potosí and Monterrey, on April 23, 1934 and in July 1935, respectively, during which the students, repre-

senting every imaginable ideological orientation, displayed their sense of unity against threats to university autonomy and academic freedom. *La Nación* (Mexico City), October 10, 1942, p. 24.

75. Ibid. For example, when Narciso Bassols attempted to introduce sex education in elementary schools, the result was a vast protest demonstration staged by mothers at the Plaza de Santo Domingo on April 23, 1934. When the mothers were beaten by the police, students of the School of Medicine promptly came to their aid. The President himself had to give a public apology for the incident.

76. In the communal *ejido* both the land parcel and the produce are jointly owned. The earlier semicommunal version at times permitted the farmer to sell whatever he produced. García Cantú, *El pensamiento de la reacción,* pp. 19–20. For authoritative data on land reform, see also James W. Wilkie, *Mexican Revolution: Federal Expenditure and Social Change since 1910* (Berkeley: University of California Press, 1970).

77. Carlos M. Velasco Gil, *Sinarquismo* (México: edición del autor, 1944), p. 65.

78. Ibid., pp. 66–67. Examples of unsuccessful opposition include the Centro Anti-Comunista, founded in Guanajuato by Hellmut Oskar Schreiter in June 1936. This center failed to gain popular support because of its name. To the masses, communism equalled *cardenismo,* and Cárdenas at that time was a mythical hero in the minds of many.

79. The word *sinarquista* is a composite of *sin* and *anarquía* (without anarchy, or, in positive terms, with order). The founders of *Sinarquismo* were José Antonio Urquiza, José Trueba Olivares, Manuel Zermeño, Juan Ignacio Padilla, and the brothers Mendoza Heredía.

80. Ben G. Burnett and Kenneth F. Johnson, *Political Forces in Latin America: Dimensions of the Quest for Stability* (Belmont, Ca.: Wadsworth Publishing Co., 1968), pp. 41–42.

81. Velasco Gil, *Sinarquismo,* pp. 69–70. The Bajío includes the central states of México, Guanajuato, Querétaro, San Luis Potosí, and Michoacán.

82. "*Sinarquismo* was born out of the forgotten lands of the Bajío. It nurtured itself from the ambitions and aspirations of our peasants, of our humble workers, of our patriots. My friend, in this movement you will not find the deceitful lawyer, the professional politician, the pedantic egg-head, nor the ideologue. You will find the warmth of the people, the spirit of a people's heart. Farmers of Mexico: come to us, join the movement of the people of the land, of those who love the soil, defend it, and, in so doing, defend the fatherland!" *El Sinarquista* (Mexico City), October 26, 1939, p. 4.

83. Velasco Gil, *Sinarquismo,* p. 108.

84. Ibid., pp. 89–93.

85. Alfonso Méndez Barraza, "Los partidos políticos en México" (Thesis, Facultad de Derecho, Universidad Nacional Autónoma de México, 1949), p. 67.

86. Velasco Gil, *Sinarquismo,* p. 360.

CHAPTER THREE

1. To qualify for registration, all political parties had to meet the prerequisites established by the most recent electoral law, since party registration was subject to yearly renewal. In 1940 it was the law of 1918, decreed by President Carranza, which was in effect, and its terms were quite liberal. It stipulated that for registration, a party needed only a minimum of 100 members, and that it had to publish a paper at least two months before the election. Unlike subsequent laws, it did not prescribe compulsory organizational standards. See Méndez Barraza, "Los partidos políticos en México," pp. 13–15.

2. Lux, "PAN: The Conservative Political Party of Mexico," p. 81.

3. Luis Calderón Vega, *Memorias del PAN,* vol. 1 (Morelia, Mich.: edición del autor, 1967), pp. 28–29.

4. Ibid.

5. Manuel Gómez Morín, *Diez Años de México* (México: Editorial Jus, 1950), p. 15.

6. Ibid.

7. "If ever there is need to label PAN's doctrine, it will have to be that of Political Humanism." Efraín González Luna, *Humanismo político* (México: Editorial Jus, 1955).

8. Brandenburg, *The Making of Modern Mexico,* p. 129.

9. Ibid., p. 127.

10. "Díaz did not dare at the end of his first four-year term as president to seek reelection. After all, 'no reelection' had been his own slogan!" José Vasconcelos, *Breve historia de México* (México: Cía. Editorial Continental, S.A., 1963), p. 410.

11. Madero, *La sucesión presidencial.*

12. Gómez Morín, *Diez Años de México,* pp. 4–6.

13. Ibid., p. x.

14. Born in Mexico City in 1876, Juan Sánchez Azcona studied philosophy in Germany and France, where he became a close friend of Madero. He was with Madero when the latter began his revolt against Díaz, and served in those moments as Madero's private secretary. Sánchez Azcona was also president of the Partido Constitucional Progresista which nominated Madero and Pino Suarez as its presidential and vice-presidential candidates. He later led the opposition to Obregón's bid for reelection. He died on May 18, 1938.

15. Juan Sánchez Azcona, *La etapa maderista de la revolución* (México: Talleres Gráficos de la Nación, 1960), p. 84.

16. *Manifiesto de Madero y Francisco Vázquez Gómez,* April 29, 1910.

17. "We Maderistas are democrats. Since 1910 we have declared, as we also do now, that the Mexican people are in principle ready to practice democracy." Sánchez Azcona, *La etapa maderista,* p. 85.

18. "We don't lack a people. What we lack, gentlemen, is a citizenry." Efraín González Luna, *Humanismo político,* p. 44.

19. *La Nación* (Mexico City), August 22, 1954, p. 7.

20. Ibid., June 16, 1957, p. 3.

21. Sánchez Azcona, *La etapa maderista,* pp. 85–86.
22. "La democracia y el pueblo," in *La Nación* (Mexico City), April 8, 1956, p. 2.
23. Sánchez Azcona, *La etapa maderista,* pp. 86–87.
24. For an excellent contemporary analysis of sector politics and the PRI, see Francisco González Pineda and Antonio Delhumeau, *Los mexicanos frente al poder* (México: Instituto Mexicano de Estudios Políticos, 1973).
25. González Luna, *Humanismo político,* p. 172.
26. Ibid., p. 185.
27. "Memorandum Addressed to the Mexican Supreme Court," in: Adolfo Christlieb Ibarrola, *Baja California: avanzada de la democracia* (México: Ediciones del PAN, 1968).
28. Ibid.
29. Sánchez Azcona, *La etapa maderista,* p. 87.
30. González Luna, *Humanismo político,* p. 98.
31. Ibid., p. 145.
32. Ibid., p. 247.
33. *Manifiesto de Francisco Madero y Francisco Vázquez Gómez.*
34. Sánchez Azcona, *La etapa maderista,* pp. 87–88. (Emphasis added.)
35. *La Nación* (Mexico City), December 30, 1944, p. 7.
36. Ibid., April 3, 1950, p. 13.
37. Ibid., December 18, 1960, p. 17.
38. Sánchez Azcona, *La etapa maderista,* p. 88.
39. *La Nación* (Mexico City), November 18, 1951, p. 21.
40. Ibid.
41. Sánchez Azcona, *La etapa maderista,* p. 90.
42. Ibid. Consult also Madero's "Plan de San Luis Potosí[1]."
43. Ibid., p. 91.
44. Ibid.
45. González Luna, *Humanismo político,* pp. 184–85
46. Ibid.
47. Wilkie and de Wilkie, *México visto en el siglo XX,* p. 148.
48. Eyler Newton Simpson, *The Ejido, Mexico's Way Out* (Chapel Hill: University of North Carolina Press, 1937).
49. Wilkie and de Wilkie, *México visto en el siglo XX,* p. 149.
50. Ibid.
51. Ibid.
52. See, for example, Jesús Silva Herzog, *Trayectoria ideológica de la revolución mexicana* (México: Cuadernos Americanos, 1963).
53. Interview with Manuel Gómez Morín, Mexico City, August 14, 1969.
54. Sánchez Azcona, *La etapa maderista,* p. 89.

Chapter Four

1. Lucio Mendieta y Núñez, *Teoría de los agrupamientos sociales* (México: Edición del Autor, 1950), p. 179.

2. Sigmund Neumann, "Toward a Comparative Study of Political Parties," in: Andrew J. Milnor, ed., *Comparative Political Parties* (New York: Thomas Y. Crowell, 1969), p. 25.

3. Manuel García Pelayo, *Derecho constitucional comparado* (Madrid, 1957), p. 191. (Emphasis added.)

4. Ivan Vallier, *Catholicism,* pp. 11–12.

5. Ibid.

6. Interview with Adolfo Christlieb Ibarrola, Mexico City, August 13, 1969.

7. *La Nación* (Mexico City,) February 17, 1957, p. 12.

8. *Ley reglamentaria del Artículo 3o. de 1939.*

9. *PAN, Principios de Doctrina,* paragraph 6 (see Appendix I).

10. Calderón Vega, *Memorias del PAN,* pp. 69–70.

11. Mayo, *La educación socialista en México,* p. 36.

12. Lyle C. Brown, "Mexican Church-State Relations, 1933–1940," *Journal of Church and State* (Spring, 1964), pp. 202–22.

13. For example, at the 1945 Inter-American Conference at Chapultepec, the official Mexican delegation declared: "Totalitarian regimes have demonstrated better than any others the efficacy of education as a political instrument to serve the ends of the state. Employing well-calculated methods, education has served to destroy gradually the personality of individuals until finally converting them into passive and servile masses, obedient only to the orders of the leaders." "Look who is talking!" was, of course, PAN's reaction. See Calderón Vega, *Memorias del PAN,* p. 134.

14. Ibid., pp. 70–71.

15. *La Nación* (Mexico City), December 22, 1945, p. 5.

16. Ibid., December 29, 1945, p. 3.

17. *Diario Oficial,* December 30, 1946.

18. Ibid. (Emphasis added.)

19. Alberto Bremauntz, *La batalla ideológica en México* (México: Ediciones Jurídico-Sociales, 1962), pp. 9, 86, 257–58.

20. This observation is supported by personal experience. This writer attended primary private schools in Mexico City from 1948 to 1955. Instructors commonly distributed pocket-sized catechisms to all the students at the beginning of every school term, but warned us that if any "unfamiliar" individual should enter the classroom (that is, a government inspector), we should promptly conceal the catechism in our desks. Such "raids" never did occur, of course, but government officials were well aware of these clandestine practices, since many of the students were themselves children of prominent *políticos.*

21. Brandenburg, *The Making of Modern Mexico,* p. 289.

22. Ibid., pp. 292–93.

23. For characteristic coverage by the Mexico City press, see *El Nacional* (September 15, 1933); *Excélsior* (September 15, 1933); and *El Universal* (September 17, 1933).

24. Calderón Vega, *Memorias del PAN,* p. 70. Consult also Mayo, *La educación socialista en México.*

25. *La Nación* (Mexico City), December 29, 1945, pp. 3, 13–16.
26. Ibid., February 25, 1962, pp. 10–11.
27. For a detailed and well-researched analysis of the role played by the UNPF in this particular confrontation, see Robert A. Monson, "Right-Wing Politics in Mexican Education: The Textbook Controversy" (Ph.D. diss., Georgetown University, 1970).
28. *La Nación* (Mexico City), February 18, 1962, p. 11.
29. Ever since the office of Secretary of Public Education was created by the Obregón administration and entrusted at that time to philosopher José Vasconcelos, Mexico, like most other Latin American countries, has followed the tradition of naming a leading intellectual to that post. Jaime Torres Bodet was both a poet and leading diplomat. A graduate of the National University, he was subsequently appointed Undersecretary of Foreign Relations in the cabinet of President Miguel Alemán. Later, he was elected Director General of UNESCO in Paris (1948–52). He was twice the titular head of the Secretariat of Public Education, in the Avila Camacho (1940–46) and in the López Mateos cabinets (1958–64). He also served as Mexican Ambassador in Belgium and France. Until his death in May 1974, he was ambassador-at-large in the Secretariat of Foreign Relations, and had recently completed a three-volume set of memoirs.
30. For example, PRI president, Alfonso Corona del Rosal, came officially to the defense of Torres Bodet, and blamed all organized demonstrations on agitation by the "extreme right." *La Nación* (Mexico City), February 25, 1962, p. 5.
31. This emphasis on the rights of small private farms, as noted in chapter 3, was consonant with Madero's own revolutionary objectives. One of the principal points raised in his platform had been "to promote large productive estates *and small farms in particular.*" *Manifiesto de Madero y Francisco Vázquez Gómez.* (Emphasis added.)
32. González Luna, *Humanismo político,* p. 185.
33. James F. Creagan, "Minority Political Parties in Mexico: Their Role in a One-Party Dominant System" (Ph.D. diss., University of Virginia, 1965), pp. 102–104.
34. Padgett, *The Mexican Political System,* pp. 111–12. See also Wilkie, *Mexican Revolution: Federal Expenditure.*
35. Calderón Vega, *Memorias del PAN,* pp. 210–11.
36. Ibid.
37. The following are illustrative of the favorable reception by the press: "Finally someone has put the leash on the growling agrarian cat." *Universal Gráfico* (Mexico City), October 18, 1946. "Within the halls of Congress, an entire political situation is being gambled: either the demagogues win out and agitators will continue to govern our fields, or we will restore to our lands the rule of law and individual guarantees." *Ultimas Noticias* (Mexico City), October 18, 1946.
38. *El Universal* (Mexico City), October 22, 1946.
39. Ibid., November 8, 1946.
40. The technical definition of *minifundio* given by the Alemanistas was

any parcel of land not exceeding one hundred *hectáreas.* A larger number of *hectáreas* was allowed for poorer lands, or in those regions where the type of agriculture so required it. For example, cotton farms were permitted up to 150 *hectáreas,* and banana and sugar plantations, up to 300. *La Nación* (Mexico City), December 14, 1946, p. 19.

41. Ibid.

42. Calderón Vega, *Memorias del PAN,* p. 217.

43. *La Nación* (Mexico City), December 21, 1946, p. 3.

44. Rupert Emerson in Roy C. Macridis, ed., *Political Parties: Contemporary Trends and Ideas* (New York: Harper and Row, 1967), pp. 255–257. Emerson notes that "guided democracies" are actually characteristic of countries where gaps "break up the homogeneity of the society," and that "it is in general more realistic to see the trend toward the authoritarian one-party system as deriving from the lack of unity rather than as an expression of it." At the same time, he adds that "a convenient device for bringing the opposition into line is the provision that the entire country forms a single electoral constituency." This hypothesis is certainly applicable to Mexico, where the Revolutionary Party has consistently regarded itself as the sole legitimate interpreter of the country's goals. Similarly, any organized opposition to the revolutionary tradition as interpreted by PRI is almost automatically labeled as anti-Mexican. This also supports Emerson's contention that in such situations the words opponent and enemy become synonymous.

45. Ibid., p. 256.

46. Roberto Pérez Patón, *Los partidos políticos y la democracia: sociología del partido único* (La Paz, Bolivia: 1961), pp. 27–28.

47. Rafael Preciado Hernández, "¿Que es la democracia?," *La Nación* (Mexico City), March 4, 1956, p. 7.

48. Rupert Emerson in Macridis, *Political Parties,* p. 254.

49. *Reglamento Interior de la Cámara Federal de Diputados,* Artículo 3o.

50. *La Nación* (Mexico City), August 28, 1943, p. 6.

51. Ibid.

52. Ibid., p. 7. In a statement supporting Estrada's contention, PAN announced: "political blocs are not legally constituted organizations, but mere party groups to which nothing has to be exposed by those who do not belong to that particular party. Acción Nacional has always opposed the so-called system of 'bloc politics', which stifles and frustrates any possibility for the normal operation of actual institutions."

53. Ibid., pp. 6–7. The credentials committee is in charge of reviewing the documentation presented by each candidate, and to make its recommendations on each case to the Federal Electoral College. Although this committee was also controlled by the PRM, PAN wished to stress that, in theory at least, the various congressional committees were legitimate legislative organizations.

54. Calderón Vega, *Memorias del PAN,* p. 101.

55. Ibid., p. 102.

56. *La Nación* (Mexico City), August 21, 1950, pp. 11–15.

57. For a detailed discussion of these two periods, see Frank Brandenburg, "Mexico: An Experiment," pp. 2–12 and 34–48.
58. *La Nación* (Mexico City), December 22, 1945, p. 6.
59. Calderón Vega, *Memorias del PAN,* p. 139.
60. Ibid., pp. 139–140.
61. Ibid., pp. 149–150.
62. Ibid., p. 140.
63. Ibid., p. 150.
64. Ibid., p. 141.
65. Ibid., p. 150.
66. *Diario Oficial,* December 30, 1945.
67. *La Nación* (Mexico City), April 27, 1946, p. 34.
68. Méndez Barraza, "Los partidos políticos en México," p. 18.
69. Ibid.
70. Ibid.
71. *Diario Oficial,* February 12, 1949.
72. *La Nación* (Mexico City), March 21, 1949, p. 4.
73. Brandenburg, "Mexico: An Experiment," p. 109.
74. *La Nación* (Mexico City), March 21, 1949, p. 4.
75. Ibid., April 11, 1949, p. 3.
76. Creagan, "Minority Political Parties," p. 63.
77. In its electoral law reform proposal, submitted to Congress in November 1954, PAN called for the creation of a Federal Council on Suffrage (*Consejo Federal del Sufragio*) as the highest tribunal in all electoral matters. *La Nación* (Mexico City), November 14, 1954, p. 6.
78. Ibid., November 21, 1954.
79. Ibid., November 14, 1954, pp. 6–7.
80. Creagan, "Minority Political Parties," p. 75.
81. *Diario Oficial,* January 5, 1973.
82. Jesús Guisa y Azevedo, *Acción Nacional es un equívoco* (México: Editorial Polis, 1966), p. 50.
83. Padgett, *The Mexican Political System,* pp. 56–57.
84. Ibid.
85. The following account was related by the late Rubén Salazar of the *Los Angeles Times,* as reported in the *Washington Post,* December 27, 1968. It should be noted that Mr. Salazar's sympathetic account of PAN's activities in the Uruapan election betrays his long-standing feud with PRI officials.
86. Ibid.
87. Ibid.
88. Ibid.

Chapter Five

1. *La Nación* (Mexico City), June 26, 1943, p. 14.
2. Gómez Morín, *Diez Años de México,* p. 15.
3. Creagan, "Minority Political Parties," p. 52.

4. Lux, "PAN: The Conservative Political Party," p. 114.
5. *La Nación* (Mexico City), April 3, 1950, pp. 12–13.
6. Calderón Vega, *Memorias del PAN,* pp. 18–19.
7. Gómez Morín, *Diez Años de México,* p. 13.
8. Calderón Vega, *Memorias del PAN,* pp. 31–32.
9. *La Nación* (Mexico City), May 8, 1943, p. 9.
10. Several prominent Mexican scholars have already commented on the insignificant role of the legislative branch in Mexico. Daniel Cosío Villegas, for one, observes: "The blackest of omens is the role played by the Congress in the revolutionary era. In the revolutionary legislatures, there has never occurred a single debate that deserves to be remembered. The revolutionary congresses have been as servile as those of the Díaz era." *American Extremes,* pp. 11–12.
11. Interview with Manuel Gómez Morín, Mexico City, August 1969.
12. It is noteworthy that PAN's regional strength has centered in those key areas which Brandenburg calls "The Big Eight": the Federal District, Guanajuato, México, Michoacán, Oaxaca, Puebla, and Veracruz. Each of these entities, plus Jalisco, has now over 1 million inhabitants. Together they comprise over half the nation's population. This area has also been a traditional stronghold of the Catholic Church. See Brandenburg, "Mexico: An Experiment," pp. 333–34. (See also Appendix III.)
13. The following assertions made by PAN illustrate this point: "In the course of this campaign, honorable and capable men set out to prove that they could indeed run for political office without being driven by selfish motives." Calderón Vega, *Memorias del PAN,* p. 99.
14. Lux, "PAN: The Conservative Political Party," p. 133.
15. *La Nación* (Mexico City), May 8, 1943; February 8, 1946; and February 28, 1949.
16. Among the more prominent personalities were Rafael Preciado Hernández, professor of law at the National University, and Luis de Garay, lawyer and founder of Editorial Jus, candidates for the VII and VIII Districts of the Federal District (Mexico City), respectively; Aquiles Elorduy, revolutionary and former deputy in the Madero administration, for Aguascalientes; González Luna, for Jalisco; and Carlos Septién García, a well-known journalist and founder of *La Nación,* for Querétaro. See *La Nación* (Mexico City), June 19, 1943, for a complete list and profile of PAN's candidates.
17. Calderón Vega, *Memorias del PAN,* pp. 96–97.
18. Ibid., p. 100.
19. *La Nación* (Mexico City), March 30, 1946; and April 6, 1946.
20. Ibid., October 5, 1946, pp. 6–7.
21. Ibid., July 6, 1946, pp. 13–17.
22. Ibid., July 13, 1946.
23. Ibid., August 17, 1946, p. 4.
24. The three were: Antonio L. Rodríguez (I District, Nuevo León); Juan Gutiérrez Lascuráin (VII District, D.F.); and Miguel Ramírez Munguía (VI District, Michoacán). On August 18, the Federal Electoral College admitted to some of PAN's charges of fraud by annulling the elections in the I District

of Aguascalientes and in the II District of Chihuahua, leaving the two seats vacant. This represented an additional moral victory for PAN. Ibid., August 13, 1946, pp. 6–9.

25. Ibid., March 7, 1949, p. 9.

26. Ibid., May 30, 1949, pp. 11–16.

27. This occurred shortly after the leaders of the UNS had been arrested for placing a black flag on the statue of Benito Juárez, in downtown Mexico City. Fuerza Popular's registration as a national party was thereupon canceled by the Secretariat of Gobernación in January 1949 following a protest campaign staged by PRI. Méndez Barraza, "Los partidos políticos en México," p. 65.

28. *La Nación* (Mexico City), May 25, 1946, p. 3.

29. Ibid., September 25, 1943, p. 7.

30. Eduardo Facha Gutiérrez (X District, D.F.). The other three were: Juan José Hinojosa (III, Nuevo León); Jaime Robles Martín del Campo (III, Jalisco); and Gonzalo Chapela, (II, Michoacán). Ibid., September 5, 1949, p. 9.

31. Ibid., August 14, 1949, pp. 3–4.

32. Brandenburg, "Mexico: An Experiment," p. 109.

33. Information provided by PAN National Committee headquarters.

34. *La Nación* (Mexico City), July 30, 1973, p. 13.

35. As a compromise to Gómez Morín's position, the delegates did not officially nominate Almazán. Instead, they merely expressed support for his candidacy. Calderón Vega, *Memorias del PAN,* pp. 33–4.

36. Gómez Morín, *Diez Años de México,* pp. 43–69.

37. Padgett, *The Mexican Political System,* p. 68.

38. *New York Times,* July 8, 1940.

39. Calderón Vega, *Memorias del PAN,* pp. 53–54. The official results gave Avila Camacho 2,476,641 votes to Almazán's 151,101.

40. The Federal Electoral Law of 1945 introduced such substantial modifications to earlier laws that PAN was required to renew its registration in order to prove that it met the stricter organizational requirements prescribed by the new law. Among other things, the law stipulated that (1) a party must have a minimum of 30,000 active members in at least two-thirds of the states, with a minimum of 1,000 members in each; (2) it must declare allegiance to the Constitution and to other national institutions; (3) it could not be affiliated to foreign political parties; (4) it could not cater to religion or to race; and (5) the organization of the party had to conform to the dictates of the law (that is, along national, regional, and local lines, in conformity with the organizational structure of the ruling party). Under the terms of Article 35 of this law, no political association could use the designation of national party unless it met the above standards. The fact that PAN did was regarded by party members as a major triumph. See Méndez Barraza, "Los partidos políticos en México," pp. 13–15.

41. *La Nación* (Mexico City), February 8, 1946, pp. 3–20.

42. Padgett, for one, contends that PAN supported Padilla in 1946. This is inaccurate, since the convention's original decision to back Cabrera was

never officially altered in the course of the presidential campaign, even after Cabrera declined PAN's nomination. See *The Mexican Political System,* p. 68.

43. *La Nación* (Mexico City), February 8, 1946, pp. 3–20.

44. Salvador Novo, *La vida en México en el período presidencial de Manuel Avila Camacho* (México: Empresas Editoriales, S.A.), p. 601.

45. *La Nación* (Mexico City), February 8, 1946, p. 1.

46. Some delegates, however, were indignant at Cabrera's refusal. An amusing incident occurred when some unidentified *Panistas* declared in the Mexico City daily, *Ultimas Noticias,* that they were seriously considering nominating comedian Mario Moreno "Cantínflas" instead. The PAN leadership had no comment, but Cantínflas did react: "I don't see why people think it funny that any citizen should aspire to become president. After all, if I were elected, things might change: I would be laughing *with* the people, not *at* them." Ibid., February, 23, 1946.

47. Ibid., April 20, 1946, p. 3.

48. Ibid. The five points included: (1) Mexico must turn away from policies of directed economics and communism and find a solution that is dependent on the country's own realities; (2) the protection of labor and peasant sectors, without prejudice for the legitimate interests of other social classes; (3) national unity is the only basis of a government capable of meeting Mexico's problems successfully; (4) increased production in the factories and the land; and (5) the elimination of creeping corruption in the rank-and-file of the regime.

49. Interview with Manuel Gómez Morín, Mexico City, August 18, 1968.

50. *La Nación* (Mexico City), September 27, 1959, p. 13.

51. Lux, "PAN: The Conservative Political Party," p. 138.

52. José Bravo Ugarte, *Efraín González Luna: abogado, humanista, político, católico* (México: Ediciones del PAN), p. 57.

53. "Un candidato insólito," *Excélsior* (Mexico City), October 7, 1964.

54. Bravo Ugarte, *Efraín González Luna,* p. 64.

55. *Diario de los Debates,* 12sp., 1952.

56. *La Nación* (Mexico City), September 27, 1959, pp. 34–35. It should be noted that PAN's representation in the Congress increased both in 1952 and 1956. In 1952, PAN won five deputy seats (Felipe Gómez Mont, Ramón Garcilita Partido, Manuel Aguilar y Salazar, Francisco Chávez González, and Eugenio Ibarrola Santoyo). In 1956, the party won six such seats (Alfonso Ituarte, Manuel Sierra, Jesús Sánz, Federico Sánchez Navarrete, Manuel Cantú Méndez, and Patricio Aguirre Andrade).

57. Lux, "PAN: The Conservative Political Party," pp. 153–54.

58. *La Nación* (Mexico City), October 27, 1957, p. 18.

59. *Tapadismo* refers to the practice of the elites within the revolutionary family (usually ex-presidents and sector leaders) of predetermining the candidate who is mutually acceptable to all. Thus, as the result of an "accidental" leak to the press, all Mexicans know months prior to the party's convention the name of the next president of Mexico.

60. Initially the list of candidates included: Luis H. Alvarez, Luis Castañeda Guzmán, Rafael Preciado Hernández, José González Torres, Miguel Estrada Iturbide, Antonio L. Rodríguez, Ernesto P. Uruchurtu, Alfonso Ituarte Servín, Juan Gutiérrez Lascuráin, and Francisco Quiroga. *La Nación* (Mexico City), December 1, 1957, p. 21.

61. Speech delivered by delegate Ignacio Arriola. Ibid. (Emphasis added.)

62. For a complete account of the convention, see *La Nación* (Mexico City), December 1, 1957, pp. 10–27.

63. Ibid., p. 23.

64. See, for example, Howard F. Cline, *Mexico: Revolution to Evolution, 1940–1960,* p. 169.

65. *La Nación* (Mexico City), December 15, 1957, p. 36.

66. Johnson, *Political Forces in Latin America,* p. 28.

67. Kenneth Johnson, "Ideological Correlates of Right-Wing Political Alienation in Mexico," *American Political Science Review* (September 1965): p. 44.

68. *La Nación* (Mexico City), April 5, 1959, pp. 19–20.

69. Creagan, "Minority Political Parties," p. 131.

70. See, for example, editorials in *El Universal* (Mexico City), November 26, 1957: *Novedades* (Mexico City), November 26, 1957; and *Excélsior* (Mexico City), November 27, 1957.

71. *La Nación* (Mexico City), July 6, 1958, pp. 10–11.

72. *Diario de los Debates,* 10sp., 1958.

73. *La Nación* (Mexico City), July 13, 1958, p. 17.

74. Ibid., June 1, 1958, and March 29, 1959.

75. Cline, *Mexico: Revolution to Evolution,* p. 170.

76. Interview with Adolfo Christlieb Ibarrola, Mexico City, August 4, 1968.

77. Interview with Adolfo Christlieb Ibarrola, Mexico City, August 12, 1969.

78. *La Nación* (Mexico City), August 1, 1970, pp. 28–31.

79. Ibid., September 27, 1959, p. 14. Born in Cotija, Michoacán in 1919, José González Torres obtained his degree in law in 1945. Earlier, he had joined the ACJM and was known as a militant spokesman for educational liberties. In 1944 he became national president of the ACJM, and in 1947 he became the first Mexican ever to be elected president of Pax Romana. His previous political experience included an unsuccessful race for the Federal District's twelfth congressional district in 1955.

80. Interview with Manuel Gómez Morín, Mexico City, August 20, 1969.

81. Ibid.

82. Adolfo Christlieb was born in Mexico City on March 12, 1919. He studied law at the National University and graduated with high honors in 1941. He joined PAN in 1942 and served in various important executive positions. He was elected federal deputy (1964–67) and served as the national president of PAN from 1962 until 1968. Stricken with leukemia, Christlieb died in Mexico City in the fall of 1969.

83. Johnson, "Ideological Correlates," p. 42.
84. Adolfo Christlieb Ibarrola, *La oposición* (México: Ediciones del PAN, 1965), pp. 12, 15.
85. Johnson, "Ideological Correlates," pp. 43–44.
86. Ibid.
87. "Declaratoria por la Cámara de Diputados," *Diario de los Debates,* 8sp., 1964.
88. The trend continues to this day for PAN candidates to win unusually high vote totals in the Federal District. In 1967, PAN polled 27.6 percent, in 1970, 33 percent, and, most recently, 38.4 percent in 1973. (See Appendix II.)
89. Scott, *Mexican Government in Transition,* p. 195.
90. This fact was recently confirmed. Interview with Arq. Fernando Ayala Carrión, member of the PAN National Council, Mexico City, August 2, 1973; and Interview with Juan Manuel Gómez Morín, Mexico City, August 1, 1973.
91. *La Nación* (Mexico City), July 30, 1973, pp. 11–13.
92. Brandenburg, "Mexico: An Experiment," pp. 364–66.
93. Ibid., p. 367. Brandenburg notes that *caciquismo* became even more entrenched in municipal politics because the local inhabitants were less disposed toward intervention by the central government than toward the periodic malpractices of their own local bosses. Departing from the Brandenburg thesis, which does not place much weight on the potential advantages of a multiparty arrangement at the municipal level, this writer agrees with PAN's position that the key to competitive politics at the national level ultimately rests in the effective democratization of smaller political units, even if, admittedly, these still remain financially dependent on the states, or, to be more exact, on the federal government.
94. *La Nación* (Mexico City), September 27, 1959, pp. 36–39.
95. Ibid., January 12 and January 19, 1946.
96. Ibid., January 26, 1946 and February 15, 1947.
97. Ibid., September 18, 1950, pp. 12–13. The states were Colima, Nuevo León, Jalisco, Michoacán, Coahuila, Tamaulipas, México, Durango, and Guerrero.
98. Ibid., September 27, 1959, pp. 36–39.
99. I personally had the occasion to evidence the strong local support enjoyed by PAN in the cities of Mexicali, Baja California, and Hermosillo, Sonora, during a lecture tour sponsored by the United States Information Agency in the summer of 1966.
100. Adolfo Christlieb Ibarrola, "Memorandum Addressed to the Supreme Court of Mexico," August 27, 1968.
101. Creagan, "Minority Political Parties," p. 122.

Chapter Six

1. Gabriel Almond and Sidney Verba, *The Civic Culture,* p. 311.
2. Ibid., p. 312.
3. Ibid.

4. La Palombara and Weiner, *Political Parties,* p. 37.

5. Ibid., pp. 24–25.

6. Ibid., p. 158.

7. Ibid., pp. 40–41. The authors suggest instead that PRI is representative of the "one-party pluralistic" pattern rather than the "one-party authoritarian." They define the former as dominated by a single party which is pluralistic in organization; pragmatic, as opposed to rigidly ideological in outlook; and absorptive, rather than ruthlessly destructive in its relationships to other groups. While it is true that PRI's relations to minority parties have become absorptive rather than ruthlessly destructive, this study challenges their contention that PRI is pragmatic, since, as the authors themselves admitted earlier, a dominant party is commonly guided by an ideology, even if the ideology is a mere defense of the status quo. One could, of course, stretch the point and argue that the defense of the status quo may be conceived in pragmatic terms, but to speak of a pragmatic ideology raises problems in logic which ultimately suggest that their effort to distinguish between "one-party authoritarianism" and "one-party pluralism" is more theoretical than practical.

8. Milnor, *Comparative Political Parties,* p. 9.

9. Sigmund Neumann, ed., *Modern Political Parties: Approaches to Comparative Politics* (Chicago: University of Chicago Press, 1955), pp. 398–400.

10. In 1969 Adolfo Christlieb suggested to me that PAN had lost substantial financial support from some of the major brewery companies in northeast Mexico. Among these was the powerful Cervecería Moctezuma.

11. *Excélsior* (Mexico City), August 2, 1973.

12. Interview with Fernando Ayala Carrión, Mexico City, August 2, 1973.

Appendixes

Appendix I

Partido Accion Nacional: Declaration of Principles

PAN's "Declaration of Principles" was approved by the Constituent Assembly of the Party in September 1939. It contains fourteen basic statements of doctrine which may be summarized as follows:

1. THE NATION: The interest of the entire nation stands above all particularistic interests. Personal human values cannot subsist if the interests of the collectivity are undermined, nor can the collectivity survive if personal values are denied. The recognition of the dignity of the human person is the essential prerequisite for the life of the Nation. The proclamation of class warfare undermines national unity and the Nation itself. The internal development of Mexico depends fundamentally on a jealous preservation of its historical and cultural ties with Spanish-America.

2. THE PERSON: The Nation is not formed by abstract individuals, nor by undifferentiated masses. Rather, it is formed by real human beings grouped together in natural communities, such as the family, the township, professional organizations, and cultural and religious institutions. The national political organization has the obligation to recognize and respect these natural communities.

3. THE STATE: Oppression and injustice run contrary to the national interest and degrade the individual. Those doctrines which propose to solve social problems through class conflict are false, and negate the most fundamental laws of social life. Social justice is what the Nation needs, not class conflict, which invariably aims to serve the interests of a given sector and to destroy or dominate other sectors. Only a truly national State can exercise authority without being tyrannical; be a mediator and not an oppressor; and bring about justice, without being subversive.

4. ORDER: Misery and ignorance are the fruits of moral and economic disorders which are introduced into society through injustice, anarchy, and oppression. These can be avoided only if the life of the Nation is based on the recognition of spiritual values, and directs its efforts toward the realization of the common good. The battle against ignorance and misery

is the duty of the State. This duty is not to be monopolized, however, as all members of the Nation must collaborate in the eradication of these ills.

5. LIBERTY: The State cannot exercise rights over individual conscience, nor prescribe and impose religious convictions. Liberty of religious conviction must become a reality in Mexico, and all laws which propose to deny the individual these rights must be eliminated.

6. EDUCATION: Liberty of research and scientific or philosophical opinion may not be restrained by the State. The State has the obligation, but not the monopoly, to procure for all its members equal opportunity in education, and to promote the cultural improvement of the Nation. But in the fulfillment of this obligation, the State may not transform itself into an agent of propaganda for specific parties or factions. Liberty in education must be guaranteed in such a way that the State does not transcend beyond its determination of technical requirements relating to method, to the extension and confirmation of a minimum education program, or the determination of the awarding of degrees which shall enable individuals to exercise a given profession or social function.

7. WORK: It is necessary, both from the national standpoint as well as from that of the individual, to proclaim the sanctity of the right and duty to work. The State and the entire community must guarantee the free exercise of this right. To regard human labor as merchandise, as a material element in production is to deny the essential dignity of the person, and runs contrary to the interest of the Nation. It becomes worse when the worker is exploited as a man for political ends, with the pretext of a need for discipline and cohesion within party-affiliated labor unions.

8. PRIVATE ENTERPRISE: Constitutes a legitimate source for social development. The State must promote and guarantee the rights of private initiative. It must see to it that the fruits of private enterprise are of a social character, and it must make certain that said enterprise will conform to the national interest and be subordinated to the Common Good.

9. PROPERTY: Private property is the most adequate means to insure national production and its constitutes a

basic guarantee of the dignity of the person, and of the existence of the fundamental human community, which is the family.

10. LAND: Perhaps the most serious of our national problems is the land question, which will never be resolved so long as the State makes use of insincere methods for political ends. The Nation requires that the State orient and make plans for the migration of the rural population into the interior; that each farming family, including the family of the *ejidatario*, might obtain full title to that amount of land which it can reasonably cultivate; that a genuine legal framework be established so as to facilitate the free and unimpeded organization of agricultural workers, and that they may enjoy proper credit, adequate markets, and so forth.

11. ECONOMY: The State has authority over the national economy but does not own it. It must advance a program of national cooperation—with the participation of all sectors—but it does not have the authority to monopolize the life of the economy.

12. MUNICIPAL GOVERNMENT: The basic unit of our national political framework is municipal government. It must be autonomous, responsible, and responsive to the will of its citizens.

13. LAW: The major attribute of the State is the attainment of justice. It is essential, therefore, that our tribunals apply laws justly. Laws should reflect justice, not run contrary to it.

14. POLITICS: The State cannot negate the existence of pluralist interests in society. Therefore, it must allow the free expression of these interests through a competitive political system, with permanently-organized political parties.

Appendix II

PAN in an Urban Context
Elections for Deputy in the Federal District: 1964–73*

Party	*1964*		*1967*		*1970*		*1973*	
	vote	*%*	*vote*	*%*	*vote*	*%*	*vote*	*%*
PAN	383,399	29.4	456,061	27.6	716,214	33.2	917,875	38.4
PRI	861,302	66.3	1,070,706	65.0	1,354,957	62.5	1,244,804	52.1
PPS	34,464	2.6	77,736	4.8	64,143	2.9	163,336	6.8
PARM	22,144	1.7	39,982	2.6	31,885	1.4	64,199	2.7
Total	1,301,309	100	1,642,485	100	2,167,226	100	2,390,214	100

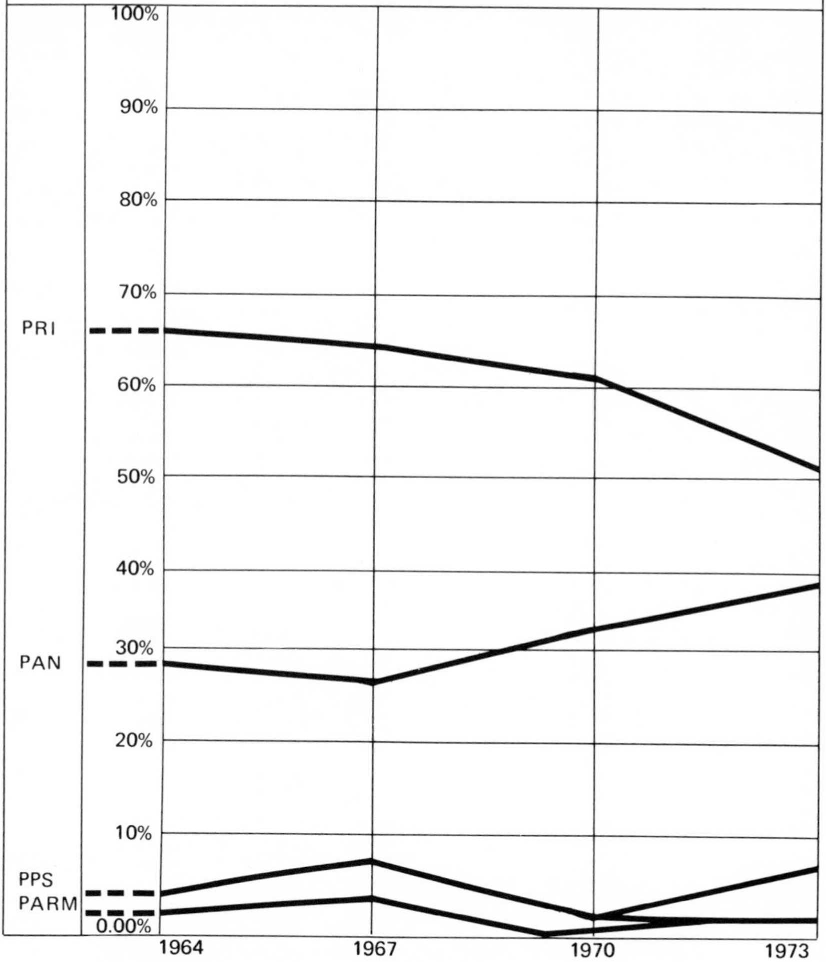

*Source: Arquitecto Fernando Ayala, *Consejo Nacional del PAN.*

Appendix III

PAN's Electoral Appeal: A Regional Analysis
Based on the Results of the 1970 Congressional Elections*
(see accompanying map)

PAN vote total: 1,893,289
Total number of congressional districts in Mexico: 178
National average of PAN vote per district: 10,636.

CATEGORY I: REGION WITH PAN VOTE TOTALS EXCEEDING THE NATIONAL AVERAGE

	State	Number of districts	PAN vote total	Average vote per district	PAN interpretation of vote
1	Distrito Federal	24	716,241	29,843	Urban-industrial; potentially competitive
2	Baja California N.	3	72,060	24,020	PRI corruption; strong PAN organization

CATEGORY II: REGION WITH PAN VOTE TOTALS WITHIN THE NATIONAL AVERAGE

	State	Number of districts	PAN vote total	Average vote per district	PAN interpretation of vote
3	México	9	135,467	15,274	Industrial; D.F. influence
4	Jalisco	12	167,253	13,938	Urban-industrial; Guadalajara
5	Nuevo León	5	67,556	13,511	Urban-industrial; Monterrey
6	Guanajuato	9	107,586	11,954	Bajío; traditional PAN strength
7	Yucatán	3	34,244	11,415	PRI abuses (Mérida); PAN mayor
8	Puebla	10	94,849	9,485	Factionalism within PRI
9	Michoacán	9	83,437	9,271	Bajío; traditional PAN strength

CATEGORY III: REGION WITH PAN VOTE TOTALS NEAR OR UNDER NATIONAL AVERAGE

	State	Number of districts	PAN vote total	Average vote per district	PAN interpretation of vote
10	San Luis Potosí	5	39,405	7,881	Bajío, but entrenched PRI rule
11	Chihuahua	6	44,240	7,373	Strong PAN organization, but PRI corruption
12	Morelos	2	14,155	7,078	Agricultural; growing PAN organization
13	Coahuila	4	28,142	7,036	Weakening PRI local organization
14	Durango	4	28,100	7,025	Weakening PRI local organization
15	Querétaro	2	12,679	6,340	PRI organization still strong
16	Tampico	5	31,589	6,318	Traditional PRI territory
17	Zacatecas	4	24,909	6,227	Weakening PRI local organization
18	Aguascalientes	2	11,238	5,619	Bajío, but entrenched PRI rule
19	Veracruz	14	73,005	5,215	PRI traditionally strong, but recent PAN gains

CATEGORY IV: REGION WITH PAN VOTE TOTALS WELL BELOW NATIONAL AVERAGE

	State	Number of districts	PAN vote total	Average vote per district	PAN interpretation of vote
20	Sonora	4	14,933	3,733	Internal PAN divisions; PAN strong in Hermosillo with mayor post
21	Sinaloa	4	13,964	3,491	Weak PAN organization
22	Tlaxcala	2	6,613	3,307	Weak PAN organization
23	Guerrero	6	18,945	3,158	Entrenched PRI organization
24	Oaxaca	9	23,027	2,559	Indigenous; low level literacy
25	Colima	2	4,784	2,392	Weak PAN organization
26	Hidalgo	5	11,455	2,291	Weak PAN organization
27	Nayarit	2	4,192	2,092	Indigenous; weak PAN organization

CATEGORY V: REGION WITH LOWEST PAN VOTE TOTALS

	State	Number of districts	PAN vote total	Average vote per district	PAN interpretation of vote
28	Tabasco	2	2,045	1,023	Indigenous; PAN organization practically nonexistent
29	Chiapas	6	3,979	663	Indigenous
30	Campeche	2	1,197	599	Indigenous; no PAN organization
31	Baja California (Territorio)	1	0	0	Uncontested
32	Quintana Roo	1	0	0	Uncontested

*Source: Fernando Ayala Carrión, member of the PAN National Council.

I
II
III
IV
V

Appendix IV

Major Offices Held by PAN - 1946 Through 1976

I. *NATIONAL: CHAMBER OF DEPUTIES*

XL	LEGISLATURE–1946-9		
III	DISTRITO FEDERAL	Ing. Juan Gutiérrez Lascuráin	Majority Deputy
I	NUEVO LEON	Sr. Antonio L. Rodríguez	"
VI	MICHOACAN	Lic. Miguel Ramírez Munguía	"
I	AGUASCALIENTES	Lic. Aquiles Elorduy*	"

*Subsequently expelled from the party because of religious differences.

XLI	LEGISLATURE–1949-52		
X	DISTRITO FEDERAL	Lic. Eduardo Facha Gutiérrez	Majority
II	JALISCO	Lic. Jaime Robles Martín del Campo	"
III	MICHOACAN	Lic. Gonzalo Chapela y B.	"
II	NUEVO LEON	Sr. Juan José Hinojosa	"

XLII	LEGISLATURE–1952-5		
II	DISTRITO FEDERAL	Lic. Felipe Gómez Mont	Majority
XI	DISTRITO FEDERAL	Lic. Eugenio Ibarrola Santoyo	"
II	JALISCO	Lic. Ramón Garcilita Partida	"
IX	MICHOACAN	Lic. Francisco Chávez González	"
III	OAXACA	Lic. Manuel Aguilar y Salazar	"

XLIII	LEGISLATURE–1955-8		
III	DISTRITO FEDERAL	Dr. Patricio Aguirre	Majority
IX	DISTRITO FEDERAL	Lic. Manuel Sierra Macedo	"
XVIII	DISTRITO FEDERAL	Sr. Alfonso Ituarte Servín*	"
III	CHIHUAHUA	Lic. Jesús Sáenz Cerrada	"
III	OAXACA	Lic. Manuel Cantú Méndez	"
I	MORELOS	Ing. Federico Sánchez Navarrete	"

*Ex-party president

XLIV	LEGISLATURE–1958-61		
II	DISTRITO FEDERAL	Lic. Felipe Gómez Mont (1)	Majority
I	ZACATECAS	Sr. Jaime Haro Rodríguez (2)	"
I	YUCATAN	Sr. Eduardo Molina Castillo (3)	"
I	PUEBLA	Sr. Antonio López y López (4)	"
II	BAJA CALIFORNIA N.	Sr. Germán Brambila (5)	"
I	CHIAPAS	Sr. Humberto Zebadua (6)	"

Numbers 1 and 2 turned down their seats in conformity with PAN's refusal to acknowledge the validity of the 1958 election results. Numbers 3, 4, 5 and 6 accepted their seats, and were consequently expelled from the party.

XLV	LEGISLATURE–1961-4		
III	DISTRITO FEDERAL	Sr. Javier Blanco Sánchez	Majority
VI	CHIHUAHUA	Sr. Carlos Chavira	"
III	MICHOACAN	Dr. Rafael Morelos Valdés	"
I	SAN LUIS POTOSI	Lic. Alfonso Guerrero Briones	"
I	COLIMA	Sr. Carlos Garibay	"

APPENDIX IV, Continued

XLVI	LEGISLATURE—1964-7		
II	CHIHUAHUA	Srta. Florentina Villalobos Chaparro	Majority
II	GUANAJUATO	Sr. Luis Aranda Torres	"
I	DISTRITO FEDERAL	Dr. Francisco Quiroga Fernández	Party Deputy
II	DISTRITO FEDERAL	Lic. Felipe Gómez Mont	"
VII	DISTRITO FEDERAL	Sr. Jesús Hernández Díaz	"
VIII	DISTRITO FEDERAL	Lic. Juan Landerreche Obregón	"
IX	DISTRITO FEDERAL	Sr. Federico Estrada Varela	"
XI	DISTRITO FEDERAL	Lic. Jorge Avila Blancas	"
XVI	DISTRITO FEDERAL	Lic. Jorge Garabito Martínez	
XVII	DISTRITO FEDERAL	Lic. Abel Vicencio Tovar	"
XIX	DISTRITO FEDERAL	Sr. Jorge Ricaut Rothicot	"
XXII	DISTRITO FEDERAL	Sr. Jacinto Guadalupe Silva	"
XXIII	DISTRITO FEDERAL	Lic. Adolfo Christlieb Ibarrola*	"
I	BAJA CALIFORNIA N.	Lic. Salvador Rosas Magallón	"
II	JALISCO	Lic. Guillermo Ruiz Vázquez	"
V	MICHOACAN	Lic. Miguel Estrada Iturbide	"
I	NUEVO LEON	Prof. Pedro Reyes Velázquez	"
I	YUCATAN	Sr. Eduardo Trueba Molina	"
VII	GUANAJUATO	Prof. Ricardo Chaurand Concha	"
I	SAN LUIS POTOSI	Lic. Antonio Rosillo Pacheco	"

*PAN President during the Session

XLVII	LEGISLATURE—1967-70		
IX	DISTRITO FEDERAL	Sr. Javier Blanco Sánchez	Majority
II	DISTRITO FEDERAL	Lic. Rafael Preciado Hernández	Party
VII	DISTRITO FEDERAL	Sr. Alfonso Ituarte Servín	"
VIII	DISTRITO FEDERAL	Lic. Efraín González Morfín (2)	"
XI	DISTRITO FEDERAL	Sr. Juan José Hinojosa	"
XII	DISTRITO FEDERAL	Sra. Graciela Acevez de Romero	"
XIII	DISTRITO FEDERAL	Sr. Adrián Peña Soto	
XVI	DISTRITO FEDERAL	Lic. Manuel González Hinojosa (3)	"
XIX	DISTRITO FEDERAL	Lic. José Angel Conchello (4)	"
XX	DISTRITO FEDERAL	Sr. Gerardo Medina Valdés	"
XXI	DISTRITO FEDERAL	Lic. Abel Martínez Martínez	"
XXIII	DISTRITO FEDERAL	Lic. Juan Manuel Gómez Morín	"
I	BAJA CALIFORNIA N.	Sr. Rigoberto López Sedano	"
II	JALISCO	Dr. Ramiro González Luna	"
VII	EDO. DE MEXICO	Sr. Astolfo Vicencio Tovar	"
I	CHIHUAHUA	Dr. Octavio Corral	"
I	NUEVO LEON	Lic. Felipe Gutiérrez Zorrilla	"
II	GUANAJUATO	Lic. Antonio Obregón Padilla	"
II	SONORA	Sr. Enrique Fuentes Martínez	"
I	MORELOS	Sr. Francisco J. Aponte Robles	"

(1) Ex-party president
(2) PAN presidential candidate, 1970
(3) Party President during the Session
(4) Present PAN president

APPENDIX IV, Continued

XLVIII	LEGISLATURE–1970-3		
I	DISTRITO FEDERAL	Lic. Jorge Garabito Martínez	Party
II	DISTRITO FEDERAL	Lic. Hiram Escudero Alvarez	"
VII	DISTRITO FEDERAL	Lic. Francisco José Peniche Bolio	"
X	DISTRITO FEDERAL	Sr. Inocencio Sandoval Zavala	"
XIII	DISTRITO FEDERAL	Lic. Juan Landerreche Obregón	"
XIV	DISTRITO FEDERAL	C.P. Magdaleno Gutiérrez Herrera	"
XVI	DISTRITO FEDERAL	Lic. Bernardo Bátiz Vázquez	"
XVII	DISTRITO FEDERAL	Ing. Ernesto Velasco Lafarga	"
XIX	DISTRITO FEDERAL	Dr. Gillermo Islas Olguín	"
XX	DISTRITO FEDERAL	Sr. Mayo A. Bravo Hernández	"
XXI	DISTRITO FEDERAL	Dr. Roberto Flores Granados	"
XXII	DISTRITO FEDERAL	Sr. Miguel Hernández Labastida	"
XXIV	DISTRITO FEDERAL	Prof. Jesús Rojo Pérez	"
I	JALISCO	Sr. Alfonso Orozco Rosales	"
III	JALISCO	Lic. Guillermo Ruiz Vázquez	"
IV	JALISCO	Lic. Guillermo Baeza Somellera	"
VII	EDO. DE MEXICO	Ing. José Melgarejo Gómez	"
IX	EDO. DE MEXICO	Prof. José Blas Briseño	"
I	PUEBLA	Lic. Miguel López González	"
II	GUANAJUATO	Dr. Juan Manuel López Sanabria	"
XLIX	LEGISLATURE–1973-6		
XI	DISTRITO FEDERAL	Sr. Juan José Hinojosa	Majority
XIII	DISTRITO FEDERAL	Sr. Javier Blanco Sánchez	"
I	PUEBLA	Sr. Miguel Fernández del Campo	"
II	PUEBLA	C.P. Alejandro Cañedo B.	"
II	DISTRITO FEDERAL	Sr. Alvaro Fernández de Ceballos	Party
VII	DISTRITO FEDERAL	Ing. Héctor González García	"
VIII	DISTRITO FEDERAL	Sra. Margarita Prida de Yarza	"
X	DISTRITO FEDERAL	Sr. Lorenzo Reynoso	"
XII	DISTRITO FEDERAL	Sra. Graciela Aceves de Romero	"
XIV	DISTRITO FEDERAL	Lic. Eugenio Ortíz Walls	"
XV	DISTRITO FEDERAL	Sr. Alberto A. Loyola	"
XVI	DISTRITO FEDERAL	Lic. José Angel Conchello	"
XVII	DISTRITO FEDERAL	Lic. Abel Vicencio Tovar	"
XV	DISTRITO FEDERAL	Sr. Federico Ruiz López	"
XIX	DISTRITO FEDERAL	Lic. José de Jesús Martínez Gil	"
XX	DISTRITO FEDERAL	Sr. Gerardo Medina Valdéz	"
XXI	DISTRITO FEDERAL	Sr. Alfredo Oropeza	"
XXII	DISTRITO FEDERAL	Lic. Manuel González Hinojosa (1)	"
XXIII	DISTRITO FEDERAL	Lic. Fernando Estrada Sámano	"
XXVI	DISTRITO FEDERAL	Sr. Armando Calzada R.	"
XXVII	DISTRITO FEDERAL	Lic. Eduardo Limón León	"
IX	EDO. DE MEXICO	Sr. Carlos Gómez A.	"
XI	EDO. DE MEXICO	Sr. Alejandro Coronel O.	"
I	JALISCO	Sr. Jorge Baeza Somellera	"
IV	JALISCO	Sr. Jesús Sánchez	"

(1) Ex-party president.

APPENDIX IV, Continued

II. *MUNICIPAL AND LOCAL*

1946–1948	*Municipio de Quiroga, Michoacán*	
	Presidente Municipal:	Sr. Manuel Torres Serrania
1946–1948	*Municipio de Llano Hondo, Oaxaca*	
	Presidente Municipal:	Sr. Jerónimo Cortés
1947–1949	*Municipio de Zamora, Michoacán*	
	Diputado Local:	Dr. Alfonso Hernández Sánchez
1949–1952	*Municipio de El Grullo, Jalisco*	
	Presidente Municipal:	Sr. Primo Pérez M.
	Munícipes:	Sr. Conrado Díaz Infante
		Sr. Hermenegildo Covarrubias M.
		Sr. José Velazco P.
		Sr. José Topete C.
1963–1966	*Municipio de Garza García, Nuevo León*	
	Presidente Municipal:	Sr. Humberto Junco
1966–1969	*Municipio de Garza García, Nuevo León*	
	Alcaldesa:	Sra. Norma Villareal de Zambrano
1967–1970	*Municipio de Mérida, Yucatán***	
	Presidente Municipal:	Victor Correa Rachó
	Munícipes:	Dr. Francisco Solís Azuar
		Lic. Héctor Bolio Pinzón
		Sr. Ignacio Milton Canto
		Sr. Raúl Alayola
		Sr. Porfirio Palma Esquivel
		Sr. Eduardo Trueba Barrera
	Diputados Locales:	Sr. Marco León Herrera
		Sr. Julio Moreno Cabrera
1967–1970	*Municipio de Teocaltiche, Jalisco*	
	Presidente Municipal:	Sr. Rafael Pérez Aguirre
1968–1971	*Municipio de Uruapan, Michoacán**	
	Presidente Municipal:	Dr. Francisco Solís Huanosto
1969–1972	*Municipio de Hermosillo, Sonora**	
	Presidente Municipal:	Sr. Jorge Valdés Muñoz
1969–1972	*Municipio de Sn. Miguel Horcasitas, Sonora*	
	Presidente Municipal:	Sr. Gerardo Tapia Limón
1969–1972	*Municipio de Bacoachi, Sonora*	
	Presidente Municipal:	Sr. Fermín Contreras Ballesteros
1969–1972	*Municipio de Cucurpe, Sonora*	
	Munícipes:	Sr. Octaviano Palomino Molina
		Sr. Francisco Palomino Molina
1969–1972	*Municipio de Cumpas, Sonora*	
	Presidente Municipal:	Sr. Francisco Sixto Agapito Félix Cubera
1969–1972	*Municipio de Abasolo, Nuevo León*	
	Presidente Municipal:	Sr. Apolonio Elizondo Cantú
1970–1973	*Municipio de Xuitetelco, Puebla*	
	Presidente Municipal:	Sr. Eliseo Córdoba Loyola
1973–1976	*Municipio de San Andrés Chilac, Puebla*	
	Presidente Municipal:	Sr. Vicente Camarilla

*Key victories in important cities.

Source: Arquitecto Fernando Ayala, *Consejo Nacional del PAN.*

Appendix V

The 1973 Congressional Elections

State	Population	Citizens	Reg. Voters	Abstentions	PAN
Aguascalientes	379,999	176,433	176,975	+542	14,894
Baja California	1,044,929	461,666	534,580	+72,914	No Reg.
Baja California T.	150,206	67,734	62,516	5,218	2,486
Campeche	290,174	137,795	133,136	4,659	1,187
Coahuila	1,199,353	601,149	621,377	+20,228	19,670
Colima	276,257	127,091	132,539	+5,448	3,009
Chiapas	1,720,195	824,232	715,968	108,264	5,774
Chihuahua	1,776,736	859,127	882,090	+22,963	61,567
Distrito Federal	7,768,033	4,023,521	4,434,173	+410,652	917,875
Durango	1,012,084	480,967	501,559	+20,592	10,711
Guanajuato	2,497,431	1,175,706	1,086,719	88,987	64,225
Guerrero	1,775,021	830,269	818,873	11,396	11,989
Hidalgo	1,273,746	632,613	597,108	35,505	29,182
Jalisco	3,666,354	1,762,135	1,617,001	145,134	222,124
México	4,919,828	1,966,828	1,666,582	300,246	298,607
Michoacán	2,513,205	1,199,888	1,158,593	41,295	54,719
Morelos	727,161	331,479	312,260	19,219	30,260
Nayarit	612,291	284,449	274,907	9,542	4,094
Nuevo León	1,989,203	934,186	845,958	88,228	67,425
Oaxaca	2,355,575	1,177,332	971,199	206,133	28,558
Puebla	2,730,791	1,363,057	1,242,733	120,324	158,592
Querétaro	542,570	251,216	253,447	+2,231	10,388
Quintana Roo T.	107,675	45,897	43,377	2,520	2
San Luis Potosí	1,376,858	675,575	607,069	68,506	28,246
Sinaloa	1,466,255	662,994	583,834	79,160	14,643
Sonora	1,238,880	592,806	610,871	+18,065	13,802
Tabasco	897,199	386,215	358,481	27,734	9,901
Tamaulipas	1,650,901	790,386	753,976	36,410	25,090
Tlaxcala	450,512	220,708	212,621	8,087	11,540
Veracruz	4,297,924	2,067,867	1,845,369	222,498	52,714
Yucatán	817,334	436,219	375,239	60,980	19,875
Zacatecas	1,003,937	470,383	450,401	19,982	18,703
Totals	54,528,617	26,017,923	24,881,531	1,136,392	2,211,852

Source: Fernando Ayala Carrión, member of PAN National Council.

APPENDIX V, Continued

Electoral Results			Non-Reg. (Cancelled Ballots)				
PRI	PPS	PARM	No Regs.	Anulds.	Total	Abstentions	Total Abst.
73,876	1,826	847	49	1,647	93,139	83,836	83,294
194,805	23,891	15,200	601	58,290	292,787	241,793	168,879
29,289	868	No Reg.	52	707	33,402	29,114	34,332
95,452	213	No Reg.	3	1,125	97,980	35,156	39,815
244,048	6,544	1,881	89	17,888	290,120	331,257	311,029
53,351	501	150	40	563	57,614	74,925	69,477
415,648	3,845	3,930	124	37,504	466,825	249,143	357,407
284,656	14,379	1,061	595	37,007	399,265	482,825	459,862
1,244,804	163,336	64,199	15,146	435,250	2,840,610	1,593,563	1,182,911
150,105	9,439	4,542	512	3,325	178,634	322,925	302,333
495,983	8,600	4,293	972	75,831	649,904	436,815	525,802
503,134	6,154	2,485	445	38,615	562,822	256,051	267,447
348,180	6,496	4,605	5,225	35,325	429,013	168,095	203,600
655,788	31,016	17,348	1,815	40,575	968,666	648,335	793,469
797,740	38,637	21,862	2,774	186,066	1,345,686	320,896	621,142
521,311	11,696	4,966	1,295	84,236	678,223	480,370	521,665
112,080	6,625	3,689	198	876	153,728	158,532	177,751
43,501	20,547	6,540	8	15,057	89,747	185,160	194,702
319,715	4,752	5,216	305	6,613	404,026	441,932	530,160
506,126	27,334	31,921	886	48,339	643,164	328,035	534,168
455,233	15,829	26,066	876	65,184	721,780	520,953	641,277
129,898	1,624	1,236	88	3,231	146,465	106,982	104,751
35,590	541	1	40	269	36,443	6,934	9,454
292,176	2,102	2,039	165	2,474	327,202	279,867	348,373
203,175	8,672	5,890	307	53,469	286,156	297,678	376,838
188,670	2,397	3,547	592	1,178	210,186	400,685	382,620
162,831	2,644	No Reg.	109	350	175,835	182,646	210,380
329,743	19,789	26,216	1,056	8,104	409,998	343,978	380,388
119,377	4,284	2,344	244	24,466	162,255	50,366	58,453
888,653	62,233	12,122	1,488	31,055	1,048,265	797,104	1,019,602
246,375	2,465	No Reg.	30	73,384	342,129	33,110	94,090
246,708	2,833	576	146	2,188	271,154	179,247	199,229
10,388,021	512,112	274,772	36,275	1,390,191	14,813,223	10,068,308	11,204,700

Bibliography

Public Documents

Constitución Política de los Estados Unidos Mexicanos.

Diario Oficial de la Federación.

Estados Unidos Mexicanos. Congreso. *Declaratoria por la Cámara de Diputados.* 8sp., 1964.

———. *Reglamento Interior de la Cámara Federal de Diputados.*

———. Cámara de Diputados. *Diario de los Debates.*

———. XLVI Legislatura de la Cámara de Diputados. *Los presidentes de México ante la nación: informes, manifiestos y documentos de 1821 a 1966.*

———. Secretaría de Gobernación. *Ley Electoral Federal* (with amendments through 1973).

México. PRI. Confederación Nacional de Organizaciones Populares. *Bases constitutivas, declaración de principios y estatutos,* 1947.

———. Confederación Revolucionaria de Obreros y Campesinos. *Declaración de principios, programa de acción y estatutos,* 1952.

Interviews

Adolfo Christlieb Ibarrola, private interviews in Mexico City, August, 1968 and 1969.

Juan Manuel Gómez Morín, private interviews in Mexico City, August 10, 1969, and August 2, 1973.

Manuel Gómez Morín, private interviews in Mexico City, August, 1968, and July, August, and December, 1969.

Fernando Ayala, private interviews in Mexico City, August, 1973.

Books

Abbott, Walter M., S. J., ed. *The Documents of Vatican II.* New York: The American Press, 1966.

Abrego Ortega, Enrique. *Algunas consideraciones en torno a los partidos políticos en México.* México: UNAM, 1959.

Alba, Victor. *Las ideas sociales contemporaneas en México.* México, 1960.

______. *The Mexicans.* New York: Praeger, 1967.

Almond, Gabriel, and Coleman, James. *The Politics of the Developing Areas.* Princeton, N.J.: Princeton University Press, 1960.

______, and Powell, G. Bingham, Jr. *Comparative Politics: A Developmental Approach.* Boston: Little, Brown, and Company, 1966.

______, and Verba, Sidney. *The Civic Culture.* Boston: Little, Brown, and Company, 1963.

Barrera Lavalle, Francisco. *En defensa del Partido Católico Nacional.* México: Juan Aguilar Vera, 1912.

Bell, Daniel. *The End of Ideology.* New York: Collier Books, 1962.

Brandenburg, Frank. *The Making of Modern Mexico.* Englewood Cliffs, N.J.: Prentice-Hall, Inc., 1964.

Bremauntz, Alberto. *La batalla ideológica en México.* México: Ediciones Jurídico-Sociales, 1962.

Burnett, Ben G., and Johnson, Kenneth F., eds. *Political Forces in Latin America: Dimensions of the Quest for Stability.* Belmont, California: Wadsworth Publishing Co., Inc., 1968.

Calderón Vega, Luis. *El 96.47 porciento de los mexicanos: ensayo de sociología religiosa.* Morelia: edición del autor, 1964.

______. *Memorias del PAN* (volume I). Morelia: edición del autor, 1967.

______. *Política y espíritu.* Morelia: Editorial Fimax, 1965.

Cline, Howard F. *Mexico, Revolution to Evolution, 1940–1960.* London: Oxford University Press, 1962.

______. *The United States and Mexico.* Cambridge, Mass.: Harvard University Press, 1953.

Cosío Villegas, Daniel. *American Extremes.* Austin: University of Texas Press, 1964.

Cué Canovas, Agustín. *El federalismo mexicano.* México: Libro Mex., 1960.

Dahl, Robert A. *Modern Political Analysis.* Englewood Cliffs, N.J.: Prentice-Hall, Inc., 1963.

Delhumeau, Antonio, *México: realidad política de sus partidos.* México: IMEP, 1970.

Denegri, Carlos. *29 estados de ánima; periplo de una campaña presidencial.* México, 1959.

Easton, David. *A Systems Analysis of Political Life.* New York: John Wiley and Sons, Inc., 1965.

Fernández Bravo, Vicente. *Política y administración.* México: Costa-Amic, 1965.

Fuentes Díaz, Vicente. *Los partidos políticos en México.* México, 1954.

García Cantú, Gastón. *El pensamiento de la reacción mexicana: historia documental, 1810–1962.* México: Empresas Editoriales, S.A., 1965.

García Pelayo, Manuel. *Derecho constitucional comparado.* Madrid, 1957.

Gómez Morín, Manuel. *Diez Años de México: informes del jefe de Acción Nacional.* México: Editorial Jus, 1950.

González Casanova, Pablo. *La democracia en México.* México: Ediciones Era, 1965.

González Genaro, María. *Catolicismo y revolución.* México: Talleres de la Imprenta Murguía, 1961.

González Luna, Efraín. *Humanismo político.* México: Editorial Jus, 1955.

González-Cosío Díaz, Arturo. *Los partidos políticos en México y su reglamentación jurídica.* México: UNAM, 1954.

Guisa y Azevedo, Jesús. *Acción Nacional es un equívoco.* México: Editorial Polis, 1966.

Johnson, John J. *Political Change in Latin America: The Emergence of the Middle Sectors.* Stanford University Press, 1958.

Kelso, Paul. *Mexico: An Emerging Democracy.* Tucson: University of Arizona Press, 1964.

Kling, Merle. *A Mexican Interest Group in Action.* Englewood Cliffs, N.J.: Prentice-Hall, Inc., 1961.

La Palombara, Joseph, and Weiner, Myron, eds. *Political Parties and Political Development.* Princeton: Princeton University Press, 1969.

Lipset, Seymour Martin, and Solari, Aldo, eds. *Elites in Latin America.* Oxford University Press, 1967.

Llano, Rodrígo de. *México y las elecciones de 1958.* México: Editorial Botas, 1957.

Mabry, Donald J. *Mexico's Acción Nacional: A Catholic Alternative to Revolution.* Syracuse, N.Y.: Syracuse University Press, 1973.

Macridis, Roy C., ed. *Political Parties: Contemporary Trends and Ideas.* New York: Harper and Row, 1967.

Madero, Francisco I. *La sucesión presidencial en 1910.*

Mayo, Sebastián, *La educación socialista en México.* Rosario, Argentina: Editorial BEAR, 1964.

Mecham, J. Lloyd. *Church and State in Latin America. A History of Politico-Ecclesiastical Relations,* rev. ed. Chapel Hill: The University of North Carolina Press, 1966.

Méndez Barraza, Alfonso. *Los partidos políticos en México.* México: UNAM, Facultad de Jurisprudencia, 1949.

Mendieta y Núñez, Lucio. *Teoría de los agrupamientos sociales.* México: edición del autor, 1950.

Milnor, Andrew J., ed. *Comparative Political Parties.* New York: Thomas Y. Crowell, Co., 1969.

Moya Palencia, Mario. *La reforma electoral.* México, 1964.

Needler, Martin C. *Politics and Society in Mexico.* Albuquerque: University of New Mexico Press, 1971.

Neumann, Sigmund, ed. *Modern Political Parties: Approaches to Comparative Politics.* Chicago: University of Chicago Press, 1955.

Novo, Salvador. *La vida en México en el período presidencial de Lázaro Cárdenas.* México: Empresas Editoriales, S.A., 1964.

———. *La vida en México en el período presidencial de Manuel Ávila Camacho.* México: Empresas Editoriales, 1965.

———. *La vida en México en el período presidencial de Miguel Alemán.* México: Empresas Editoriales, 1967.

Olivera Sedano, Alicia. *Aspectos del conflicto religioso de 1926 a 1929. Sus antecedentes y consecuencias.* México, D.F.: INAH, 1966.

Padgett, L. Vincent. *The Mexican Political System.* Boston: Houghton-Mifflin, 1966.

Pereyra, Carlos. *México falsificado.* México: Editorial Polis, 1948.

Pérez Patón, Roberto. *Los partidos políticos y la democracia: sociología del partido único.* La Paz: Bolivia: edición del autor, 1961.

Pineda, Francisco y Delhumeau, Antonio. *Los mexicanos frente al poder.* México, D.F.: Instituto Mexicano de Estudios Politicos, A.C., 1973.

Pye, Lucian W. *Aspects of Political Development.* Boston: Little, Brown, and Company, 1966.

______, and Verba, Sidney, eds. *Political Culture and Political Development.* Princeton, N.J.: Princeton University Press, 1965.

Quirk, Robert E., in: *Religion, Revolution, and Reform.* William V. D'Antonio and Frederick B. Pike, eds. New York: Praeger, 1964.

Ramos, Samuel. *Profile of Man and Culture in Mexico.* Trans. by Peter G. Earle. New York: McGraw-Hill, 1962.

Ricasens Siches, Luis. *Tratado general de sociología.* México: edición del autor, 1958.

Ríus Facius, Antonio. *Méjico cristero.* México: Editorial Patria, S.A., 1960.

Roa Hernández, Antonio. *La doctrina de los partidos políticos y el Partido Revolucionario Institucional.* México: UNAM, Facultad de Derecho, 1961.

Rokeach, Milton. *The Open and Closed Mind.* New York: Basic Books, 1960.

Ross, Stanley R. *Is the Mexican Revolution Dead?* New York: Alfred A. Knopf, 1966.

Sánchez Azcona, Juan. *La Etapa Maderista de la Revolución.* México: Talleres Gráficos de la Nación, 1960.

Scott, Robert E. *Mexican Government in Transition.* Urbana: University of Illinois Press, 1959.

Segovia, Rafael, "Mexican Politics and the University Crisis." *Political Power in Latin America: Seven Confrontations.* Richard R. Fagen and Wayne A. Cornelius, eds. Englewood Cliffs, N.J.: Prentice-Hall, Inc., 1970.

Silva Herzog, Jesús. *Inquietud sin tregua.* México: Cuadernos Americanos, 1965.

______. *Trayectoria ideológica de la Revolución Mexicana.* México: Cuadernos Americanos, 1963.

Simpson, Eyler Newton. *The Ejido, Mexico's Way Out.* Chapel Hill: University of North Carolina Press, 1937.

Solís Quiroga, Héctor. *Los partidos políticos en México.* México: Editorial Orión, 1961.

Tannenbaum, Frank. *Mexico, The Struggle for Peace and Bread.* New York: Alfred A. Knopf, 1951.

______. *Peace by Revolution.* New York: Columbia University Press, 1933.

Taracena, Alfonso, *La revolución desvirtuada.* México: Costa-Amic, 1966.

Tucker, William P. *Mexican Government Today.* Minneapolis: University of Minnesota Press, 1957.

Vallier, Ivan. *Catholicism, Social Control, and Modernization in Latin America.* Englewood Cliffs, N.J.: Prentice-Hall, Inc., 1970.

______, in: *Elites in Latin America.* Seymour Martin Lipset and Aldo Solari, eds. Oxford University Press, 1967.

Vasconcelos José. *Breve historia de México.* México: Compañía Editorial Continental, S.A., 1963.

Velasco, Gil, Carlos. *Sinarquismo.* México: edición del autor, 1944.

Wilkie, James W. *Mexican Revolution: Federal Expenditure and Social Change Since 1910.* Berkeley: University of California Press, 1970.

Wilkie, James W., and Edna Monzón de. *México visto en el Siglo XX: entrevistas de historia oral.* México: Instituto Mexicano de Investigaciones Económicas, 1969.

Williams, Edward J. *Latin American Christian Democratic Parties.* Knoxville: University of Tennessee Press, 1967.

Monographs and Pamphlets

Acción Nacional. *Ayuntamiento de Garza García: primer año de servicio,* 1967–1969. Garza García; Nuevo León, 1969.

Acevedo Amaya, Valmore. *Democracia cristiana en America Latina.* Caracas: Publicaciones de la Fracción Parlamentaria, Partido Social-Cristiano COPEI, 1965.

Alisky, Marvin. *Governors of Mexico.* El Paso: Texas Western Press, 1965.

______, ed. *Who's Who in Mexican Government.* Tempe: Center for Latin American Studies of Arizona State University, 1969.

Bravo Ugarte, José. *Efraín González Luna: abogado, humanista, político, católico.* México: Ediciones de Acción Nacional, 1968.

Christlieb Ibarrola, Adolfo. *Baja California, avanzada de la democracia,* México: Ediciones de Acción Nacional, 1968.

______. *Crónicas de la no-reelección.* México: Ediciones de Acción Nacional, 1965.

______. *La oposición.* México: Ediciones de Acción Nacional, 1965.

______. *¿Monopolio educativo o unidad nacional?* México: Editorial Jus, 1962.

______. *Temas políticos.* Mèxico: Ediciones de Acción Nacional, 1963.

______. *Acción Nacional: convergencias y divergencias.* México: Talleres de la Editorial Jus, 1966.

______. *Comentarios sobre el Proyecto de Reformas al Artículo 123 de la Constitución.* México: Talleres de la Editorial Jus, 1962.

______. *Construcciones en el Distrito Federal: reglamento nuevo, vicios nuevos y viejos.* México: Imprentas del PAN, 1966.

______. "Discurso pronunciado en la sesión solemne celebrada por la Cámara de Diputados el día primero de diciembre de 1966 para conmemorar la instalación del Congreso Constituyente de 1916–1917 en Querétaro." México: Talleres de la Editorial Jus, 1966.

______. *Inversiones extranjeras en México.* México: Imprentas del PAN, 1965.

______. *La iniciativa privada y la política.* México: Talleres de la Editorial Jus, 1966.

______. *Partido y Gobierno.* México: Talleres de la Editorial Jus, 1968.

______. *Presencia viva de la juventud.* México: Talleres de la Editorial Jus, 1966.

______. *Sindicatos, política y clausula de exclusión.* México: Imprentas del PAN, 1965.

______. *Transformación de los empresarios.* México: Talleres de la Editorial Jus, 1962.

Emerson, Rupert. *Political Modernization: The Single-Party System.* Denver: The Social Science Foundation and Department of International Relations Monograph Series in World Affairs, University of Denver, 1963.

Gómez Morín, Manuel. *Seguridad Social.* México: Ediciones de Acción Nacional, 1966.

González Flores, Anacleto. *El Plebiscito de los mártires.* México: Comité Central de la Asociación Católica de la Juventud Mexicana, 1961.

González Luna, Efraín. *El fétiche de la estabilidad política.* Guadalajara, Jal.: Centro Jalisciense de Productividad, A.C., 1965.

______, *et. al. La democracia en México.* México: Editorial Jus, 1962.

González Morfín, Efraín. *El puño y la mano tendida.* México: Ediciones de Acción Nacional, 1965.

______. *Justicia y reforma social.* México: Ediciones de Acción Nacional, 1967.

______, *et. al. Cuestiones políticas y sociales.* México: Ediciones de Acción Nacional, 1965.

Madero, Francisco I. *Plan de San Luis Potosí.*

Martínez Domínguez, Alfonso. "Una nueva política y un nuevo tipo de políticos." México: Comisión Nacional Editorial, 1970.

México. Partido Revolucionario Institucional. "El estado debe ser una organización dinámica: discurso pronunciado por el Sr. Lic. Luis Echeverría Alvarez." México: Comisión Nacional Editorial, 1970.

______. Comité Ejecutivo Nacional. *Ideario Luis Echeverría,* Volumes 1–7. Mexico: Polémica (Organo Teórico del PRI), 1970.

Partido Acción Nacional. *Informes de las Convenciones Nacionales del PAN.* México: Editorial Jus, 1970.

______. *Informes del Presidente del Partido al Consejo Nacional de Acción Nacional.* México: Editorial Jus, 1969.

______. "La Batalla . . . '70." (Suplemento de Campaña de *Acción Nacional.* México, D.F., Agosto 1, 1970.

______. *Plataforma Política y Social 1967–1970.* (Also all party platforms since 1939.)

______. "Principios de doctrina: su proyección en 1965." *XVIII Convención Nacional del PAN.* México, May 16, 1965.

Preciado Hernández, Rafael. *Discursos parlamentarios.* México: Editorial Jus, 1968.

Simposio. *Seis estudios sobre Baja California.* México: Ediciones de Acción Nacional, 1964.

ARTICLES

Aberbach, Joel D. "Alienation and Political Behavior." *The American Political Science Review* 58 (1969): 86–99.

Albores Guillén, Roberto. "La dinámica de los partidos políticos en México." *Pensamiento Político* 3, No. 9 (1970): 69–90.

Alisky, Marvin. "Budgets of State Governments in Mexico." *Public Affairs Bulletin* 5, No. 2 (1966).

———. "Provision for Municipal Government in Latin American Constitutions." *Public Affairs Bulletin* 7, No. 1 (1968).

Anderson, Bo, and Cockcroft, James D. "Control and Cooptation in Mexican Politics." *International Journal of Comparative Sociology* 7, No. 1 (1966): 16–22.

Arendt, Hannah. "Ideology and Terror: A Novel Form of Government." *The Review of Politics,* July 1953.

Ashby, J. C. "Labor and the Theory of the Mexican Revolution under Lázaro Cárdenas." *Americas* 20 (1963): 158–99.

Brown, Lyle C. "Mexican Church-State Relations, 1933–1940." *Journal of Church and State,* Spring, 1964, pp. 202–22.

Davis, Harold E. "Enigma of Mexican Sinarquism." *Free World* 5, May 1943, pp. 410–16.

Duff, Ernest A., and McCamant, John F. "Measuring Social and Political Requirements for System Stability in Latin America." *The American Political Science Review* 57 (1968): 1125–43.

Ebenstein, William. "Public Administration in Mexico." *Public Administration Review* 5 (1945): 102–12.

Fitzgibbon, Russell H. "The Party Potpourri in Latin America." *Western Political Quarterly,* March, 1957, pp. 3–22.

Gil, Federico G. "Responsible Parties in Latin America." *Journal of Politics* 15 (1953): 333–348.

González Avelar, Miguel. "La sucesión presidencial y el problema educativo." *Pensamiento Político* 3, No. 12 (1970): 445–60.

Guzmán, Martín Luis. "Orígenes del partido de la revolución." *Pensamiento Político* 3, No. 11 (1970): 375–96.

Hidalga, Luis de la. "Sistemas electorales en el constitucionalismo mexicano." *Pensamiento Político* 3, No. 12 (1970): 493–536.

Huntington, Samuel P. "Political Development and Political Decay." *World Politics* 17 (1965): 393.

Johnson, Kenneth F. "Ideological Correlates of Right-Wing Political Alienation in Mexico." *American Political Science Review,* September 1965, p. 44.

———, and Hill, Duane W. "A Cross-Cultural Approach to Political Alienation." *The Rocky Mountain Social Science Journal,* May 1965.

Kling, Merle. "Toward a Theory of Power and Political Instability in Latin America." *The Western Political Quarterly* 9 (1956): 21–35.
Martz, John D. "Dilemmas in the Study of Latin American Political Parties." *Journal of Politics* 26 (1964): 509–31.
Mecham, J. Lloyd. "Mexican Federalism—Fact or Fiction?" *Annals of the American Academy of Political and Social Sciences* 208 (1940): 23–38.
Michaels, Albert L. "Fascism and *Sinarquismo:* Popular Nationalisms Against the Mexican Revolution." *Journal of Church and State,* Spring 1966, pp. 234–50.
Needler, Martin C. "Political Development in Mexico." *American Political Science Review* 55 (1961): 306–12.
Ochoa Campos, Moisés. "Causas políticas de la revolución mexicana." *Pensamiento Político* 3, No. 9 (1970): 91–104.
Padgett, L. Vincent. "Mexico's One-Party System: A Reevaluation." *American Political Science Review* 51 (1957): 995–1008.
Parsons, Talcott. "On the Concept of Influence." *Public Opinion Quarterly* 27 (1963): 37–62.
Pinney, E. L., and Conley, J. E. "On Political Modernity in Mexico: Consensus and Recruitment." II. *South West Social Science Quarterly* 44 (1963): 225–36.
Sánchez Azcona, Jorge. "Carismo y liderazgo." *Pensamiento Político* 3, No. 11 (1970): 301–22.
Sartori, Giovanni. "Politics, Ideology, and Belief Systems." *American Political Science Review* 63, No. 2 (1969): 398–411.
Schmitt, Karl M. "The Mexican Positivists and the Church-State Question, 1876–1911." *Journal of Church and State,* Spring 1966, pp. 200–13.
Spain, August O. "Mexican Federalism Revisited." *Western Political Quarterly* 9 (1956): 620–32.
______. "En Torno a la Iglesia de hoy." *El Dia* 8, July 1969.
Taylor, Philip B. "The Mexican Elections of 1958: Affirmation of Authoritarianism?" *Western Political Quarterly* 13 (1960): 722–44.
Vallier, Ivan. "Church 'Development' in Latin America: A Five-Country Comparison." *Journal of Developing Areas* 1, No. 4 (1967): 461–76.
Villaseñor, Antonio. "La continuidad de las ideas revolucionarias en la obra constructiva de México." *Pensamiento Político* 2 (1970): 323–32.
Wilkie, James W. "The Meaning of the Cristero Religious War Against the Mexican Revolution." *Journal of Church and State,* Spring 1966, pp. 214–33.
______. "New Hypotheses for Statistical Research in Recent Mexican History." *Latin American Research Review* 6 (1971): 3–17.

Newspapers

Boletín de Acción Nacional. (Mexico City)
Christian Science Monitor.
El Nacional (Mexico City).

El Sinarquista (Mexico City), October, 1939.
El Universal (Mexico City).
Excélsior (Mexico City).
La Nación (Mexico City). Detailed examination of all issues from 1943 to 1973.
L'Osservatore Romano (Rome), August 11, 1926.
Novedades (Mexico City).
The New York Times.
The News (Mexico City).
Últimas Noticias (Mexico City).
Universal Gráfico (Mexico City).
Washington Post, December 27, 1968.

UNPUBLISHED MATERIALS

Beals, Ralph C. "Bureaucratic Change in the Mexican Catholic Church, 1926 to 1950." Unpublished Ph.D. dissertation, University of California, Berkeley, 1966.
Brandenburg, Frank R. "Mexico: An Experiment in One-Party Democracy." Unpublished Ph.D. dissertation, University of Pennsylvania, 1955.
Brown, Lyle C. "General Lázaro Cárdenas and Mexican Presidential Politics, 1933–1940: A Study in the Acquisition and Manipulation of Political Power." Unpublished Ph.D. dissertation, University of Texas, 1967.
Carlson, Harry J. "The Impact of the Cárdenas Administration on Mexican Education." Unpublished Ph.D. dissertation, University of Arizona, 1964.
Creagan, James F. "Minority Political Parties in Mexico: Their Role in a One-Party Dominant System." Unpublished Ph.D. dissertation, University of Virginia, 1965.
Lux, William Robert. "PAN: The Conservative Political Party of Mexico." Unpublished Ph.D. dissertation, University of Southern California, 1967.
Monson, Robert A. "Right-Wing Politics in Mexican Education: The Textbook Controversy." Unpublished Ph.D. dissertation, Georgetown University, 1970.
Padgett, L. Vincent. "Popular Participation in the Mexican 'One-Party' System." Unpublished Ph.D. dissertation, Northwestern University, 1955.

Index